BIOTERROR

BIOTERROR

Anthrax, Influenza, and the Future of Public Health Security

R. William Johnstone

James Dutton, Imprint Adviser

PRAEGER SECURITY INTERNATIONAL
Westport, Connecticut • London

Library of Congress Cataloging-in-Publication Data

Johnstone, R. William, 1953–
    Bioterror : anthrax, influenza, and the future of public health security / R. William Johnstone.
       p. ; cm.
    Includes bibliographical references and index.
    ISBN 978–0–275–99326–9 (alk. paper)
    1. Bioterrorism—United States.   2. Anthrax—United States.   I. Title.
    [DNLM: 1. Bioterrorism—United States.   2. Anthrax—United States.   3. Disease Outbreaks—United States.   4. Public Health Administration—United States.   5. Public Policy—United States. WA 295 J73b 2008]
    HV6433.35.J64   2008
    363.325′30973—dc22   2008020105

British Library Cataloguing in Publication Data is available.

Library of Congress Catalog Card Number: 2008020105
ISBN-13: 978–0–275–99326–9

First published in 2008

Praeger Security International, 88 Post Road West, Westport, CT 06881
An imprint of Greenwood Publishing Group, Inc.
www.praeger.com

Printed in the United States of America

The paper used in this book complies with the
Permanent Paper Standard issued by the National
Information Standards Organization (Z39.48–1984).

10 9 8 7 6 5 4 3 2 1

CONTENTS

ILLUSTRATIONS

TABLES

FIGURES

PREFACE

On the morning of September 11, 2001, I was working as the legislative director for U.S. Senator Max Cleland (D-GA) in the Dirksen Senate Office Building in Washington, DC when four planes were hijacked by foreign terrorists. After the crashes of the aircraft into the World Trade Center in New York and the nearby Pentagon, I helped evacuate the Senator's office. In the days and weeks that followed the shock of those events, our office, like most of Capitol Hill, focused on responding to them.

A little over a month later, on October 15, 2001, the Capitol and nation were hit by another attack, this one involving the opening of a letter containing anthrax spores in the Hart Senate Office Building suite of U.S. Senator Tom Daschle (D-SD) that was only about a hundred yards away through an open passageway from my own room. Along with many other Senate workers, a few members of Senator Cleland's staff (not including me), who were thought to have possibly been exposed, were tested and put on ciprofloxacin, which was the preferred treatment for inhalational anthrax. The Hart Building was closed on October 17. As the seriousness of the situation and the extent of the contamination became better understood (including the discovery that the mailroom in the Dirksen basement had traces of anthrax), the Dirksen Building was shuttered on October 20, 2001 and our staff had to "telecommute" from our widely dispersed homes.

Although none of the Cleland staff members tested positive, and none of the few dozen Senate workers who were found to have been exposed subsequently developed an infection, and though the Dirksen Building was opened several weeks later (with the Hart Building following in January

2002), the physical disruption was real and the psychological impact was palpable.

Subsequently, I had the privilege of serving on the staff of the National Commission on Terrorist Attacks Upon the United States (the 9/11 Commission), and thus had the opportunity to participate in that effort to understand and explain the September 11 hijackings, while making recommendations designed to prevent a reoccurrence.

There was no such body created to perform an authoritative and comprehensive examination of the anthrax attacks and to help produce public and congressional consensus behind appropriate policy responses. The genesis of this work was, thus, the notion to attempt to create, on a much humbler scale, a 9/11 Commission-like look at the anthrax crisis, including consideration of the attacks themselves, the evolution and performance of the defenses against them, and suggestions for policy improvements to reduce the probability of future such attacks.

Lacking the resources of the 9/11 Commission, it was clear that some choices were going to have to be made in narrowing the scope somewhat to allow for the desired comprehensiveness in treatment of the chosen subjects. Therefore, though many other relevant topics presented themselves (including, among the defensive entities involved in some way in the anthrax case, the intelligence community and the Environmental Protection Agency), a decision was made to focus primarily on the public health system, which was the most directly implicated in the response. In providing a more thorough view of the anthrax attacks themselves, it was also determined that a limited look at the criminal investigation conducted by law enforcement agencies would be included.

Having decided to center on the public health system, however, it quickly became apparent that limiting my survey to anthrax alone would not allow for a true assessment of that system, which was, and is, faced with a large number of ongoing challenges, including one—the threat of pandemic influenza—that has emerged since 2001 as perhaps an even greater concern than bioterrorism in the eyes of many in the public health community, the administration, the Congress, and the general public. In the end, the determination was made to broaden this study to include pandemic flu, in addition to anthrax and other biological weapons threats. And since the notion of infection is central to most of those threats, the more general topic of infectious disease control was also added.

The primary point of analysis in the present work is at the policy level rather than on the medical side, so that, for instance, much more attention is given to the legislative and administrative authorization and funding of public health policies and programs than to the clinical descriptions of diseases and treatments.

The goal herein was to assess the capability of the public health system to address the anthrax attacks and the ongoing challenges of bioterrorism and naturally occurring pandemics, to offer some suggestions for remedying major deficiencies, and to do so in a manner that is accessible to policy makers, public health officials, and the interested public. Extensive endnotes are provided to help direct readers seeking more information on specific topics to additional sources.

CHAPTER 1

The Anthrax Attacks of September / October 2001

Though significantly less so than in earlier times, the threat of infectious disease has been substantial and ongoing throughout modern American history. For example, every year an estimated 36,000 Americans die and another 226,000 hospitalizations occur as the result of flu epidemics in the United States.[1] Three times during the twentieth century, the extent and severity of an influenza outbreak reached the level termed "pandemics"[2] by health authorities: the *1918 Spanish Flu*, estimated to have killed between 20 and 100 million people worldwide, including 500,000 or more in the United States; the *1957 Asian Flu*, which killed approximately 70,000 in the United States; and the *1968 Hong Kong Flu*, which produced an estimated 34,000 American fatalities.[3]

On the other hand, the danger from biological weapons has been far less apparent. With respect to anthrax, while research on using it as a weapon dates back more than eighty years, most of the national programs conducting such research (including the American program) were terminated in the early 1970s following the ratification of the Biological Weapons Convention. However, some nations, most notably Iraq and the former Soviet Union, continued such research after that time, and it has been reported that at least thirteen countries had, or were suspected of having, anthrax weapons programs as of 2001.[4]

Even with the apparent existence of such programs, however, experience with their actual usage was extremely limited. The most serious case, by far, was the 1979 accidental release of anthrax spores into the area surrounding the Soviet bioweapons complex in Sverdlovsk, Russia. Though information on this event is still somewhat limited and contradictory in places, it appears that the Sverdlovsk accident produced an anthrax epidemic in the area with as many as 250 infections and 100 deaths. Aside from this, Aum Shinrikyo—the same Japanese cult responsible for the 1995 release of sarin gas into the Tokyo subway system—released aerosols of anthrax and botulism in Tokyo on at least eight occasions in that same year. However, the type, or strain, of anthrax they employed was not a significant risk to humans and it is probable that these attacks produced no illnesses.[5]

The name "anthrax" is derived from the Greek word for coal because of the dark black skin lesions associated with the onset of what has historically been the most prevalent form of the disease. The infecting agent itself is a bacterium called *Bacillus anthracis* that is rod-shaped in appearance under a microscope. The usual means by which the disease is transmitted is the spore, typically produced when the bacterium is exposed to oxygen or receives insufficient nutrients. The anthrax spore is highly resistant to destruction and can remain dormant in the environment for many years while retaining its infective ability when introduced into the body of a susceptible host.[6]

Anthrax infection in humans can be produced through three types of contacts: cutaneous, gastrointestinal, and inhalational. Cutaneous anthrax, which is generally produced by physical exposure to infected animals, is easily the most common form of the disease, with an estimated 2,000 cases a year globally. In the United States, there were 224 reported cases between 1944 and 1994, and a single case reported in 2000. Gastrointestinal anthrax is usually contracted through ingestion of insufficiently cooked contaminated meat. It is much rarer than cutaneous anthrax, but small-scale outbreaks are reported from time to time, especially in Africa and Asia.

By 2001, the third form, inhalational anthrax, had become very rare as a naturally occurring disease in the United States. Only eighteen cases—mostly involving special kinds of occupational exposure, such as goat hair milling, tannery work, or laboratory exposure—were reported in the United States during the twentieth century, the last occurring in 1976.[7]

THE SEPTEMBER ATTACKS

On Tuesday, September 11, 2001, nineteen men from Middle Eastern countries succeeded in hijacking four transcontinental flights within the United States. The first two hijacked flights were deliberately crashed into the two World Trade Center tower buildings in New York City, killing all on board the two aircraft and subsequently causing the collapse of the two towers and the deaths of those trapped in the two buildings. The third plane was used to crash into the Pentagon across the river from the nation's Capitol, while the fourth crashed into a field in western Pennsylvania because of a revolt by the passengers. According to the 9/11 Commission, excluding the hijackers, 2,749 people were killed because of the New York crashes, another 184 perished as a result of the attack on the Pentagon, and 40 died in the Pennsylvania crash. That death toll of 2,973 represented the largest loss of life, ever, on American soil as a result of hostile external attack.[8]

After this "day of unprecedented shock and suffering,"[9] the attention of the federal government was rapidly redirected toward assessing and preparing to deal with the terrorist threat. The Atlanta headquarters of the Centers for Disease Control and Prevention (CDC), the country's chief agency responsible for dealing with infectious disease from whatever source, was evacuated on 9/11 itself because of concerns about another potential hijacking aimed at it. Though this proved to be unfounded, officials at CDC were focused on the possibility of a quick, follow-on attack utilizing biological or chemical weapons.[10]

Among other actions taken by the public health system right after the hijackings, CDC's Health Alert system was implemented, putting state and local health departments and health laboratories on notice to watch for suspicious or unusual illnesses, and thirty-five CDC epidemiologists were sent to New York City to assist in this effort. Five teams of medical professionals from the National Disaster Medical System were dispatched to New York, and two others went to the Pentagon. In addition, for the first time, CDC deployed one of its "push packs" of medical supplies, which were prepositioned at several locations around the country and were designed to arrive at any place in the United States within twelve hours. In this case, 50 tons of supplies arrived in New York City within seven hours.[11]

Another part of this response was a Sunday, September 16, 2001 meeting between the Secretary of the U.S. Department of Health and Human Services (HHS), Tommy Thompson, and infectious disease expert and former HHS Deputy Assistant Secretary in the Clinton administration, Donald A. Henderson.

Many months later, Henderson recalled the discussion.

> We sort of worked our way through the conversation. Doing something with an airplane again was going to be much harder now than it had been, we decided. I think we all came to the conclusion that it could very well be a biological event. And it was quite apparent to me that this was Thompson's view too . . . He was obviously extremely distressed. "They [his contacts in the White House] just don't understand." What don't they understand, [I] asked. "Biological weapons . . . [The country is] unprepared, grossly unprepared for a biological attack," [Thompson said].[12]

Just after the Thompson–Henderson meeting, and most likely on either Monday, September 17 or Tuesday, September 18, 2001, a person or persons mailed letters containing anthrax spores addressed to Tom Brokaw of National Broadcasting Company (NBC) News and to the Editor of the *New York Post*, both in New York City.[13] These were later recovered and the

Federal Bureau of Investigation's (FBI) analysis of the handwriting used in addressing the envelopes and in writing the one-page message inside concluded, "It is highly probable, bordering on certainty, that [these] letters were authored by the same person."[14]

Further investigation of the two recovered letters indicated that they were processed at the U.S. Postal Service Trenton Mail Processing and Distribution Center in Hamilton Township, New Jersey (located 10 miles from Princeton, New Jersey), which affixed a "Trenton, New Jersey" postmark on the letters, dated September 18, 2001. These and the subsequently revealed anthrax letters to New York City addresses were sent to the Morgan Central Postal Facility in New York City for final sorting and delivery.[15]

Because of subsequent investigations of the locations from which mail was delivered to the Hamilton Township office, it is very likely that these letters (and the other September 2001 anthrax letters) were mailed from a mailbox on Nassau Street in Princeton, New Jersey.[16]

The message inside each letter was identical—a copy of a one-page, handwritten note in all capital letters, as follows (with the word "penicillin" misspelled):

> 09-11-01
> THIS IS NEXT
> TAKE PENACILIN NOW
> DEATH TO AMERICA
> DEATH TO ISRAEL
> ALLAH IS GREAT[17]

At or around this same time, at least three other letters containing anthrax were mailed to ABC (American Broadcasting Company) News and CBS (Columbia Broadcasting System) News in New York City, and to the building in Boca Raton, Florida owned by American Media, Inc. (AMI),[18] most likely addressed to the *National Enquirer*.[19] None of these has been recovered but their existence has been inferred from the pattern of anthrax infections subsequently discovered at the three locations. Furthermore, similarities in that infection pattern and in the targets selected strongly suggest that the ABC and CBS letters were identical to the Brokaw letter in content, authorship, and mailing date.

The Florida case likely fits this same profile, too, given the timing of the onset of anthrax symptoms and infection. The National Anthrax Epidemiologic Investigation Team, headed by CDC and charged with examining the epidemiological aspects of the 2001 anthrax attacks, concluded, "The dates of illness onset in AMI media company employees in Florida suggest possible exposure to envelopes mailed in mid-September 2001."[20]

According to coworkers of Robert Stevens,[21] a photo editor at AMI in Florida who would become the first fatality of the 2001 attacks, on September 19, 2001 a letter or package addressed to Jennifer Lopez in care of the AMI *Sun* and containing some form of powder was opened in the AMI building.[22] However, the disconnect between the recollected content of the Lopez letter (which pertained to her forthcoming marriage) and the four recovered anthrax letters, plus the subsequent environmental testing of the AMI building (which showed a heavy concentration in the mailroom and surrounding first floor rooms, but very limited contamination on the third floor, where Stevens worked and the Lopez letter was said to have been circulated) have led many to conclude that this communication was not involved in the anthrax attacks.

Sometime between September 19 and September 25, 2001, the letter to Brokaw was received and processed at NBC. When it was opened by a clerical worker, a brownish, granular substance fell out. The worker brushed as much of that material as she could into a nearby trash can, and then placed the letter into another envelope and added it to a group of "hate mail" that the company periodically sends along to law-enforcement authorities.[23]

On September 25, another letter that released a powdery substance upon being opened was processed in the AMI building in Florida. The worker who opened it recalled discarding the letter in the trash without reading it. She reported to investigators that it could have arrived anytime during the preceding two weeks when she had been on vacation. Given that, aside from Robert Stevens, the only other AMI employee who contracted anthrax worked in the mailroom and the first floor (which included the mailroom) displayed by far the highest levels of anthrax contamination,[24] many have surmised that this was the most likely source of the anthrax used in the Florida attack.[25]

Starting on September 22 and continuing until October 1, 2001, nine individuals (five in New York, two in New Jersey, and two in Florida) who either worked at one of the targets of the five anthrax-attack letters, or with entities associated with mail delivery to those facilities, contracted anthrax and began to exhibit symptoms, though none were correctly diagnosed at this point.[26]

Early on the morning of October 2, 2001, Robert Stevens checked into JFK Medical Center in Atlantis, Florida, with "a severe illness that began 2 days earlier, characterized by fever, chills, sweats, fatigue, and malaise, which progressed to vomiting, confusion, and incoherent speech."[27] He was initially diagnosed as suffering from meningitis, but shortly thereafter one of the Center's infectious disease specialists, Dr. Larry Bush, began to suspect that he had been infected with anthrax, based on the hospital's lab results. That afternoon, a Ft. Lauderdale laboratory to which Bush had sent a sample of the bacteria infecting Stevens reported back to him that its test results were consistent with anthrax.[28]

Bush next contacted Philip Lee, head microbiology technician at the Florida Department of Health Bureau of Laboratories in Jacksonville, which was coincidentally part of the CDC-established Laboratory Response Network (LRN) recently created to establish uniform testing methods for suspected biological weapons. In addition, Lee himself had recently completed a CDC-training program on recognition of bioweapons. Also on October 2, the CDC was notified of Dr. Bush's suspicions by Florida's state epidemiologist, Steven Wiersma.[29]

The Jacksonville lab received a sample of the suspect bacterium by noon, the next day, October 3, 2001. Its initial tests were "equivocal" as to the presence of anthrax, and Lee sent a sample to CDC. However, Dr. Jean Malecki, the director of the Palm Beach County health department was already sufficiently convinced of the likelihood of anthrax that she opened a formal investigation. By late in the evening on October 3, Lee had obtained more definitively positive results, which he relayed to the CDC.[30]

Also on October 3, HHS Secretary Thompson testified to Congress about the nation's preparedness to deal with bioterrorism in the wake of the 9/11 attacks.

> Our response encouraged me. It should encourage...the Congress. And it should encourage the American public that we do have the ability to respond. Now I do not by any means contend that our system is perfect or without weaknesses. We have gaps. We can, indeed, make our response stronger and it is imperative we do so. We must continue to accelerate our preparedness efforts...Frankly, bioterrorism preparedness hasn't been the highest fiscal priority in the past as it competed with other public needs. My hope is that will change as a result of greater awareness of our needs.[31]

On Thursday, October 4, 2001, the Jacksonville lab confirmed that Robert Stevens had inhalation anthrax, the first identified victim of the 2001 anthrax attacks.[32] On that date, HHS circulated a press release drafted by CDC, which indicated that CDC itself had confirmed the Stevens diagnosis, noting that "So far this appears to be an isolated case." The release went on to make a number of additional points.

- Right now, there is no suggestion of other possible cases, but we are aggressively checking to see if other people are similarly ill.
- The Florida State health department and a team from CDC are aggressively investigating the source of infection. They are reconstructing the patient's schedule for the last few weeks to attempt to determine the location where the patient may have been exposed.
- A team of CDC epidemiologists were sent to Florida to look for any indications of exposure to this disease. Medical teams and supplies are prepared to be moved quickly if needed.

- CDC and state health officials are alerting health care providers to look for unusual cases of respiratory diseases. Although anthrax starts out with flu-like symptoms, it rapidly progresses to severe illnesses, including pneumonia and meningitis.
- If anyone has been exposed, antibiotics are the appropriate preventive treatment. CDC has an emergency supply of antibiotics readily available for distribution. If the investigation of the cause of the illness indicated that you need antibiotics, your state and local health department will notify you and your physician and will assure you receive the drugs.
- Based on what we know right now, there is no need for people to take any extraordinary actions or steps. They should not go to a doctor or hospital unless they are sick. They should not buy and horde medicines or antibiotics. They should not buy gas masks.
- The public needs to understand that our public health system is on a heightened sense of alert for any diseases that may come from a biological attack. So we may have more reports of what may appear to be isolated cases. We're going to respond more aggressively to these cases than in the past.[33]

Also on October 4, at a press briefing at the White House, HHS Secretary Thompson reiterated the point that it appeared the Stevens infection was "an isolated case," and added "there is no evidence of bioterrorism."[34] In Florida, state epidemiologist Wiersma similarly told the news media, "We have no reason to believe at this time this was an attack at all." Late in the afternoon on that same day, CDC officials arrived in South Florida, and began establishing investigatory teams of federal, state, and local health authorities "to determine how the exposure occurred and . . . to identify other possible cases."[35]

Robert Stevens died on October 5, becoming the first fatality from the anthrax letters.[36] The CDC-led teams began their epidemiological investigation, starting with Stevens' residence and continuing on to the AMI building. Another CDC group was searching places visited by Stevens just prior to his hospitalization.[37] In addition, surveillance was initiated for other potential anthrax cases via a review of intensive-care unit (ICU) records, from September 11 forward, for Palm Beach County, Florida and for certain parts of North Carolina (where Stevens had recently been), and alerts to the relevant medical examiners and laboratory directors requesting that they forward to the Florida Department of Health any cultures suspicious for anthrax.[38]

As a result of the reports of Robert Stevens' illness and subsequent death, and the public health surveillance undertakings, six potential anthrax exposures at AMI were reported to CDC and Florida health authorities shortly thereafter. One of them was AMI mail distributor Ernesto Blanco, who had originally become ill on September 28, and was admitted to Cedars Medical Center in Miami, Florida on October 1. After his case was reported by his doctor to the public health authorities, he was tested for anthrax on October 5, but initial results were inconclusive.[39]

On Sunday, October 7, 2001, CDC reported that testing at AMI had detected anthrax in one nasal sample (later identified as Blanco's) and in one of the numerous workplace environmental samples that had been collected in the building. The release continued, "The current risk of anthrax among employees and visitors to the building is extremely low. However, as a preventive measure, public health officials have begun to contact personnel who worked in the building since August 1, 2001, to provide antibiotics."[40] Late that afternoon, the Palm Beach County health department ordered the AMI building to be closed.[41]

More intensive environmental testing of the AMI building commenced on October 8,[42] as did the testing and treatment (a ten-day supply of antibiotics) of approximately 1,000 individuals considered at-risk because of their presence in the AMI facility.[43] On the same day, the President established the Office of Homeland Security to develop and coordinate the national strategy for addressing the threat of terrorism within the United States.[44]

Although not known at the time, sometime in this period (October 6–9, 2001) a second set of letters containing anthrax was sent via US Mail.

Speculation that the anthrax present in Florida had been transmitted via contaminated mail began by October 10, 2001.[45]

On October 12, substantial new evidence emerged about the extent and method of the anthrax outbreak. Early that morning, the CDC reported to the New York City health department that Erin O'Connor, an editorial assistant to Tom Brokaw of NBC News, had tested positive for cutaneous anthrax, the second confirmed case of anthrax resulting from the September letters.[46]

O'Connor indicated she had first noticed symptoms on September 25, when she developed a sore on her chest. She went to see her physician on October 1, who thought she might be suffering from a spider bite. However, after hearing the reports on the two Florida cases, he recalled she told him that she had opened a threat letter containing some type of powder. As a precaution, he then decided to call the New York City health department and sent them the skin sample. The health department sent the skin sample to CDC for testing and contacted the FBI, which sent agents to NBC to retrieve the suspect letter. The Bureau found the letter, postmarked September 25 from St. Petersburg, Florida, but subsequent testing was negative for anthrax.

Once CDC had confirmed O'Connor's anthrax infection on October 12, health department staff went to the NBC workplace for further investigation, and was directed to a second threat letter, which they returned to their lab for testing. This was the September 18 letter to Tom Brokaw, with a Trenton, New Jersey postmark—the first of the September attack letters to be recovered—and it tested positive for anthrax.[47]

Though not generally reported at the time, another NBC worker, a news intern who helped process the mail and who reported first developing symptoms on September 28, also tested positive for cutaneous anthrax on October 12. This never received all of the clinical verification to be classified as a "confirmed" case, but test results were sufficient to qualify as a "suspect" case, and suspicions were strong enough for it to be included in CDC's ultimate list of twenty-two cases of "bioterrorism-related anthrax" from the 2001 attacks.[48]

On October 15, 2001, CDC finally confirmed that Ernesto Blanco, who remained hospitalized, was infected with inhalational anthrax, and the New York City health department announced another case of confirmed cutaneous anthrax—a seven-month old child of an ABC News producer who had visited the workplace on September 28 and developed a lesion on the arm the next day.[49] Thus, as of that day, four cases of anthrax were confirmed and another was highly suspected.

Also on October 15, the Florida Department of Health announced that anthrax spores had been discovered in the Boca Raton post office in an area that sorted mail for pickup by AMI and other nearby buildings.[50] Therefore, by this time, much—though not all—was known about the method, targets, and victims of the September attacks. Events on that same day in Washington, DC, however, were to begin to make clear the full extent of the plot.

THE OCTOBER ATTACKS

At some time on or just before October 9, 2001, a person or persons mailed letters containing anthrax spores to U.S. Senators Tom Daschle (D-SD) and Patrick Leahy (D-VT) and addressed to their offices in Washington, DC. Both letters were later recovered and FBI and other experts expressed a near "certainty" that they were written by the same individual who wrote the September anthrax letters to news media representatives.[51]

The letters to the Senators were postmarked "Trenton, New Jersey," on October 9, 2001, likely mailed from the Trenton–Princeton area. They were processed at the Hamilton, New Jersey Processing and Distribution Center and then sent to the Brentwood Mail Processing and Distribution Center in Washington, DC.[52]

Unlike the September letters, the October ones had a return address, which proved to be fictitious.

4th GRADE
GREENDALE SCHOOL
FRANKLIN PARK NJ 08852

And the content—identical in both of the letters to the Senators—differed somewhat from the September 2001 letters.

```
        09-11-01
YOU CAN NOT STOP US.
WE HAVE THIS ANTHRAX.
YOU DIE NOW.
ARE YOU AFRAID?
DEATH TO AMERICA.
DEATH TO ISRAEL.
ALLAH IS GREAT.[53]
```

Though unrecognized at the time, the first health impact from the newly mailed letters occurred on October 14, when two workers at the Hamilton, New Jersey postal facility (Patrick O'Donnell and Norma Wallace) began exhibiting disease symptoms. A day later, a third Hamilton postal worker (Jyotsna Patel) also experienced an onset of illness.[54]

At approximately 9:45 A.M. on Monday, October 15, 2001, an intern working in the sixth floor Hart Senate Office Building suite of Senator Daschle cut open the taped business envelope containing the letter to the Senator that had been postmarked "Trenton, New Jersey," on October 9. As it was opened, a fine white powder escaped from the envelope. The U.S. Capitol Police were summoned at once, and officers arrived at the Daschle office within five minutes. The FBI and the Office of the Attending Physician of the U.S. Capitol were also notified and dispatched representatives to the scene.

Upon the arrival of the law-enforcement and health authorities, the area was vacated and secured, the office ventilation system was deactivated (to reduce the spread of the suspected anthrax spores), the Capitol Hill Police officers took some samples of the powder, and the letter and carpet upon which the powder had fallen were removed and sent for testing.[55]

The initial investigation indicated that two floors in the southeast quadrant of the Hart Building in and around the Daschle suite were potentially contaminated and approximately 340 Senate staff and visitors might have been exposed. (Senator Daschle was away from his office, and thus was not exposed.[56]) Beginning on October 15, nasal swab testing was performed on these individuals, as well as another approximately 5,000 persons who were in the vicinity of the Daschle office and referred themselves for testing. (Ultimately, twenty-eight of those tested had some evidence of exposure to anthrax: thirteen from the Daschle mailroom, nine from adjacent areas in the Hart Building, and six from first responders. However, these individuals immediately began receiving antimicrobial treatment and none subsequently contracted anthrax.)[57]

On October 16, four postal workers from the Brentwood facility in Washington, DC (Leroy Richmond, Thomas Morris, Joseph Curseen, and a colleague) began displaying signs of mild illness. (Because of the dates of onset, it is likely that they and the three other postal workers who became ill on

October 14–15 were victims of the October anthrax letters.)[58] In addition, a public-opinion survey conducted for ABC and the *Washington Post* was released, indicating that 54 percent of the American public was "very" or "somewhat" worried that they or a relative, or friend might be the victim of an anthrax attack.[59]

Linda Burch, who was a bookkeeper at a New Jersey accounting firm that received mail directly from the Hamilton postal facility, became the next anthrax victim to display symptoms of the onset of disease on October 17. (Epidemiologic investigators were not able to determine definitively whether the ultimate source of her exposure was from the September or October anthrax letters.)[60]

Concerned about additional anthrax letters, also on October 17 the FBI quarantined all unopened mail in the U.S. Capitol complex, transferring it into 635 plastic garbage bags that were placed into sealed drums. These drums were moved to a government warehouse in northern Virginia, which was then sealed in plastic to prevent hazardous materials from escaping.[61] And the remainder of the Hart Building was closed on that day.[62]

On October 18, lab results confirmed two additional cases of cutaneous anthrax: Teresa Heller, a mail carrier based in West Trenton, New Jersey, and Claire Fletcher, an employee of CBS News in New York who handled mail, and they thus became the fifth and sixth confirmed cases of anthrax from the 2001 attacks. Heller had started to develop symptoms on September 29, whereas Fletcher reported that she became ill on October 1. Also on October 18, Hamilton postal worker Richard Morgano, who first developed symptoms on September 26, was recorded as the second "suspect" for cutaneous anthrax based on lab results, and the Hamilton postal processing center was closed.[63]

Because of when they first showed signs of their exposure to anthrax, which all occurred prior to the postmarking of the Daschle and Leahy letters, it is almost certain that Fletcher, Heller, and Morgano were victims of the September 2001 attacks. More importantly, Heller and Morgano represented the first diagnosed cases involving those who delivered unopened mail, rather than individuals exposed in workplaces where the letters had been opened.

The newly appointed head of the White House Office on Homeland Security, Tom Ridge, held his first briefing on October 18 at which he provided an update on the anthrax situation.

There is a great deal of speculation out there. There is obvious concern to most Americans—all Americans. And instead of speculating, we would like to focus on the facts. First, thousands and thousands and thousands have been tested for anthrax exposure, and thousands of environmental samples have been taken as well. Yet only five people have tested positive at this time for anthrax. I will tell you we are in the process of confirming a sixth . . . Two of these cases have tested positive for inhalation anthrax. While one gentleman unfortunately passed away, the other is expected to make a full recovery . . . The only death at this point, as we all know, happened in Florida.[64]

Also on October 18, Postmaster General John Potter visited the Brentwood postal facility to reassure the workers there, telling them that the letter to Senator Daschle "was extremely well-sealed and there is only a minute chance that anthrax spores escaped from it into the facility."[65]

On October 19, the September 9 letter to the editor of the *New York Post* was recovered unopened and was found to be identical to the letter to Tom Brokaw. On that same day, an employee of the *Post* who handled mail there, Johanna Huden, was listed by the CDC as a "suspect" for cutaneous anthrax, bringing the total to six confirmed and three suspected cases of anthrax. Huden was actually the first to experience the onset of the disease, on September 22, and thus like all of the previous eight, her case too was linked to the September 2001 attack.[66]

The first confirmed case resulting from the October letters also emerged on October 19, when Hamilton, New Jersey postal employee Patrick O'Donnell was confirmed as having cutaneous anthrax.[67] And in his press briefing on that day, Director Ridge indicated that tests of the anthrax from the AMI building, the Brokaw letter, and the Daschle letter "have concluded that the strains are indistinguishable. They are similar."[68]

Having by this time become aware of some of the developing cases involving Brentwood employees, in part as a result of "enhanced regional [disease] surveillance activities" by health authorities in Washington, DC, Maryland, and Virginia, as well as the fact that, "although no specific exposure event was identified [at Brentwood], the contaminated tightly sealed letter that was mailed to [Senator Daschle's office] was processed at this facility," on October 20, CDC and the Washington, DC Department of Health "initiated an investigation [of the Brentwood facility]."[69]

Early on the morning of October 21, Brentwood postal worker Thomas Morris was admitted with suspected inhalational anthrax to Greater Southeast Hospital in Washington, DC, "with persistent symptoms, including chills, vague chest tightness, and temperature of 102 F." His condition deteriorated and he died less than six hours after having been admitted. (Formal confirmation of inhalational anthrax came two days later, on October 23.)[70]

Also on October 21, Leroy Richmond was confirmed as having inhalational anthrax, and the mail-processing area on the first floor of the Brentwood Mail Processing and Distribution Center was closed and "antimicrobial prophylaxis was recommended to employees working in proximity to the same mail sorting area [as Richmond]."[71] As a precautionary measure, the postal facility in Anne Arundel County, Maryland, where

Richmond also worked, was closed and certain employees there were tested and given antimicrobial treatment.[72]

The following day, Brentwood worker Joseph Curseen became the third fatality of the anthrax attacks just a few hours after having been admitted to Southern Maryland Hospital in Clinton, Maryland with suspected inhalational anthrax (which was confirmed by laboratory analysis on October 26).[73]

Two more diagnoses for anthrax infection were made on October 22. The first was for one of Richmond's Brentwood coworkers, who was confirmed as having inhalational anthrax, and the other was for a mail handler at the *New York Post* in New York. This last was something of an anomaly given that the date of disease onset was October 19, but the identity of the workplace as well as "suspect" diagnosis for cutaneous, rather than inhalational, anthrax strongly suggested that this individual was a victim of the September 2001 attacks.

"Because of concern about the potential for unrecognized aerosol exposures among postal workers," on October 22, "antimicrobial therapy was recommended for all workers and visitors to nonpublic areas in [the Brentwood] postal facility."[74]

The subject of the federal response to contamination at Brentwood was a major topic of the October 22 press conference hosted by Director Ridge.

Question: Some of the workers, the postal workers who worked at the Brentwood facility, are asking two questions. Number one, since the Daschle letter would have originated there, they want to know why this facility wasn't closed sooner. And they also want to know why the workers themselves weren't tested sooner. And the Postal Service spokeswoman, I think earlier, said that they were following the advice of the Centers for Disease Control. So were federal officials a little slow in responding to the threat here?

Ridge: I think we can always look to, whether it's this threat or any other threat, move to hasten, move as quickly as we possibly can. But let me give you the sequence of events as I know them . . . They [the CDC and the Postal Service] followed the line back as aggressively, as quickly as they could. If the envelope was in the Senator's office, that means it went to—it came out of the Dirksen Building. If it came out of the Dirksen Building, previous to that it had been at the Post Office on P Street. P Street, as I understand it, was tested environmentally, but the tests were negative. In order to get to P Street, it has to come through the Brentwood Post Office. Thereafter, immediately, they put everybody—the hospitals and everybody else—on alert to see if anybody presented themselves with symptoms. So I think they moved back, followed the chain as quickly as they possibly can. Obviously we are going to do everything we can every time to expedite that, but I think they moved quickly, as quick as they could.[75]

David Hose, who supervised mail sorting at the State Department annex in northern Virginia, became ill with anthrax symptoms on October 22, as did another *New York Post* employee on October 23.[76] As with the other *Post* employees, it is likely that the latter was the victim of the September 2001 anthrax letter to that publication. Hose's infection was subsequently linked to the yet-to-be-discovered Leahy letter.[77]

By this point, there were nine confirmed and six suspect cases of anthrax infections, including three fatalities. Five others (Hamilton postal workers Norma Wallace and Jyotsna Patel, New Jersey bookkeeper Linda Burch, Hose and the *New York Post* employee) had in fact developed what was later confirmed to be anthrax.

At his October 25 press conference, Director Ridge reported that further testing had revealed the anthrax spores in the Daschle letter to be "more dangerous" than those in the other recovered letters because they were more concentrated, purer, and smaller in size. However, the tests had also shown that the anthrax in all three letters was treatable with existing antibiotics. He also provided an update on the situation with respect to postal workers and facilities.

> As of this morning, health officials have tested and treated more than 4,000 postal workers in the impacted areas. In addition, the Postal Service, working with federal, state, and local officials, have begun environmental testing at the 200 postal facilities along the Eastern corridor. The Postal Service will also conduct random environmental testing at major postal facilities nationwide.[78]

October 25 also witnessed the beginning of medical surveillance of all postal workers in Palm Beach County, Florida (through examination of all reports on recent postal worker illnesses and hospitalizations and the activation of a toll-free hotline for postal employees),[79] and the laboratory confirmation of David Hose as suffering from inhalational anthrax.[80]

Norma Wallace was formally confirmed with inhalational anthrax, and the *New York Post* employee was officially recorded as a confirmed case of cutaneous anthrax on October 28. On the following day, Jyotsna Patel (inhalational anthrax) and Linda Burch (cutaneous anthrax) were both confirmed as having an infection, bringing the total to twenty either confirmed or suspected cases of anthrax resulting from the September and October 2001 attacks.[81]

Also on October 29, at Director Ridge's briefing a representative from the postal service reported that 6,000 postal employees in the Baltimore–Washington area and 7,000 in New York–New Jersey were on antibiotics. Ridge was asked about the possibility of an undiscovered anthrax letter as well as cross-contaminated mail.

Question: Governor Ridge, Dr. Koplan from the CDC said late last week that it was his belief, given the pattern of exposure of anthrax, that there had to be another letter that had not been discovered yet, making its way through the postal system. I'd like your thoughts on that...

Ridge: With regard to the investigation surrounding the Brentwood Post Office and the one letter to Senator Daschle's office, the FBI has secured its own independent facility to run the mail that had been basically sequestered, after we discovered that they had—there was anthrax contained in one letter [the Daschle letter]. And they are in the process of investigating to determine whether or not there are additional letters...

Question: The issue of a second letter you've already spoken to. What is the latest theory as to the nature of these additional hot spots within the Brentwood facility, and how cross-contamination might have occurred? In other words, is other mail affected that's now being sterilized as a precaution? Or—and all going to the point of whether or not there's mail arriving at people's home, particularly in this city, that might somehow be tainted?

Ridge: The belief within the administration is that we need to isolate all the mail that was on the Hill to determine whether there was more than one letter, and that process is being done and that's part of the investigation the FBI is running... The commitment within the administration is to do as much environmental testing as we possibly can to determine whether or not there are other environmental indications of anthrax. And then we would proceed accordingly to determine the medical sufficiency in dealing with people who may have been exposed to it...

Question: Can I follow on one point? In other words, what I'm asking is almost mechanically, what would happen—in other words, if nobody within Daschle's office got the inhaled form of anthrax, is that because once it aerosolizes, your biggest hot spot is going to be within the processing center or where it's going through various equipment and so forth?

Ridge: It seems to me that the inhalation anthrax that took some lives of a couple postal workers came at a point where there was obviously maximum exposure. What caused it, whether or not it was spraying the strappers with—again, it's an investigation dealing with frankly, perhaps a universe of unknowns that we're trying to narrow down...

THE LAST TWO CASES AND THE LEAHY LETTER

On October 28, hospital supply worker Kathy Nguyen checked in at the emergency department of Lenox Hill Hospital in New York City and indicated that she had been suffering from weakness, heaviness in the chest, cough, chills, and other symptoms for the past three days. She was admitted to the hospital's intensive care unit and initially treated for congestive heart failure, pneumonia, as well as for the possibility of inhalational anthrax because, in the words of her doctors, "of the widespread publicity surrounding previous cutaneous anthrax cases in New York City and the alerts issued to the medical community by the New York City Department of Health." Her condition continued to deteriorate and on October 30, lab results confirmed she had inhalational anthrax. She died from that cause the next day, the fourth fatality of the 2001 anthrax attacks.[82]

Nguyen's infection was made public by New York City Mayor Giuliani on October 30, and because of her lack of ties to any of the previously confirmed or suspected cases of anthrax infection, concern was especially widespread.[83]

All subsequent tests for anthrax at her residence, workplace, and along her regular subway route to work were negative, as were tests of her regular contacts and coworkers. A cross-contaminated envelope has been proposed, but never confirmed, as the source of her infection.[84]

The twenty-second and final case of anthrax associated with the attacks of September and October of 2001 was that of Ottillie Lundgren from Oxford, Connecticut, who first went to her local hospital on November 16, with fever, fatigue, coughing, and shortness of breath that had begun two or three days before. She was ninety-four years old, and suffered from chronic obstructive pulmonary disease and hypertension. The initial diagnosis was viral syndrome and dehydration, and she was treated with intravenous hydration, with antibiotics added on the second day. On November 18, her condition began to significantly weaken and by November 19, analysis of her test results produced suspicion that she might have anthrax. By November 21, she was confirmed as suffering from inhalational anthrax. She died that same day.[85]

As with Kathy Nguyen, environmental samples of Lundgren's home and all other places she was known to have recently visited were negative. However, testing at the southern Connecticut postal center that processed her mail did discover anthrax spores on three of its high-speed mail sorters, and at least one of her neighbors was found to have received a letter contaminated with anthrax. Thus, as reported by her doctors, "These findings do not provide definitive evidence of the route of exposure . . . , but they are consistent with the hypothesis that the exposure to *B anthracis* may have resulted from receipt of mail that was cross-contaminated with spores."[86]

On the same day that Ottillie Lundgren went to her local hospital, the letter to Senator Patrick Leahy that had been postmarked back on October 9 at the Hamilton postal facility was finally discovered. Though the letter had arrived and been processed at the Brentwood facility at the same time as the Daschle letter, the zip code on the address had been incorrectly read as "20520" rather than as the correct zip code for the U.S. Senate, "20510." Therefore, the Leahy letter had been transported to the mail-processing facility for that zip code, the U.S. State Department's annex in Winchester, Virginia, where David Hose worked.

Apparently, at that point, the Leahy letter was then correctly rerouted to the U.S. Capitol complex, where it was caught in the October 17 FBI quarantine of unopened mail, and transferred to the General Services Administration (GSA) warehouse in Springfield, Virginia. That is where it was uncovered on November 16 by FBI and Environmental Protection Agency (EPA) agents in protective clothing, who were cutting a slit and performing quick swab tests for anthrax in each of the garbage bags sealed back in October.

The bag containing the Leahy letter recorded 20,000 anthrax spores in the test and was then opened for inspection of the envelopes within. Bearing the same handwriting, return address, and postmark as the Daschle letter, the suspect letter was quickly spotted, sealed (unopened), and forwarded to U.S. Army Medical Research Institute of Infectious Diseases (USAMRIID) for further testing.[87]

Based on the material that had leaked out of the envelope, it was quickly determined that the anthrax spores in the Leahy letter were similar to those in the Daschle letter, and this was confirmed when the Leahy envelope was finally opened and the anthrax inside tested on December 5, 2001.[88]

SUMMARY

Other than a March 2002 case of cutaneous anthrax contracted by a laboratory worker who was handling anthrax samples in connection with the investigations of the 2001 anthrax attacks, the Lundgren case was the last one arising from those attacks. Between October 2 and November 20, 2001, as shown in Table 1.1, twenty-two individuals were diagnosed with either confirmed or suspected anthrax infections, evenly split between the cutaneous and inhalational forms. Five of the eleven individuals with inhalational anthrax died, representing a mortality rate of 45 percent, whereas none of those with cutaneous anthrax did. Most of the victims were either mail handlers (twelve) or employees of media companies (six).[89]

The survival rate for inhalational anthrax was considerably higher than what had been anticipated based on prior experience, "perhaps due to rapid diagnosis, aggressive therapy with multidrug antibiotic regimens, and state-of-the-art general medical supportive care."[90]

On the other hand, prior knowledge of exposure risks was clearly inadequate, as reported by the National Anthrax Epidemiologic Investigation Team.

> Investigators did not anticipate the exposures and [inhalational] disease in those exposed to aerosols of B. *anthracis* spores from unopened envelopes along the path of the mail... Cutaneous and inhalational disease in postal workers in our investigation clearly shows that sealed, B. *anthracis*-positive,

TABLE 1.1

Summary of Confirmed and Suspected Cases of Anthrax from Bioterrorist Attack, Fall 2001.

Name	Occupation; location	Onset date	Diagnosis date	Type/status	Outcome
Johanna Huden	NY Post employee; NYC	09/22/01	10/19/01	Cutaneous/S	Survived
Erin O'Connor	NBC TV News assistant; NYC	09/25/01	10/12/01	Cutaneous/C	Survived
Richard Morgano	USPS machine mechanic; Hamilton, NJ	09/26/01	10/18/01	Cutaneous/S	Survived
Ernesto Blanco	AMI mailroom worker; Boca Raton, FL	09/28/01	10/15/01	Inhalational/C	Survived
Teresa Heller	USPS mail carrier; W. Trenton, NJ	09/28/01	10/18/01	Cutaneous/C	Survived
	NBC TV News intern; NYC	09/28/01	10/12/01	Cutaneous/S	Survived
(Infant)	Child of ABC News employee; NYC	09/29/01	10/15/01	Cutaneous/C	Survived
Robert Stevens	AMI photo editor; Boca Raton, FL	09/30/01	10/04/01	Inhalational/C	Died 10/05/01
Claire Fletcher	CBS TV News assistant; NYC	10/01/01	10/18/01	Cutaneous/C	Survived
Patrick O'Donnell	USPS mail processor; Hamilton, NJ	10/14/01	10/19/01	Cutaneous/C	Survived
Norma Wallace	USPS mail processor; Hamilton, NJ	10/14/01	10/28/01	Inhalational/C	Survived
Jyotsna Patel	USPS mail processor; Hamilton, NJ	10/15/01	10/29/01	Inhalational/C	Survived
Leroy Richmond	USPS mail worker; Brentwood, DC	10/16/01	10/21/01	Inhalational/C	Survived
Thomas Morris	USPS mail worker; Brentwood, DC	10/16/01	10/23/01	Inhalational/C	Died 10/21/01
Joseph Curseen	USPS mail worker; Brentwood, DC	10/16/01	10/26/01	Inhalational/C	Died 10/22/01
	USPS mail worker; Brentwood, DC	10/16/01	10/22/01	Inhalational/C	Survived
Linda Burch	Bookkeeper; Hamilton, NJ	10/17/01	10/29/01	Cutaneous/C	Survived
	NY Post mail handler; NYC	10/19/01	10/22/01	Cutaneous/S	Survived
David Hose	State Dep mail processor; Winchester, VA	10/22/01	10/25/01	Inhalational/C	Survived
	NY Post employee; NYC	10/23/01	10/28/01	Cutaneous/C	Survived
Kathy Nguyen	Hospital supply worker; NYC	10/25/01	10/30/01	Inhalational/C	Died 10/30/01
Ortrillie Lundgren	Retiree; Oxford, CT	11/14/01	11/21/01	Inhalational/C	Died 11/21/01

Notes:
Names, occupation locations, and dates of deaths obtained by matching data in Table 1 in "Demographic, Clinical, and Exposure Characteristics of 22 Cases of Bioterrorism-Related Anthrax, United States, 2001," in Jernigan, Raghunathan, et al., with other published accounts. NYC = New York City. For *Status,* S = suspect, C = confirmed. Diagnosis Date based on lab results.

Sources:
Daniel B. Jernigan, Pratima L. Raghunathan, et al., "Investigations of Bioterrorism-Related Anthrax, United States, 2001: Epidemiologic Findings," *Emerging Infectious Diseases,* Vol. 8, No. 10, October 2002, p. 1021, supplemented by Leonard A. Cole, *The Anthrax Letters: A Medical Detective Story* (Washington, DC: Joseph Henry Press, 2003), and Marilyn W. Thompson, *The Killer Strain: Anthrax and a Government Exposed* (New York: HarperCollins Publishers, 2003).

powder-containing envelopes can be a source of infection... The possibility of B. *anthracis* exposure from envelopes secondarily contaminated from implicated postal facilities greatly extended the group of potentially exposed persons in our investigation. Experience with anthrax related to agricultural or industrial sources indicated that direct exposure to animals, animal products, and wool-producing facilities accounted for most reported cases... From our investigation, B. *anthracis*-positive powder appears capable of contaminating other mail during processing, leading to exposure and subsequent development of cutaneous and possibly inhalational anthrax.[91]

In the words of Dr. Anthony Fauci, head of the National Institute of Allergy and Infectious Diseases, "In addition to the human toll of the anthrax attacks, the fear and disruption they engendered were extraordinary, as were the associated economic costs related to prophylactic antibiotic treatment, the law enforcement efforts, the clean-up of anthrax-contaminated buildings, and other activities... The anthrax attacks of 2001... have revealed significant gaps in our overall preparedness against bioterrorism, and have given a new sense of urgency to biodefense efforts. Clearly, there is a need to improve the ability to protect our citizens from potential bioterror threats, and to increase our capacity to deal with the medical and public health consequences of any future attacks."[92]

CHAPTER 2

Threats and Risks

The anthrax attacks awakened the nation to the threat of bioterrorism, whereas a sharp rise in the death rate from infectious diseases beginning around 1980[1] as well as periodic worries about pandemic outbreaks (such as the Swine Flu scare of 1976 and the Russian Flu scare of 1977[2]) reminded the public and policy makers of the continuing danger from naturally occurring diseases.

INFECTIOUS DISEASES

As far back as can be traced in the archaeological and historical records, infectious diseases have been major causes of death and illness among human populations.

Measles may have been the source of the "plague" that killed an estimated 25 percent of the population of Athens, Greece (including its leader Pericles) in 430–429 B.C. A smallpox epidemic in Rome between 165 and 180 A.D. is also thought to have led to the deaths of a quarter of that city's population.[3]

The most famous, and one of the most deadly, source of premodern pandemics was the bubonic plague (caused by the bacterium *Yersinia pestis*), which was responsible for two distinct disease cycles during the Middle Ages, the first of which resulted in the death of between 50 and 60 percent of Europe's population between 541 and 750 A.D., and the second (known to history as the Black Death) that produced approximately 25 million deaths in Europe in the six-year period from 1347–1352 A.D.[4]

European colonization of the western hemisphere during the fifteenth and sixteenth centuries carried with it "the introduction of smallpox, measles, and typhus to South American and Central American human populations, who had no natural resistance or immunity to these diseases, [and] led to appalling numbers of deaths." As one example, it has been estimated that the population of Mexico fell from 20 million in 1518 to 3 million in 1568, and to just 1.6 million only fifty years after that.[5]

The 1918–1919 Spanish Flu pandemic produced between 20 and 100 million fatalities globally, including at least 500,000 in the United States. According to the U.S. Department of Health and Human Services (HHS), "the severity of that virus has not been seen again."[6] Nutritional deprivation attributable to conditions during World War I and the return home of infected soldiers who fought in that conflict are thought to have contributed to the high mortality rate.[7]

In the United States, infectious diseases remained the leading cause of death until the early twentieth century, when, in the words of a 1988 report from the Institute of Medicine (IOM), "the identification of bacteria [as the cause of many infectious diseases][8] and the development of interventions such as immunization and water purification techniques provided a means of controlling the spread of disease and even of preventing disease."[9] In 1900, infectious diseases were the number one cause of fatalities in the United States, and accounted for almost a quarter of all deaths. By 1910 these illnesses had been supplanted by heart disease as the leading killer, and by 1933 they had dropped to third, behind both heart disease and cancer.[10] The downward trend in deaths from infectious diseases continued and reached an all-time low in 1980.[11]

By the latter part of the twentieth century, however, a number of factors led to a resurgence in the health threat from naturally occurring infectious diseases. According to the 2003 RAND report, "The Global Threat of New and Re-emerging Infectious Diseases," chief among these causes were globalization, certain contemporary medical practices, urbanization, environmental changes, and alterations in social and other behavioral patterns.

Globalization has been fueled by improvements in transportation technology and liberalization of the international economic system, resulting in faster and more extensive movement of people, goods, and services across national borders. Over 500 million airline passengers cross international boundaries every year, and international travel has been linked to the spread of malaria, typhoid fever, and tuberculosis, among other diseases. Global trade in food products has resulted in the transmission of illnesses such as Rift Valley Fever and West Nile virus.[12]

The second key factor in the increased threat from infections concerns contemporary medical practices, and in particular those that have contributed to the emergence of drug-resistant infectious agents. The very effectiveness of the antibiotic treatments developed over the past 100 years led to their overuse and misuse in both humans and livestock, and other agricultural products consumed by humans. That, in turn, produced "'pathogenic natural selection,' which is helping to generate ever more resilient, resistant, and powerful disease strains...that either offer resistance to several families of antibiotics at any one time or confer greater powers of infectivity and virulence." Examples include certain strains of *streptococcus* and *staphylococcus* infections, tuberculosis, malaria, cholera, and influenza.[13]

Other modern medical practices that have inadvertently contributed to the reemergence of infectious diseases in the late twentieth and early twenty-first centuries include invasive surgical and other treatment procedures that have exposed more people to hospital-acquired infections, the use of undetected contaminated blood in transfusions, and changes in medical research that seek to eradicate rather than control microbial diseases and that may "upset the delicate balance between microbes and their human hosts, and, in so doing, exacerbate overall individual vulnerability to pathogenic infections and mutations."[14]

A third factor is the increasing concentration of the world's population in large cities. This has especially occurred in less economically developed countries, whose urban populations rose from 18 percent of their total inhabitants in 1950 to 40 percent by 2000. Much of this growth has taken place on the fringe of major cities in so-called shantytowns that lack adequate housing, water and food supplies, sanitation, and medical services, and thus are particularly susceptible to infectious diseases.[15]

Environmental changes have also played a part in the renewed infectious disease threat. Higher rainfall in arid regions in Ethiopia, India, Madagascar, and Peru has been linked to malaria outbreaks there caused by sudden increases in mosquito populations. Other epidemics involving cholera, typhoid, and dengue fever have also been associated with changed weather patterns that have altered the distribution of insects and other disease carriers. Many of these environmental shifts have been the result of global warming, and with further projected temperature increases in coming years, millions more individuals in temperate regions could be exposed to insect-borne diseases heretofore largely confined to tropical areas.[16]

The final causative item cited in the RAND report was changes in social and behavioral patterns. Alterations in sexual behavior, for instance, played a major role in the rapid spread of the human immunodeficiency virus (HIV)/acquired immunodeficiency syndrome (AIDS), which has been particularly devastating in sub-Saharan Africa, a region that now accounts for approximately 70 percent of total AIDS cases and 75 percent of AIDS-related deaths. Increased intravenous drug use has also contributed to the spread of AIDS, especially in Asia.[17]

These and other developments led the U.S. National Intelligence Council to produce an analysis in January 2000 on "The Global Infectious Disease Threat and Its Implications for the United States," which indicated, "New and reemerging infectious disease will pose a rising global health threat and will complicate U.S. and global security over the next 20 years."

The following were among the report's key findings.

- Infectious diseases are a leading cause of death, accounting for a quarter to a third of the estimated 54 million deaths worldwide in 1998.
- Annual infectious disease-related death rates in the United States have recently doubled to some 170,000 annually after reaching an historic low in 1980.
- Twenty well-known diseases—including tuberculosis (TB), malaria, and cholera—have reemerged or spread geographically since 1973, often in more virulent and drug-resistant forms.
- At least thirty previously unknown disease agents have been identified since 1973, including HIV, Ebola, hepatitis C, and Nipah virus, for which no cures are known.
- The economic costs of infectious diseases—especially HIV/AIDS and malaria— are already significant and their increasingly heavy toll on productivity, prof- itability, and foreign investment will be reflected in growing gross domestic product (GDP) losses as well that could reduce GDP by as much as 20 percent or more by 2010 in some sub-Saharan countries, according to recent studies.[18]

It has been estimated that over 300,000 species of bacteria and more than 5,000 kinds of viruses potentially threaten human beings.[19] According to data compiled by the World Health Organization (WHO), the infectious diseases that caused the most deaths in 1998 were acute respiratory in- fections (especially pneumonia and influenza), which were responsible for 3.5 million deaths in that year; AIDS (2.3 million); diarrheal diseases, such as *e coli* and cholera (2.2 million); TB (over 1.5 million); malaria (1.1 million); measles (900,000); and hepatitis B and C (over 600,000). The National Intel- ligence Council's (NIC) 2000 estimate reported that, of these, TB, malaria, hepatitis, and especially HIV/AIDS were expected to continue to increase as threats, whereas the others (including influenza) "appear to have peaked at high incidence levels."[20]

In 2005, WHO revised its International Health Regulations, which "are an international legal instrument designed to achieve maximum security against the international spread of diseases." This effort singled out a few such illnesses for special attention by the creation of two categories of diseases that trigger different reporting responsibilities among WHO's member nations.

Four diseases comprise the first group, in which the occurrence of a single case "is unusual or unexpected and may have serious public health impact," and thus the national authorities where such a case occurs are mandated to report it to WHO. Those four diseases are smallpox, poliomyelitis due to "wild-type" poliovirus, human influenza caused by a new subtype, and severe acute respiratory syndrome (SARS).

The second WHO category includes diseases that "have demonstrated the ability to cause serious public health impact and to spread rapidly interna- tionally," but such impact is regarded as "not inevitable." The occurrence of a case in this category requires the relevant national authority to utilize a specified decision-making process "that permits evaluation of the risk of international spread." Reporting to WHO is to take place when an international risk is identified. Diseases placed in this grouping include cholera, pneumonic plague, yellow fever, viral hemorrhagic fevers (Ebola, Lassa, and Marburg), West Nile fever, and certain other diseases of regional or special concern (currently including dengue fever, Rift Valley fever, and meningococcal disease; see Table 2.1).

For all other diseases (including those caused by acts of bioterrorism) "that could spread internationally or might require a coordinated international response," the affected national health authorities are to utilize the same decision-making process as employed for diseases in the second category to determine whether or not they are required to report.[21]

BIOLOGICAL WEAPONS

Before the scientific breakthroughs in bacteriology in the late nineteenth century that led to the first true understanding of the nature and causes of many infectious diseases, not many well-documented cases of the intentional usage of bioweapons exist.

One of the few such instances occurred at the outset of the Black Death, in 1346–1347, when invading Mongol armies catapulted corpses contaminated with plague over the walls of Kaffa in the Crimea, leading to the city's surrender. In a similar tactic, in 1710 Russian troops sent the corpses of plague victims over the wall of the Swedish city of Reval during a war between those two nations. In 1767, a British general provided smallpox-contaminated blankets to Native Americans allied with the French, triggering an epidemic among those tribes and contributing to some British successes during the French and Indian (or Seven Years) War.[22]

The possibilities for biological weaponry began to be realized by the early twentieth century. During World War I German agents in Baltimore, Maryland employed anthrax and glanders to infect 3,000 livestock and feed exported to Allied forces in Europe, allegedly resulting in the infection of several hundred soldiers. Japan employed a biological weapons program during World War II, which resulted in the reported death of over 10,000 prisoners in experiments, poisoned the water supply of Soviet forces stationed at the former Mongolian border with intestinal typhoid bacteria, and dropped plague-infected rice and wheat over China.[23]

As is made clear by this short listing of the best-known cases of twentieth-century bioweapons use, as well as by the previously mentioned 1979 accidental release of anthrax spores from the Soviet biological weapons facility in Sverdlovsk, Russia, most of the pre-2001 threat from such weapons was believed to come from national bioweapons programs. An October 2000 RAND report listed twelve countries that the United States suspected of having a biological weapons capability as of that date: China, Egypt, India,

Iran, Iraq, Israel, Libya, North Korea, Pakistan, Russia, Syria, and Taiwan, with the Russian program (the successor to the extensive Soviet effort) being by far the most sophisticated.[24]

The Soviet Union's biological weapons program was established in 1928 and by the start of World War II had developed the capability to produce and disseminate biological weapons employing typhus, tularemia, and Q fever. As the program continued to grow in size and scope, by the end of the 1960s, it also had developed smallpox, Ebola fever, Lassa fever, and monkeypox as bioweapons.

Though the Soviets ratified the Biological Weapons Convention of 1972, which prohibited the development, production, and stockpiling of biological weapons, its bioweapons program continued clandestinely and eventually involved fifty-two facilities and over 50,000 researchers that were officially claimed to be a part of the legitimate biotechnology and pharmaceutical industry.

By the end of the 1980s the Soviet program had produced and stockpiled several hundred tons of weaponized plague, tularemia, glanders, anthrax, smallpox, and Venezuelan equine encephalomyelitis (VEE). Delivery systems included crop duster planes, bombers, cruise missiles, and intercontinental ballistic missiles or ICBMs.

In 1992, Russian President Boris Yeltsin announced that the Soviet offensive bioweapons program had ceased when the Soviet Union was dissolved and that its facilities and workers would be redirected toward peaceful purposes.

Though several accidental releases of Soviet-produced bioweapons occurred over the years (most notably the Sverdlovsk incident), there is no evidence that these weapons were ever intentionally used. Questions exist, however, about the security of the still-existing biological weapons stockpiles, the possible continuation of a scaled-back, clandestine Russian bioweapons program, and the whereabouts and employment of some of the Soviet-trained bioweapons researchers.[25]

The United States also operated a large biological weapons program, which was established early during World War II and continued until November 1969 when President Richard Nixon cancelled the program and declared the United States would destroy its entire inventory of biological munitions. The program operated a research facility at Fort Detrick, Maryland and two open-air testing facilities at Dugway Proving Ground, Utah and Horn Island, Mississippi. During the war, it developed large supplies of anthrax and virulent brucellosis strains that could be disseminated by bombs. Before its termination, the U.S. effort also produced tularemia, Q fever, VEE, and botulinum toxin bioweapons.

Like the Soviets, the United States never intentionally employed its biological weapons, but has retained a large and sophisticated biodefense program after the offensive program was closed. For example, the U.S. Army unit

TABLE 2.1
Major Potential Infectious Disease Threats

Disease (agent)	Description	Status
Smallpox (variola virus)	An acute, contagious disease marked by fever and a distinctive skin rash, which killed as many as 30 percent of those infected.	Declared eradicated in 1980 following worldwide vaccination program, but is considered a possible bioweapon.
Poliomyelitis (wild-type) (poliovirus)	A highly infectious disease that can produce permanent muscle weakness, paralysis, and other symptoms within a matter of hours.	Cases have declined by over 99 percent since 1988 (to 1,951 reported cases in 2005); global eradication may be achieved within next ten years.
Human influenza (new sub-type) (influenza virus)	A contagious respiratory illness that can cause mild to severe illness, and sometimes death marked by fever, cough, headache, and other symptoms.	Between 5 and 15 percent of world population gets the flu each year, with 250,000–500,000 fatalities. Concerns exist that avian flu strain H5N1 has potential to cause a pandemic.
Severe acute respiratory syndrome (SARS) (SARS-associated coronavirus)	A contagious respiratory illness that is sometimes fatal and begins with a high fever, sometimes followed by headache, body aches, and/or diarrhea.	First reported in Asia in February 2003, and spread to more than two dozen countries by the end of the year, causing over 8,000 infections and 774 deaths. Limited occurrences since then, with no fatalities to date in United States.
Cholera (bacterium *Vibrio cholera*)	An acute infection of the small intestine that is often mild but sometimes can be severe, characterized by diarrhea, vomiting, leg cramps, and if untreated, death.	Rare in industrialized nations for past 100 years, but reemerging in developing countries. Number of reported cases rose by 79 percent (compared to 2005) to 236,896 in 2006, with 6,311 fatalities.
Pneumonic plague (bacterium *Yersinia pestis*)	An acute, highly contagious infection of the lungs that produces fever, chills, cough, difficulty breathing, followed by rapid shock and death if untreated. Least common but most virulent form of plague (bubonic and septicemic are the other forms).	Plague is endemic in parts of Africa, the former Soviet Union, the Americas, and Asia. In 2003, there were a total of 2,718 reported cases of all forms of plague, with 182 deaths.

(*continued*)

TABLE 2.1
(Continued)

Disease (agent)	Description	Status
Ebola hemorrhagic fever (Ebola filovirus)	A severe hemorrhagic fever, which often results in headache, stomach pain, intense weakness, and sore throat, followed by vomiting, rash, diarrhea, and bleeding. Death rate is 50 to 90 percent of clinically ill cases.	First recognized in 1976 in central Africa, and has appeared sporadically since then. Approximately 1,850 cases, with over 1,200 deaths, have been documented to date.
Lassa fever (Lassa arenavirus)	An acute illness that produces mild or no symptoms in 80 percent of cases, but in the remaining cases produces severe multisystem disease.	Discovered in 1969 in Nigeria, and is now considered endemic in parts of west Africa. Some studies indicate that 300,000 to 500,000 cases occur each year in west Africa, resulting in 5,000 deaths.
Marburg hemorrhagic fever (Marburg filovirus)	A rare, severe, and highly fatal type of hemorrhagic fever that affects many organs, and is marked by severe headache and severe malaise.	First recognized in 1967 in Germany, but subsequently traced to parts of eastern and southern Africa. The two largest outbreaks to date were in the Democratic Republic of Congo from 1998–2000 (154 cases, 128 fatalities) and Angola from 2004 to the present (163 cases, 150 fatal as of 3/05).
West Nile Virus (West Nile flavivirus)	Potentially serious illness, which produces severe symptoms in approximately one out of every 150 infected persons that can include high fever, headache, disorientation, coma, and paralysis	Commonly found in Africa, Asia, the Middle East, and has probably been present in eastern United States since 1999, and is now regarded as permanently established as a seasonal epidemic in North America that flares in summer.

Sources:
1. World Health Organization, http://www.who.int/mediacentre/factsheets: Smallpox; Poliomyelitis (Fact sheet No. 114, revised September 2006); Influenza (Fact sheet No. 211, revised March 2003); Cholera (Fact sheet No. 107, revised September 2007); Plague (Fact sheet No. 267, revised February 2005); Ebola haemorrhagic fever (Fact sheet No. 103, provisional revision September 2007); Lassa fever (Fact sheet No. 179, revised April 2005); Marburg haemorrhagic fever (fact sheet, March 2005).
2. Centers for Disease Control and Prevention, "Fact Sheet: Basic Information about SARS," January 13, 2004.
3. Centers for Disease Control and Prevention, "Fact Sheet: WNV Fact Sheet," September 27, 2005.

responsible for developing biological weapons was renamed the U.S. Army Medical Research Institute of Infectious Diseases (USAMRIID) and assigned to develop vaccines and other countermeasures.[26]

Questions have been raised about possible weapons applications of a number of current U.S. nonlethal biological programs, particularly those involving genetically altered microbial agents. However, given that many of these initiatives are highly classified, it is difficult to evaluate such claims.[27]

At present, no national government admits to possessing an offensive biological weapons program and there is no evidence of any preparations for usage of such weapons by any government. As Professor Barry Kellman, Director of the International Weapons Control Center of DePaul University College of Law, has written,

> Of course, virtually any State with a reasonably sophisticated bioscience sector has the wherewithal to make bioweapons . . . but capability does not unequivocally lead to a [bioweapons] program . . . What purpose would such weapons achieve? Just because a weapon can be easily, safely, and cheaply built does not answer whether it is worthwhile to do so. This is especially true for bioweapons that are universally condemned. For a State (unlike a terrorist organization), an offensive bioweapons program could jeopardize its diplomatic status. It is unlikely that any State would make that decision lightly.[28]

Nonetheless, there are concerns that existing clandestine national bioweapons programs could pose a threat through unacknowledged covert use,[29] transfer (whether intentional or not) of bioweapons to terrorist organizations, and/or provision of the necessary training to individual scientists and technicians who could in turn pose individual threats (the latter being similar to one of the leading theories about the perpetrator of the anthrax attacks).[30]

The absence of state-sponsored use of bioweapons after World War II, the curtailment (if not full abandonment) of the large American and Soviet bioweapons efforts, and the rising concern about terrorism in the 1990s led to an increasing focus on the bioterrorist threat. A study of bioterrorist acts from 1900 to 1999 found a total of 180 incidents involving biological agents over that entire period, but only 27 of these were traceable to terrorist groups, 56 were linked to traditional criminal motives and over half (97) were undertaken for other or unknown purposes. However, the vast majority of these cases occurred between 1990 and 1999, with 153 of the total incidents and 19 of the terrorist acts occurring then. Additionally, of the 27 substantiated instances involving terrorism, 13 were simply hoaxes or threats, six involved an expression of interest in bioweapons, in three cases the terrorists actually acquired biological agents, and in only five did they actually acquire and use such weapons.[31]

Of the five terrorist uses of biological weapons during the twentieth century, only one produced casualties. It happened in September of 1984 in Oregon when the religious cult Rajneesh employed *Salmonella typhimurium* to contaminate restaurant salad bars. An estimated 751 individuals became ill with food poisoning, and approximately forty-five were hospitalized, though no fatalities resulted. The true cause of the illnesses was not known at that time, but was discovered a year later when some of the cult members disclosed the group's involvement and indicated that the goal had been to influence the outcome of a local election.[32]

Evaluating the threat in December of 1999, the Advisory Panel to Assess Domestic Response Capabilities for Terrorism Involving Weapons of Mass Destruction reported that

> The dangers posed specifically by chemical and biological weapons have become increasingly apparent. In part, this is a function of the demise of the Cold War preoccupation with the nuclear dimension of international relations. Perhaps more significant, however, is the possibility that, given the ongoing travails of the Russian economy, poorly paid, disgruntled former Soviet scientists might attempt to sell their expertise in chemical, biological and nuclear weapons on the "open market" to terrorists or rogue states. Finally, a precedent for mass destruction may have been set in the guise of the 1995 Aum [Shinrikyo] nerve gas attack. That incident . . . represented the first widely known attempt by a nonstate group to use a [chemical, biological, radiological, or nuclear] weapon with the specific intent of causing mass civilian casualties.[33]

In its 2004 report, the 9/11 Commission observed, "The greatest danger of another catastrophic attack in the United States will materialize if the world's most dangerous terrorists acquire the world's most dangerous weapons." It went on to note al-Qaeda's biological weapons program and the Central Intelligence Agency's (CIA) assessment that "more than two dozen other terrorist groups are pursuing [chemical, biological, radiological, and nuclear weapons] materials."[34]

Another federally mandated threat analysis—this one a March 2005 report by the Commission on the Intelligence Capabilities of the United States Regarding Weapons of Mass Destruction—observed that, although a number of nations as well as perhaps some terrorist groups have had access to biological weapons, no significant bioweapons attack has occurred since the anthrax incidents in late 2001. However, the report went on to warn that impediments that may have prevented such attacks were eroding.

> Some terrorist groups may have the financial resources to purchase scientific expertise. Even without sophisticated expertise, a crude delivery system would be sufficient to inflict mass disruption and economic damage. Moreover, extremists willing to die in a suicide bombing are not likely to be deterred by

the dangers of working with biological weapons. As a result, a senior intelligence official told the Commission that we should consider ourselves "lucky" we have not yet suffered a major biological attack. And the terrorist threat will only grow, as biological weapons are rapidly becoming cheaper, easier to produce, and more effective.[35]

As expressed in a 2004 WHO publication, "While . . . hundreds of pathogenic microorganisms have been investigated for their potential utility as military weapons, relatively few have been found capable of meeting military requirements . . . and fewer still have found their way into weapons and actually been used."[36]

In 1998 the Working Group on Civilian Biodefense, composed of leading American governmental and academic authorities on the subject, set out to "identify the pathogens that, if used as bioweapons against civilian populations, might cause illness and death on a large scale." Among the factors considered in this study of biological agents were lethality, person-to-person transmissibility, availability of effective vaccines and treatments, availability of the pathogen or toxin, feasibility of large-scale production of the pathogen or toxin, and capacity for aerosol delivery and infection. From this analysis, the Working Group selected anthrax, smallpox, plague, tularemia, botulinum toxin, and viral hemorrhagic fevers as the greatest threats. The U.S. Centers for Disease Control and Prevention (CDC) subsequently designated the same set of potential bioweapons, which it termed "class A agents," as the major dangers.[37]

The World Health Organization sought to cast a somewhat wider net in identifying potential biological threats because of the greater uncertainties about the calculations of non-state entities (such as terrorists) in choosing biological agents. The WHO criteria included:

- The Biological Weapons Convention (BWC) definitions of biological weapons.
- The list of biological agents that have been proposed for inclusion in efforts to implement the BWC.
- Publicly available information about which biological agents have been recently weaponized or stockpiled.
- Agents known to have been used as bioweapons.
- Other specific considerations about the intentions and capabilities of non-state entities with respect to biological weapons.[38]

Employing these considerations, the WHO analysis identified eleven infective biological agents as the "representative group" of the most threatening potential bioweapons.

1. Anthrax (*Bacillus anthracis*),
2. Brucellosis (*Brucella suis* and *Brucella melitensis*),
3. Glanders (*Burkholderia mallei*),

4. Melioidosis (*Burkholderia pseudomallei*),
5. Tularemia (*Francisella tularensis*),
6. Plague (*Yersinia pestis*),
7. Q Fever (*Coxiella burnetii*),
8. Epidemic typhus (*Rickettsia prowazekii*),
9. Coccidioidomycosis (*Coccidioides immitis* and *Coccidioides posadasii*),
10. Venezuelan equine encephalitis (VEE), and
11. Smallpox (*variola* virus).[39]

In addition, WHO identified several toxins (poisonous substances) produced by biological organisms that have been weaponized in the past, including *staphylococcus aureus* enterotoxin, *clostridium botulinum* neurotoxin (which was also designated as a Class A agent by CDC), aflatoxins, trichothecenes, saxitoxin, and ricin (see Table 2.2).[40]

Risk

The ongoing threat to global health from infectious disease outbreaks is undeniable. Every year such illnesses account for a quarter or more of all deaths worldwide, and for over 40 percent of the international "disease burden," which factors in disabilities as well as deaths. In the United States, the rising death rates from infectious diseases cause approximately 170,000 annual fatalities.[41]

The dangers from the more unpredictable pandemics and acts of bioterrorism are far more difficult to quantify.

As the 2005 WHO Global Influenza Preparedness Plan indicates, "It is impossible to anticipate when the next pandemic might occur or how severe its consequences." It went on to note, however, that "on average three pandemics per century have been documented since the 16th century, occurring at intervals of 10–50 years," including the three outbreaks during the twentieth century (1918, 1957, and 1968).[42] The same organization's World Health Report for 2007 cited expert estimates that the next influenza pandemic could cause illness in around 25 percent of the world's population, which would amount to over 1.5 billion victims, and result in severe harm not only to public health, but to economic and political security, and social stability as well.[43]

In a 2004 emergency planning exercise involving various mass-casualty scenarios, Department of Homeland Security (DHS) officials calculated that the greatest impact would occur from pandemic influenza, rather than from a nuclear or biological weapon, with deaths in the United States alone ranging from 87,000 (if 15 percent of the population gets infected) to 207,000 (35 percent infection rate), and with economic damage amounting to between $71 billion and $166 billion.[44]

On an even more dire note, CDC's December 2006 Influenza Pandemic Operation Plan reported, "Based on current models of disease transmission,

TABLE 2.2
Major Potential Biological Weapons Threats

Disease (agent)	Lethality	Transmission	Designation
Anthrax (bacterium *Bacillus anthracis*).	*If untreated*, Cutaneous: 5–20% Inhalational: over 90% Gastrointestinal: highly variable.	Only cutaneous form is contagious via human-to-human transmission. Most infections result from contact with infected animals or animal products.	BWC, CDC, WHO
Botulinum Toxin (from bacterium *Clostridium botulinum*).	6% *if treated*, nearly 100% *if untreated*.	Not contagious via human-to-human transmission, but extremely poisonous if ingested or inhaled.	CDC, WHO
Brucellosis (bacteria *Brucella suis* and *Brucella melitensis*).	*If untreated, B. suis*: 2% or less *B. melitensis*: somewhat higher.	Not readily contagious via human-to-human transmission. Likely to be infectious via contact with diseased animals.	BWC, WHO
Coccidioidomycosis (fungi *Coccidioides immitis* and *Coccidioides posadasii*).	Rarely fatal, except in cases of extrapulmonary dissemination (1% of all infections), which has mortality rate of 50–100%.	Not contagious via human-to-human transmission. Infection caused by inhalation of airborne fungi.	WHO
Ebola Hemorrhagic Fever (Ebola filovirus).	50–90%.	Moderately contagious via direct human-to-human transmission. Also may be spread via handling of infected primates.	CDC
Glanders (bacterium *Burkholderia mallei*).	50% *if treated*.	Not readily contagious via human-to-human transmission. Likely to be infectious via aerosol exposure to infected animals.	BWC, WHO
Marburg Hemorrhagic Fever (Marburg filovirus).	25–100%.	Moderately contagious via human-to-human transmission, requiring extremely close contact with infected person.	CDC

(Continued)

TABLE 2.2
(Continued)

Disease (agent)	Lethality	Transmission	Designation
Melioidosis (bacterium *Burkholderia pseudomallei*).	Over 90% *if untreated*, 10–80% *if treated*.	Not readily contagious via human-to-human transmission. Most infections via contact with contaminated soil and water.	BWC, WHO
Plague (bacterium *Yersinia pestis*).	*If untreated*, Bubonic: 60% Pneumonic: nearly 100% Septicemic: 30–75%.	Pneumonic form highly contagious among humans. Bubonic form spread mainly by flea bites transmitting bacteria from infected rodents.	BWC, CDC, WHO
Q Fever (bacterium *Coxiella burnetii*).	Less than 1%.	Not readily contagious via human-to-human transmission. Infection usually occurs via inhalation of materials from infected livestock.	BWC, WHO
Smallpox (*Variola* virus).	*Variola minor*: less than 1% *Variola major*: 20–40%.	Moderately high contagion via human-to-human transmission of saliva droplets or nasal secretions from infected persons.	CDC, WHO
Tularemia (bacterium *Francisella tularensis*)	*If untreated*, Ulceroglandular: 5% Pleuropulmonary: up to 40–60%.	Not contagious via human-to-human transmission. Highly infectious via insect bites and contact with infected animals or contaminated food or water.	BWC, CDC, WHO
Epidemic Typhus (bacterium *Rickettsia prowazekii*).	*If untreated*: 10–40%.	Not contagious via direct human-to-human transmission. Infection occurs via contact with lice or fleas that have bitten infected humans.	BWC, WHO

TABLE 2.2
(Continued)

Disease (agent)	Lethality	Transmission	Designation
Venezuelan Equine Encephalitis (*VEE* virus)	Less than 1%.	Not contagious via human-to-human transmission. Infection occurs via bite of infected mosquitos.	BWC, WHO

Notes: BWC = UN compilation of declarations of information by BWC state parties (1992); CDC = CDC Class A Agents (2000); WHO = WHO representative biological and toxin agents (2004).
Sources: World Health Organization, *Public Health Response to Biological and Chemical Weapons: WHO Guidance* (Geneva: WHO, 2004), pp. 214–274; and Barry Kellman, *Bioviolence: Preventing Biological Terror and Crime* (New York: Cambridge University Press, 2007), pp. 22–23.

a new pandemic could result in the deaths of 200,000 to two million residents," and pointed to a Congressional Budget Office estimate "that an influenza pandemic on the scale of the 1918 outbreak could result in a loss of five percent of gross domestic output, or a loss of national income of about $600 billion." However, just as WHO acknowledged the large uncertainties involved in gauging the probable severity of the next pandemic, the CDC plan noted, "Historically, the number of deaths during an influenza pandemic has varied greatly... Accurate predictions of mortality cannot be made before the pandemic influenza virus emerges and begins to spread."[45]

Uncertainties surrounding the bioterrorism threat are even greater. In the words of national security analyst Anthony Cordesman,

> There is no valid way to quantify actuarially the risk posed by biological terrorism. There is far too little history of successful attacks to estimate their future frequency and lethality. There is equally little meaningful history of the level of technical competence demonstrated in planning and executing past attempts and even less historical information on why so many threats and low-level attempts have failed or produced bioweapons with little or no lethality.[46]

The Commission on the Intelligence Capabilities of the United States Regarding Weapons of Mass Destruction highlighted the "intelligence gap" with respect to bioterrorism.

> The Intelligence Community has struggled to understand the biological weapons threat. According to a senior official in CIA's Counterproliferation Division, "We don't know more about biological weapons than we did five

years ago, and five years from now we will know even less." Assessments of state and non-state [biological weapons] programs rely heavily on assumptions about potential biological weapons agents, biological weapons-adaptable delivery systems, and fragmentary threat reporting. Unsurprisingly, this leads to faulty assessments.

The Commission went on to cite the 2002 Intelligence Community's "highly confident" estimate that Iraq had an active bioweapons program and its evaluation that al-Qaeda's biological weapons efforts were somewhat limited in scope, which proved to be inaccurate or misleading.[47]

Such limitations, combined with the proliferation of *potential* perpetrators (especially among non-state groups and properly trained and supplied individuals) and the sure but uncertain pace of advances in biotechnology, have yielded a wide variety of views as to the extent of the bioterrorism threat.

For example, a 2004 CIA report to Congress stated, "The threat of terrorists using chemical, biological, radiological, and nuclear (CBRN) materials remained high [during the last half of 2003]. Many of the 33 designated foreign terrorist organizations and other non-state actors worldwide have expressed an interest in using CBRN; however, most attacks probably will be small-scale, incorporating improvised delivery means and easily produced or obtained chemicals, toxins, or radiological substances."[48]

March 2007 testimony by bioweapons expert Dr. Tara O'Toole is representative of the view that bioterrorism already constitutes a serious threat to United States and international security.

A covert bioterror attack on U.S. citizens or, even worse, a campaign of such attacks, is within the capability of terrorist groups today and could potentially cause tens of thousands of casualties and immense social and economic disruption. The scope and seriousness of the bioterror threat has been emphasized and verified by multiple U.S. government agencies and analyses . . . It is important to recognize that the technical barriers to building bioweapons that faced the superpowers in the 1970's have been overtaken by the rapid advancements in bioscience. There are today no significant technical barriers to terrorists seeking to conduct large-scale bioattacks.[49]

A different perspective on the current state of affairs was offered by Milton Leitenberg, another authority in the field, who wrote in December 2005 that

"Bioterrorism" may or may not develop into a serious concern in the future, but it is *not* "one of the most pressing problems that we have on the planet today." The production and distribution of a dry powder anthrax product in the United States in 2001 is the most significant event [in demonstrating non-state/terrorist biological weapons capabilities]. However, understanding to what degree that competence is relevant to "traditional" terrorist groups is impossible until the perpetrator(s) of the anthrax events are identified... The steps taken by the al Qaeda group in efforts to develop a BW [biological weapons] program were more advanced than the United States understood prior to its occupation of Afghanistan in November–December 2001. Nevertheless, publicly available information, including the somewhat ambiguous details that appeared in the March 31, 2005 report of the Commission on Intelligence Capabilities, indicates that the group failed to obtain and to work with pathogens. Should additional information become available regarding the extent to which the al Qaeda BW effort had progressed, that assessment might have to be changed... For the past decade, the risk and immanence of the use of biological agents by non-state actors/terrorist organizations—"bioterrorism"—has been systematically and deliberately exaggerated.[50]

As federal policy makers focused increased attention and resources on countering terrorism (including bioterrorism) during the late 1990s, and especially after 2001, there were growing concerns about the basis of its priority-setting efforts. Cordesman has observed, "Bioterrorism is only one of many threats, and no nation can afford to implement every useful program to deal with even one such threat. Moreover, when costs approach the levels they have in the United States, the question has to be asked about whether counterterrorism programs justify their costs relative to a host of other public policy needs."[51]

In these circumstances, a number of independent organizations, including GAO and the 9/11 Commission, called for the federal government's homeland security programs to employ a risk management approach: "a systematic process to analyze threats, vulnerabilities, and the criticality of assets to better support linking resources with prioritized efforts for results."[52] Though progress in implementing this approach has been somewhat problematic in other sectors,[53] the uncertainties and divergent assessments with respect to bioterrorism have presented particular challenges in this regard.

A November 2004 paper prepared for the U.N.-chartered Weapons of Mass Destruction Commission observed "that inadequate threat assessment leads to sub-optimal policy decisions," and continued,

> In the absence of a structured threat assessment, most of the current discourse surrounding bioterrorism focuses almost solely on the harm potential of biological weapons. Less quantifiable aspects such as the strength of the terrorist's motivation to use such weapons and the psychological vulnerability of various societies to bioterrorism are just as important. Perhaps even more consequential than the de-emphasis of the non-physical effects of bioterrorism is the tendency to infer intention from capability, and vice versa. While these factors certainly influence one another, they also must be considered separately.[54]

Under Homeland Security Presidential Directive 10 (HSPD-10), "Biodefense for the 21st Century," issued on April 28, 2004, the DHS was required to conduct a risk assessment of the biological weapons threat in coordination with other federal agencies. The department contracted with Batelle to produce a computer-based system for assessing the relative risk of terrorist use of twenty-eight pathogens in terms of illness, death, and direct economic costs. The first DHS Bioterrorism Risk Assessment was finished on January 31, 2006, with supporting documentation published nine months later.[55]

As described by the National Research Council (NRC) committee tasked by DHS with analyzing and recommending improvements in its methodology, the Bioterrorism Risk Assessment includes the following features:

- Employs probabilistic risk assessment (PRA), "which is particularly well adapted for low-frequency, high-potential-consequence events for which there is no database sufficient to assess risk using statistical analysis of historical data."
- Utilizes scenarios, and for each provides an estimate of the probability of occurrence, consequences, and risk.
- Breaks down each scenario into as many as seventeen separate events, including those related to the terrorist group's motivations, goals, methods of operation, and ability to acquire, produce, and transport the biological agent, as well as others concerning the attack itself and the subsequent response.
- Calculates a range of consequences (in terms of illnesses, fatalities, and economic losses) for each scenario, based on the properties of the pathogen, the scenario details, and the hypothesized U.S. response to the attack.[56]

Beyond the specific components of risk assessment, perhaps even more fundamental issues about addressing threats and risks were raised in a report by the British Nuffield Trust Global Programme on Health, Foreign Policy and Security. The study observed, "there has been a change in the *perception* of risk. We have moved to a risk perception society where what is important is not whether the number or nature of risks have increased in their seriousness, but that people *believe* that this is so and act accordingly. This clearly has important implications both in the manner in which health issues might be deemed as risks, and how such risks might be mitigated [*emphasis in the original*]."[57]

The British report contrasted the manner in which public health authorities ascertain risk ("an objective, measurable phenomenon with a distinct methodology for assessment involving 'risk factors' and empirical evidence") with the public's perceptions of risk, which are influenced primarily by such factors as geographic distance, novelty, and personal control over exposure to the source of the threat. The key role of communication was emphasized.

Mass communication can heighten levels of anxiety or it can provide reassurance; authorities can use it, but can rarely control it; and there is a difficult balance to be struck over the amount of information to release, particularly early on in an emergency, when saying too much may lead to an overreaction and appear panicky, while too little can appear complacent or conspiratorial...The demand for information about risks is such that when none is provided through official channels, then it will be filled from elsewhere. Doing or saying nothing has therefore become a dangerous strategy for those in authority, even when there is nothing to say.[58]

The challenge of gauging the right governmental response is especially acute with respect to unlikely but high impact events, in which category both bioterrorism and pandemics would fall. As one expert noted, "They [the public] delegate the problem of low-probability, high consequence risks to their government."[59] The Nuffield Trust analysis concluded that in these cases, "the demand for government action is likely to be high. Actions taken may reassure anxious publics, possibly despite limited epidemiological effectiveness. Inaction is not advisable."[60]

CHAPTER 3

The Pre-9/01 Public Health System

The public health system is the portion of the health care sector that is concerned with the prevention of disease within whole populations.[1] And given that a goal of bioterrorism is to inflict mass casualties, it is thus the key component of the medical defenses against the terrorist threat.

HISTORY OF THE U.S. PUBLIC HEALTH SYSTEM

Public health efforts in the United States date back to the colonial era, and a number of local health boards and the federal Marine Hospital Service (which provided health services to seamen) were established at the end of the eighteenth century. Throughout the nineteenth century, there was a growing organization of public health activities at the local, regional, and state levels, and by 1900, forty states had established health departments.[2]

During this period, public health measures such as sanitation and quarantines were more effective than the available medical treatments in dealing with the communicable diseases (including tuberculosis, influenza, and pneumonia) that were the major causes of death and disability.[3]

As in many other areas, the federal role in public health care evolved considerably over the course of the twentieth century. In 1902, the Marine Hospital Service was renamed as the Public Health and Marine Hospital Service in recognition of its growing responsibilities in quarantines. The agency's designation was again altered in 1912 when it became the U.S. Public Health Service (PHS) and received additional responsibilities for investigating disease outbreaks, providing health information to the public, giving medical examinations to arriving immigrants, assisting in local disease control, and conducting health research.[4]

Along with the changing federal organizational structure, Congress began to provide federal financial assistance to state and local health departments through grants aimed at combating specific diseases or aiding particular population groups. These "categorical" grants started during World War I with assistance to states for treatment of U.S. military personnel with sexually transmitted diseases. This was followed over the next thirty years by targeted grant programs for maternal and child health, disabled children, tuberculosis, mental health, industrial hygiene, and dental health. A 2004 analysis of the public health system and bioterror defense highlighted the consequences of this approach.

> The emergence of federally funded state public health programs in the early 20th century contributed little to the development of a coherent public health system nationally. Rather, because of political forces and special interests, distinct and multiple funding streams had a fragmenting effect on state and local public agencies, facilitating the creation of isolated and insular programs and organizational "silos." Funneling money into silos became the dominant solution to a given public health problem instead of supporting an entire public health system capable of responding to new threats. In public health, therefore, it became an axiom that the initiatives that get done are those that get funding, the initiatives that get funding are those that have political backing, and the initiatives that have political backing fall into narrowly focused silos.[5]

World War II witnessed the creation of the Office of Malaria Control in War Areas as a federal agency tasked with limiting the impact of malaria and similar diseases that could hamper the war effort. In 1946, this office was renamed as the Communicable Disease Center (CDC) and placed within the U.S. Public Health Service, but located in Atlanta, GA rather than Washington, DC because malaria (which was still to be the agency's primary focus) was most prevalent in the southeastern United States.[6] Further name changes followed, first to the Center for Disease Control in 1970, and then to the Centers for Disease Control and Prevention in 1992, reflecting its ever-expanding role in national public health care.[7]

Over the course of the last century the role of public health itself was considerably altered. Vastly improved medical treatments for individual patients (including vaccinations, antitoxins, and antibiotics) assumed the major role in responding to infectious diseases, which in turn diminished as leading sources of serious illness. The public health system increasingly focused on measures, such as immunizations, that were targeted at individuals as a means of disease prevention for entire communities. In addition, public health agencies came to see themselves as the health-care provider of last resort for such groups as low-income individuals and rural residents that lacked access to private health-care providers, and began to offer services like prenatal care and disease screenings. Finally, with chronic diseases, such as heart disease, cancer, and diabetes, supplanting infectious diseases as the nation's chief health concern, the public health system directed an increasing portion of its efforts toward prevention of the behavioral factors (such as smoking) associated with these maladies.[8]

A December 1999 CDC publication prophetically declared, "Public health is a complex partnership among federal agencies, state and local governments, nongovernment[al] organizations, academia, and community members. In the twenty-first century, the success of the U.S. public health system will depend on its ability to change to meet new threats to the public's health."[9]

PUBLIC HEALTH SYSTEM AS OF SEPTEMBER 2001

The "essential services" of public health were identified in a 1995 report by the Public Health Services Steering Committee established by the Department of Health and Human Services (HHS).

- Monitoring health status to identify community health problems
- Diagnosing and investigating community health problems and health hazards
- Informing and educating people about health needs
- Mobilizing community partnerships to identify and solve health problems
- Developing policies and plans that support individual and community health efforts
- Enforcing laws and regulations to protect health and ensure safety
- Establishing linkages between personal health services and those needing such services but who otherwise would lack access to them
- Assuring the competence of the public health system and its workforce
- Evaluating the effectiveness, accessibility and quality of both personal and population-based health services
- Conducting research to develop new insights and solutions to health problems.[10]

Most of the legal authority to carry out public health activities is vested in state governments, which exercise it in a wide variety of ways, including enforcing sanitary and safety codes, conducting health inspections, mandating health professionals to provide reports to health authorities on certain diseases, imposing quarantines, and licensing health care workers and facilities.[11]

At the state level, a number of different organizational approaches have been adopted for public health, often involving several state agencies. Freestanding health agencies have been established in thirty-five states, while in the others this function is administered as part of a larger agency that has wider responsibilities. Furthermore, certain key public health activities, including environmental health and emergency medical services, are separated organizationally from the primary state health agency in many states.[12]

There is also considerable variation in the degree to which state governments delegate public health responsibilities to local authorities. Eleven states have adopted a *centralized* approach, under which state agencies maintain extensive control over local health authorities, another seventeen have opted for a *decentralized* method that allows much of the control to be exercised at the local level, and the other twenty-two states employ a *hybrid* system in which responsibility is shared between state and local governments.[13]

The same diversity of approach found among the states exists to an even greater degree at the local level. According to a 2000 survey by the National Association of County and City Health Officials (NACCHO), there were then 2,912 local health departments across the United States, 60 percent of which were county based, with the rest divided between township (15 percent), city (10 percent), multicounty (8 percent), and consolidated city–county organization (7 percent).

The NACCHO survey similarly revealed considerable variety in the kinds of services offered by local public health agencies. While most of these were involved in epidemiology and disease surveillance (84 percent) and communicable disease control (94 percent), far fewer had responsibilities for laboratory services (45 percent), or emergency medical response (61 percent).[14]

Regardless of the kind of state and local organizational arrangements, the initial response to any type of public health emergency was viewed as primarily a local responsibility in which individuals exposed to a disease would seek out local health providers, such as their own physician or doctors in hospital emergency rooms. These providers would be expected to discern and then report to their local or state health departments on any illness patterns or other clues that might indicate an unusual disease outbreak.

Those state and local health departments were to collect and monitor such reports and other relevant data for evidence of an outbreak, and then to direct the collection of environmental and clinical samples for laboratory testing for disease identification and determination of individual exposures. At that point, state or local epidemiologists—who were responsible for analyzing the distribution of disease in populations and the factors that influence such distribution—were to determine whether an outbreak had occurred. If so, the relevant state and/or local health authorities were to communicate the necessary information to health-care providers, other government agencies, and the general public, and to take appropriate action to treat affected individuals and prevent the spread of the disease.

State and local health departments could request federal assistance, typically provided by CDC in such areas as laboratory testing, epidemiological investigation, and treatment advice.[15]

By 2001 the federal government had come to play a significant role in public health, through such instruments as the previously discussed categorical grant programs, tax incentives (such as the deduction for employer health care costs) and excise taxes (like the cigarette tax), control of the entry into the country of persons and goods, and the enactment of laws and enforcement of regulations concerning public health policy. The major policy areas where the federal government has played a significant role in recent years include financing, public health protection, collection and dissemination of information on health and healthcare delivery systems, capacity building, and direct management of certain services.[16]

Health and Human Services served as the federal lead for public health matters. Within HHS, the chief public health role was played by CDC, which was responsible for working with state, local, and international health authorities in detection, investigation, and prevention of disease and injury. In carrying out these assignments, CDC provided training programs, technical assistance, advanced laboratory services, research, standards development, and financial assistance. One of the most important of the latter was the state and local preparedness grant program created in 1999 to help boost the capacity of these public health systems.[17]

In 2000, HHS released "Healthy People 2010," which set forth ten-year objectives for improving both individual and public health care ("healthy people in healthy communities") and was subsequently "endorsed as national policy at the highest levels of government and by most states, many localities, and a large coalition of business and non-profit organizations."[18] The plan called for improvements in the public health system's organizational effectiveness and accountability, data and information systems, workforce training, and prevention research efforts.[19]

Among other HHS components with significant public health roles were the Health Resources and Services Administration (HRSA), which was charged with improving public health systems and enhancing workforce development (including by providing training in emergency medicine and trauma treatment), and the Food and Drug Administration (FDA), which worked to ensure the safety and efficacy of drugs, vaccines, and medical devices. The National Institutes of Health (NIH) conducted and supported biomedical research, including for the detection, prevention, and treatment of biological, chemical, or radiological threats, whether natural or manmade. The Agency for Healthcare Research and Quality (AHRQ) sponsored and performed research related to health care quality, including for the clinical preparedness of health-care providers.[20]

When the Bush administration and its new Health and Human Services Secretary Tommy Thompson took over in 2001, HHS headquarters sought to exert more control over its component agencies, especially in the areas of legislative activities, planning, budget, and communications.[21]

Outside HHS, other federal departments with sizeable pre-September 2001 public health-related duties included

- Federal Emergency Management Agency (FEMA), which coordinated federal assistance in major disasters;

- Environmental Protection Agency (EPA), which responded to incidents involving chemicals or other hazardous materials;
- U.S. Department of Agriculture (USDA), which dealt with public health emergencies involving food safety or plant, or animal disease;
- Department of Veterans Affairs (VA), which operated one of the nation's largest health care systems and purchased drugs for the National Pharmaceutical Stockpile and for National Medical Response Teams;
- Department of Defense (DOD), which provided research, training, and civil support in cases of public health emergencies; and
- Department of Justice (DOJ), which sponsored research, training, and grants for such emergency responders as police, fire, and rescue personnel.[22]

Attempts to determine the composition and total amount of spending on public health activities have been complicated by the definitional challenges in separating "individual" from "population-based" health services, the complex intergovernmental relationships involved, and differences in accounting procedures. This led to large variations in estimates concerning pre-2001 public health spending in the United States, with an HHS report calculating that in 1999, $41.1 billion was spent on all governmental, population-based health services, only 11 percent of which was contributed by the federal government (the rest coming from state and local sources). On the other hand, a different analysis (based on a more detailed examination of 1996 spending by two state and two local public health systems) put the national total of population-based health expenditures at just $17.1 billion, with Washington supplying 29 percent. That same survey indicated that less than one-third of this public health spending actually went for population-based services, with the remainder used for providing personal health care.[23] A more comprehensive look at total national health care spending (including federal, state, and local expenditures, private health insurance, and patient fees) found that, in 2000, just over 3 percent of the total of $1.35 trillion was used for public health purposes.[24]

PRE-9/01 INFECTIOUS DISEASE CONTROL INITIATIVES

The foregoing description of the evolution of the U.S. public health system makes clear that concerns about infectious diseases played a major part in that evolution, particularly through the middle of the twentieth century.

Several American port cities plus the colony of Massachusetts had instituted measures to quarantine and isolate individuals suffering from such illnesses as smallpox by the early 1700's, and by the end of that century many municipalities in the newly established United States had created organizations to enforce these measures and hospitals to provide care for the ill.[25]

During the period between the end of the Civil War and 1900, forty states and a number of localities had established health departments, some of which instituted such communicable disease control activities as immediate case reporting, investigation of health complaints and disinfection of home and work environments.[26] In 1878 Congress enacted legislation authorizing the collection of data on quarantines of cholera, smallpox, plague, and yellow fever patients.[27]

Local and state health departments began, in the 1890's, to establish laboratories in order to make use of newly discovered information about the role of bacteria in causing diseases. The results were impressive, as recounted in a 1988 Institute of Medicine report.

> Rapid advances in scientific knowledge about causes and prevention of numerous diseases brought about tremendous changes in public health. Many major contagious diseases were brought under control through science applied to public health.[28]

By the beginning of the twentieth century every state had a law requiring that local health authorities be notified about the occurrence of specified infectious diseases, such as cholera, smallpox, and tuberculosis.[29]

In this period and in the years immediately following, state and local public health agencies expanded significantly, including in the production and dispensing of antitoxins, the establishment of disease registries, the provision of immunizations, the establishment of clinics and the development of public education programs.

With the advent of the Public Health Service in 1912, the federal role also began to grow. In 1930, the National Hygienic Laboratory (which had been established in 1887) was renamed as the National Institute of Health, and in 1937 its role was expanded to include research on all diseases. The federal effort with respect to infectious diseases was given particular focus by the creation of CDC during World War II.[30]

At the international level, the World Health Organization (WHO) undertook to develop an effective global framework to prevent the transnational spread of disease by developing International Health Regulations (IHR) in 1969 to promote the monitoring, reporting and control of cholera, plague, yellow fever and smallpox (the last of which was removed in 1981 after the successful global campaign to eradicate it). The regulations were designed "to ensure the maximum security against the international spread of diseases with a minimum interference with world traffic" and "to encourage epidemiological activities at the national level so there is little risk of outside infection establishing itself."[31]

The success against smallpox marked the culmination of a long period of dramatic advances in reducing the threat of infectious diseases. For example, in the United States, infectious respiratory diseases (including influenza, pneumonia and tuberculosis) were the leading cause of death in 1900, but except during the Spanish flu pandemic of 1918–1920, the death

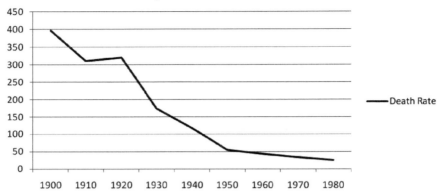

Figure 3.1 Death Rate from Influenza, Pneumonia, and Tuberculosis in United States, 1900–1980 (per 100,000 Population). *Sources:* U.S. Public Health Service, *Vital Statistics of the United States, Annual, Vol. I and Vol. II;* and U.S. National Center for Health Services, *Vital Statistics of the United States, Annual.*

rate from these sources steadily declined over the next eighty years as shown in Figure 3.1.

The situation was summarized in a 1995 report.

> Modern scientific advances, including antibiotic drugs, vaccines against childhood diseases, and improved technology for sanitation, had facilitated the control or prevention of many infectious diseases, particularly in industrialized nations.

However, the report continued,

> As it turned out, our understandable euphoria was premature. It did not take into account the extraordinary resilience of infectious microbes, which have a remarkable ability to evolve, adapt, and develop resistance to drugs in an unpredictable and dynamic fashion. It also did not take into account the accelerating spread of human populations into tropical forests and overcrowded mega-cities where people are exposed to a variety of emerging infectious agents.[32]

The Centers for Disease Control and Prevention responded to the threat of "emerging infectious diseases" (defined by the agency as those infectious diseases "whose incidence in humans has either increased within the past two decades or threatens to increase in the near future") by developing a strategic plan in 1994 that focused on surveillance, research, and prevention activities.

Citing newly identified infections (such as HIV/AIDS, Legionnaire's disease, and hepatitis C), increases in the incidence of certain other diseases (including tuberculosis) presumed to have been under control, and a series of Institute of Medicine reports documenting deficiencies in the public health system, the CDC blueprint concluded, "The public health infrastructure is insufficiently prepared to confront today's emerging disease problems." To address the situation, the CDC plan identified four goals "for revitalizing the ability to identify, contain, and most importantly, prevent illness" from such diseases.

1. Enhance and expand local, state, national, and international disease surveillance programs to "detect, promptly investigate, and monitor emerging pathogens, the diseases they cause, and the factors influencing their emergence."
2. Integrate laboratory science and epidemiology by focusing on applied research, such as evaluating the cost-effectiveness of infectious disease control strategies and developing improved laboratory detection techniques.
3. Improve communication about emerging diseases and ensure prompt implementation of prevention strategies, including through creation of an "accessible and comprehensive infectious disease database."
4. Strengthen public health infrastructure at all levels, particularly with respect to personnel, and facilities and equipment.

It was, however, noted that "implementation will be based on public health priorities and resource availability."[33]

A few months after the CDC plan was unveiled, President Clinton's National Science and Technology Council convened a federal interagency working group under the auspices of its Committee on International Science, Engineering and Technology Policy (CISET), which was to address "the global threat of emerging and re-emerging infectious diseases." The working group's report, "Global Microbial Threats in the 1990s," issued in September 1995, stated

> To address the growing threat of emerging infectious diseases the U.S. Government must not only improve its public health infrastructure, but also work in concert with other nations and international bodies, particularly WHO. The work and cost of protecting the world's people from infectious diseases must be shared by all nations.

The report took note of a project recently endorsed by President Clinton and the other leaders of the Group of Seven (G7) nations[34] called "Toward a Global Health Network," which was designed to "help public health institutions in their fight against infectious diseases and major health hazards." It went on to make nineteen recommendations to "improve worldwide disease surveillance, reporting and response," and "strengthen the U.S. capacity to combat emerging infectious diseases." Among these proposals were the following:

- Establishing regional disease surveillance and response networks linking national health ministries, WHO regional offices, U.S. government laboratories and field stations abroad, foreign laboratories and medical centers, and WHO Collaborating Centers.
- Developing a global alert system whereby national governments can inform appropriate worldwide health authorities of outbreaks of infectious diseases in a timely manner, and whereby individual health authorities can access regional centers.
- Preserving existing U.S. government activities that enhance other countries' abilities to prevent and control emerging and reemerging health threats.
- Rebuilding the U.S. infectious disease surveillance public health infrastructure at the local, state, and federal levels.
- Providing accurate and timely health information to private citizens and health-providers, both in the United States and abroad, when a disease outbreak occurs.[35]

A Presidential Decision Directive (PDD) was issued in June 1996 based on the interagency working group's recommendations. Taking particular heed of the fact that, even excluding HIV/AIDS, the death rate in the United States from infectious diseases had risen 22 percent between 1980 and 1992, the PDD sought to implement and build upon the group's proposals by directing U.S. government agencies to work with other countries and international organizations to create a global infectious disease surveillance and response system, and to strengthen federal research, countermeasures, and public information efforts with respect to these diseases. More specifically, it gave CDC responsibility for coordinating federal activities to strengthen surveillance and response capabilities at all levels, and designated NIH as the lead for the research components. The Directive also clarified CDC's mandate to make explicit the agency's authorization to conduct surveillance and response activities, including abroad, and committed the United States to support a strengthening of the existing International Health Regulations and other WHO efforts to control infectious disease.[36]

In 1997, a new avian strain of influenza was detected, which had never before infected humans and resulted in fatalities in Hong Kong. This raised fears of a possible influenza pandemic that could rival the impact of the 1918 pandemic that killed 20 million individuals. Those concerns, combined with other recent trends in microbial resistance to antibiotics, health care delivery and technological advances, plus ongoing funding challenges—as of fiscal year (FY) 1997, CDC estimated that only about one-third of its 1994 infectious disease plan had been implemented due to funding constraints—led CDC to revise its 1994 strategic plan.

The resulting "Preventing Emerging Infectious Diseases: A Strategy for the 21st Century," was made public on September 11, 1998. The 1994 plan's goals and objectives were reorganized, expanded, and focused more specifically on concrete actions that would be necessary to implement the plan. The objectives this time were grouped under the categories of surveillance and response, applied research, infrastructure and training, and prevention and control.

To facilitate implementation, the 1998 strategy identified its "anticipated outcomes," including

- A nationwide network for surveillance and response will ensure the prompt identification of emerging infectious diseases. State and local health departments will have the equipment and trained personnel needed to provide the frontline public health response to infectious disease threats.
- Countries in all regions of the world will participate in a global system for surveillance and response that includes surveillance for infectious agents that are resistant to antimicrobial drugs.
- Enhancement of the public health infrastructure will help prepare the United States to respond to bioterror incidents.
- The next generation of epidemiologists and laboratorians will be trained and prepared to respond to emerging infectious disease threats.[37]

A 2002 analysis by the RAND Corporation concluded that, "despite these initiatives . . . the public health infrastructure across the United States remains variable and in many cases inadequate."[38]

PRE-9/01 BIOTERROR DEFENSE INITIATIVES

American concerns about bioterrorism, and attempts to prepare for it, long predated the September 2001 anthrax attacks.

International efforts to prevent the use of both biological and chemical weapons date back at least as far as the early seventeenth century. Heightened concerns after the extensive use of chemical weapons during World War I culminated in the "Protocol for the prohibition of the use of asphyxiating, poisonous or other gases and of bacteriological methods of warfare," usually referred to as the Geneva Protocol of 1925. The United States was an original signatory of the treaty, which went into effect in 1928.[39]

Though the Geneva Protocol was considered an important statement of an international consensus against the wartime use of biological and chemical weapons, it did not address the issue of their possession. In addition, many of the signatories reserved the right to use such weapons in retaliation against their first use by an adversary, or against countries that had not signed the treaty.[40]

The treaty's limitations were recognized from the start, and negotiations to prohibit the production and stockpiling of biological and chemical weapons began in earnest in the 1930s. As progress proved difficult in the years that followed, some governments (led by Great Britain, subsequently joined by the United States) indicated that one of the most serious obstacles in the negotiations was the continued linkage between chemical weapons—which had actually been used in war and were even then still in the defense arsenals of many nations—and biological weapons—much less prevalent and thus felt to present a much less "intractable" problem. This position ultimately prevailed and, following a delinkage of the two sets of weapons, and the 1969 unilateral renunciation of biological and toxin weapons by the United States, the "Convention on the prohibition of the development, production and stockpiling of bacteriological (biological) and toxin weapons and on their destruction," also known as the Biological Weapons Convention (BWC), was completed in 1972. The treaty was ratified by the U.S. Senate in December 1974 and entered into force in 1975.

Under the BWC, signatories agreed to "never in any circumstances" develop, produce, stockpile, or acquire biological agents or toxins "that have no justification for prophylactic, protective, or other peaceful purposes," as well as weapons and means of delivery involving such substances. This approach was taken so as to not interfere with biomedical and other non-hostile uses of microbial or other biological agents and toxins, on the one hand, while allowing the Convention to cover any such substances that in the future might be developed as weapons. Another key provision required all signatories to destroy, or convert to peaceful uses, all covered biological agents and toxins, weapons, and means of delivery within nine months. The U.S. government certified that it was in full compliance with the BWC as of December 1975. While regarded as an improvement over the Geneva Protocol with respect to biological weapons, concerns about verification of compliance with its provisions have yet to be successfully addressed.[41]

In an attempt to improve verification, an ad hoc group was formed in the mid-1990s. A draft, 210-page document was presented at the group's July 2001 meeting, and contained language under which suspect countries would have to submit to international inspections of relevant facilities to assure the international community they were not in violation of the Convention. However, the representative of the United States led the opposition to the proposal because of the Bush administration's views that cheating would still not be adequately detected, that U.S. biodefense efforts might be harmed, and that U.S. companies' proprietary data could be compromised. These objections blocked further progress on verification efforts.[42]

Domestically, during the Cold War the CDC's attention to the potential threat of biological weapons had a substantial impact on the agency's evolution.

[Alexander Langmuir, CDC's chief epidemiologist from 1949–1970] brilliantly exploited an earlier generation's fear of biological warfare to revitalize the CDC in the postwar period, design a system of disease reporting, and create the Epidemic Intelligence Service (EIS), a practical training program for young epidemiologists. The EIS in turn served as educational preparation for many national and international public health leaders who would spread the Langmuir philosophy of surveillance and disease control.[43]

However, it was not until the 1990s that the federal government directed sustained attention to the issue of bioterrorism.

Concerns about Iraq's possible use of anthrax or botulinum toxin against American forces during the 1991 Persian Gulf War led the United States to vaccinate approximately 150,000 servicemen and women deployed in the region against both diseases. (Renewed worries about Iraq's bioweapons program caused the Defense Department to expand the anthrax immunization to cover all U.S. service personnel in 1998.)[44]

In 1992, the Federal Response Plan was drafted in order to specify how the federal government was to respond once the President declares an emergency requiring federal disaster assistance. A terrorism-specific annex was added in 1997, and a further update was made in 1999. The Plan was to serve as the single source for an all-hazards approach[45] to domestic disasters, including terrorism, and it designated primary and supporting federal agencies for each emergency support function. The Health and Medical Services Annex named HHS as the lead agency in coordinating the federal response to public health and medical care needs following a major emergency or disaster.

The year 1995 was a pivotal one with respect to the U.S. government's perceptions about the potential of biological attack. That year, Saddam Hussein's son-in-law Hussein Kamel Hassan, who had been in charge of Iraq's biological, chemical, and nuclear weapons programs, defected, leading to claims of a larger Iraqi biological weapons effort than had been previously admitted. In addition, disclosures by defectors from the old Soviet biological weapons program revealed more details about its size and scope. Finally, members of the Aum Shinrikyo cult killed twelve and caused the hospitalization of 5,000 when they released sarin gas into the Tokyo subway system. Though the agent in this case was a chemical one, it was felt the attack suggested a means and a target that could be utilized by biological weapons as well.[46]

Partly in response to such concerns as well as to the Oklahoma City bombing,[47] Presidential Decision Directive 39 (PDD-39) was issued by President Clinton in 1995, outlining how the federal government was to respond to terrorism incidents within the United States that involved the use of Weapons of Mass Destruction (WMD). Under this document, the Federal Bureau of Investigation (FBI) was designated as the lead agency for crisis management in such cases, whereas FEMA was given the lead for consequence management.[48]

In reaction to the Presidential directive, CDC, joined by the FBI and the Association of Public Health Laboratories, established the Laboratory

Response Network (LRN). This network of federal, state, and local facilities, was to provide for the collection, transport, and testing of suspect substances, the development of a surge capacity in emergencies, and the training of lab personnel in identifying key biological and chemical agents.[49]

The Department of Health and Human Services presented its internal plan for managing the public health response to chemical and biological terrorism in July 1996. The Centers for Disease Control and Prevention was tasked with identifying biological agents and conducting the epidemiological investigations, whereas FDA was to provide pharmaceutical support and the National Disaster Medical System (NDMS)[50] was to coordinate mortuary services, transportation, supplies, pathology, and public affairs functions. By 2001, the HHS plan had been elaborated into a strategy centering on five basic components.

- Tightened controls on shipment of biological agents to prevent or deter bioterrorism;
- Upgraded state and local disease surveillance capabilities;
- Improved public health and medical responses to bioterrorism;
- An expanded national pharmaceutical stockpile; and
- Increased research on vaccines and rapid screens for toxic agents.[51]

As part of the development of the HHS plan, the department's Office of Emergency Preparedness took on significant responsibilities. In addition to housing the NDMS, this office provided assistance to cities for the development of action plans and the creation of Metropolitan Medical Response System (MMRS) teams for responding in the immediate aftermath of acts of chemical or biological terrorism. A prototype team was deployed in Atlanta during the July 1996 Summer Olympics. As of 2000, seventy-two of these entities had been created, with an ultimate goal of 120 teams. In 1997, four National Medical Response Teams were established to provide assistance to areas not covered by the metropolitan teams.[52]

Two pieces of significant bioterrorism legislation were adopted by the Congress in 1996. The Antiterrorism and Effective Death Penalty Act (PL 104-132) required HHS to create a program to identify and list specific infectious agents that could be used in biological weapons, and to register facilities (primarily laboratories) involved in shipping such materials. The Centers for Disease Control and Prevention was made responsible for this "select agent" program.[53]

The Defense Against Weapons of Mass Destruction Act (Title XIV of the National Defense Authorization Act for Fiscal Year 1997, PL 104-201) authorized $97 million for domestic emergency assistance programs. In addition, the act authorized the DOD to form military rapid response teams, which were to provide support to the lead federal agency (as designated by the Federal Response Plan) in cases of domestic terrorism (including bioterrorism), and to provide training on how to deal with such terrorist acts to first responders in the 120 largest U.S. cities. (It was estimated that, as of 2001, 38,500 emergency responders and medical personnel had received some degree of training as a result of these provisions.) Lastly, it called for periodic exercises to test and improve the responses of government agencies at all levels to emergencies involving biological or chemical weapons.[54]

In spite of such initiatives, some of those involved at that time in the U.S. effort to prepare against bioweapons were not fully satisfied. For example, Dr. Donald A. Henderson, who had worked at the CDC, the World Health Organization (WHO), and as deputy assistant secretary for health in HHS during the Clinton administration, commented, "It became apparent to me that the responses were being crafted by police and chemical and military people. It was all focused on 'bang' or on gas release. There was very little attention being paid to biological [weapons]."[55]

Growing concern about the terrorist threat caused President Clinton to issue another Presidential Decision Directive on terrorism (PDD-62) in 1998. This guidance sought to further organize and clarify the roles and responsibilities of federal agencies involved in terrorism preparedness and response. Of particular relevance to the efforts against bioterrorism, PDD-62 directed that the necessary training and equipment be provided to state and local responders, and that stockpiles of vaccines and specialized medicines be created to address the threat.[56] This latter requirement led to the 1999 establishment of the Strategic National Stockpile (originally called the National Pharmaceutical Stockpile), which was to ensure that sufficient amounts of antibiotics, antidotes, antitoxins, and other medical and surgical supplies were available to respond to an act of bioterrorism or other mass-casualty event.[57]

PDD-62 also provided for the establishment of federal rapid response teams to assist local agencies in dealing with acts of biological or chemical terrorism. However, it offered no guidance as to which federal agencies were to be involved, with "predictable repercussions: virtually every agency had license to enter the hottest game in town."[58]

Congress moved more specifically to address the issue of bioterrorism as well as newly emerging infectious diseases by passing the Public Health Threats and Emergencies Act (Title I of the Public Health Improvement Act of 2000, PL 106-505). This 2000 law included provisions to reauthorize and expand a number of CDC programs to enhance the capacity of the public health system, including CDC's own facilities, its state and local government preparedness grants, the Laboratory Response Network, and the grants to states for epidemiology and laboratory capacity.[59] In addition, it required the General Accounting Office[60] (GAO) to provide Congress with a detailed description of federal programs concerning the public health and medical consequences of a bioterrorist attack.[61]

A plan for training public health and medical professionals in bioterrorism preparedness and response was established by CDC in November 2000. By October 2001, approximately 12,000 health professionals had completed the program.[62]

In January 2001, the U.S. Government Interagency Domestic Terrorism Concept of Operations Plan (CONPLAN) was ratified as a follow-up to the Federal Response Plan's Terrorism Incident Annex. It was developed primarily through discussions involving DOD, the Department of Energy, HHS, DOJ, EPA, and FEMA and was meant to provide more detail as to the responsibilities of the primary and supporting federal agencies designated by the Federal Response Plan for the various categories of emergency support. At the time of the September 2001 anthrax attacks, HHS was developing a bioterrorism annex to CONPLAN that was to address specific issues about the appropriate response to bioterrorist attacks.[63]

By the late 1990s, a number of exercises were being sponsored by the federal government and others to improve the readiness of the U.S. government and its partners to respond to bioterrorism. As previously noted, the FY 1997 Defense Authorization bill contained language authorizing such activities. By 2001, approximately 240 of these "tabletop" exercises had taken place. For example, the DOJ reported that in FY 2001, it facilitated fifty-two training exercises on bioterrorism for state and local public health, fire, law enforcement, and emergency personnel. The DOJ programs were one-day simulations of a bioterrorism incident addressing medical surveillance, epidemiological investigation, quarantine management, remediation, and mass-fatality management.[64]

Among the largest of the federally sponsored training exercises was the Top Officials 2000 (TOPOFF 2000) exercise in May 2000. A part of this[65] was a simulated release of a biological agent in Denver, Colorado, and involved state, local, and private sector representatives as well as officials from HHS, DOD, FEMA, the FBI, and EPA.[66]

But perhaps the most notable pre-September 2001 tabletop exercise on bioterrorism preparedness was the "Dark Winter" simulation, conducted on June 22–23, 2001 by the Johns Hopkins Center for Civilian Biodefense Strategies in collaboration with the Center for Strategic and International Studies (CSIS), the Analytic Services Institute for Homeland Security (ANSER), and the Oklahoma National Memorial Institute for the Prevention of Terrorism.

Dark Winter simulated a bioterrorist attack employing smallpox against shopping malls in three American cities (Atlanta, Oklahoma City, and Philadelphia) and covered a two-week period, broken down into three separate segments. Twelve individuals were chosen to play the part of senior government officials (for example, former U.S. Senator Sam Nunn played the role of President of the United States), and five members of the news media participated in a mock press conference during the simulation. According to its designers, "Dark Winter was constructed to examine the challenges that senior-level policy makers would face if confronted with a bioterrorist attack that initiated outbreaks of highly contagious disease."[67]

ASSESSMENTS OF PUBLIC HEALTH SECURITY BEFORE SEPTEMBER 2001

For many years prior to the events of September 2001, worries had been expressed about the condition of the American public health system. For example, during the 1950s there were sharp declines in enrollments in schools of public health and a number of experts offered pessimistic forecasts about the field's future.[68] However, it was not until 1988 that a comprehensive assessment was undertaken by the Institute of Medicine (IOM) of the National Academies of Science because of "a growing perception among the [Institute's] membership and others concerned with the health of the public that this nation has lost sight of its public health goals and has allowed the system of public health activities to fall into disarray."[69]

The IOM report highlighted the lack of consensus on the proper mission of the public health system, and the resulting widespread variability in the "mix and intensity" of public health services and in the training and expertise of the public health workforce around the country.[70]

Coinciding worries about newly emerging, naturally occurring diseases (such as Ebola virus and West Nile virus) and potential acts of bioterrorism led to a series of governmental and private analyses of the U.S. public health system in 2000 and 2001. Almost without exception, these assessments found serious shortcomings in that system in general, and in its bioterrorism preparedness programs in particular. For instance, a March 2001 CDC report concluded that, in spite of some improvements, "the U.S. public health infrastructure . . . is still structurally weak in nearly every area."[71] The following are some of the most significant flaws noted in the various reports.

Fragmentation of Effort

Coordination between the various public health and bioterrorism response programs was seriously complicated by the multiplicity of federal, state, and local entities involved, resulting in duplication, lack of unity of effort, and diminished accountability. Furthermore, efforts to overcome this fragmentation varied widely across agencies and jurisdictions, and were virtually nonexistent in certain states and localities. The result was an overall system for both infectious disease control and bioterror defense that lacked clearly defined leadership, sufficient coordination mechanisms, and adequate internal communication capabilities.[72]

A September 2001 GAO report on federal bioterrorism activities found "different agencies have developed separate threat lists of biological agents, several agencies have not been included in bioterrorism-related policy and response planning, and agencies have developed programs to provide assistance to state and local governments that are similar and potentially duplicative." In addition, it noted that attempts to coordinate these efforts "are not always clear and sometimes overlap, leading to a fragmented approach."[73]

Fragmentation was further evident in the existence of fifty to sixty different infectious disease surveillance systems across the country. A 2000 workshop organized by the Institute of Medicine to assess the capabilities of the public health system to deal with emerging infections observed that such multiplicity "is not necessarily desirable, and, in fact, can be detrimental when it concerns disease surveillance. The need to integrate national, state, and local public health systems, including those from the private sector, is one of the most daunting challenges confronting epidemiological investigations and laboratory surveillance. An unexpected disease outbreak or act of bioterrorism . . . stress an already fragmented public health system."[74]

Another key factor inhibiting effective coordination was the categorical aid programs, which, for example, were a principal funding source for the many disease-monitoring systems across the United States, producing "disease-specific" surveillance and "resulting in disjointed programs and unsustainable systems."[75]

And even though in the 1990s Congress began to fund efforts to broadly upgrade public health infrastructure, at least in part because of concerns that categorical assistance programs tended to "limit flexibility and elasticity within the public health system, resulting in suboptimal performance when resources are redeployed in response to an emergency," the categorical programs continued to be the dominant form of federal funding for public health.[76]

The coordination problems between federal, state, and local authorities were accompanied by similar difficulties within states. In some cases, there was "a serious tension at the [state–local] interface, with poor working relationships between local and state officials." Such problems were "sometimes most prominent between states and large municipalities that have fairly well-developed public health and emergency response infrastructures and that are accustomed to working with little support from state resources."[77]

Inadequate Staffing and Training of Workforce

Insufficient staffing and staff training was observed at all levels and among all sectors of the public health community. GAO documented a number of indicators pointing to particular shortages of nurses, nurse aids,[78] and laboratory personnel.[79] The 2000 IOM workshop found, "Local public health departments . . . are often plagued with a high rate of staff turnover, poor pay, intermittent calls for individuals with unique skills, and inadequate financial support, thus making maintenance and continuity of skills difficult and training essential."[80]

In spite of the urgency of training, the 2001 CDC status report indicated less than half of the total public health workforce had "formal, academic training in public health and those with graduate public health degrees were an even smaller fraction." It went on to observe, "The statistics highlight the gap between the increasing demands placed on the highly dedicated and motivated public health workforce and the increasing complexity of disease patterns, interventions, and partnerships and the technology, tools, and training necessary to meet these escalating demands." The result, in the words of CDC, was a situation in which "Our public health physicians and nurses are untrained in new threats like West Nile Virus and weaponized microorganisms."[81]

Similarly, a 1998 survey of emergency medicine physicians found that over 70 percent rated their own ability to recognize the clinical signs of bioterrorism as inadequate.[82] More generally, the 2000 IOM workshop indicated, "Many physicians often are not sure when or whether to report suspicious cases of infection, are unaware of the need to collect and forward clinical specimens for laboratory analysis, and may not be educated regarding the criteria used to launch a public health investigation."[83]

The potential consequences of such shortcomings were highlighted by one of the major lessons learned from the June 2001 Dark Winter exercise.

After a bioterrorist attack, leaders' decisions would depend on data and expertise from the medical and public health sectors. In Dark Winter, even after the smallpox attack was recognized, decision makers were confronted with many uncertainties and wanted information that was not readily available.[84]

Outdated Information Systems

In a series of 1999 assessments, CDC determined that less than half of local health departments had continuous, high-speed access to the Internet, just 45 percent of these agencies had "fax" capability, and only one-third of them could be reliably contacted by e-mail.[85] Another report in 2000 observed that many states still employed paper-based disease reporting systems. That same document noted "Too often . . . communications systems at the state and local levels are outdated, situational, and low budget. Few assessments of their sufficiencies have been conducted, and no standards or guidance for the development of such standards exist."[86]

The 2000 Stimson Center report on chemical and biological terrorism found "Despite universal recognition among rescuers and health care providers that communications problems are chronic in every sizable emergency, communications is one of the most neglected areas of emergency response."[87] The Centers for Disease Control and Prevention concluded, "These gaps in the basic information infrastructure are troubling because not only do they prevent public health agencies from communicating with each other in a timely manner, but they also hinder communication between public health staff, private clinicians, or other sources of information about emergency health problems."[88]

Insufficient Capacity for Mass-Casualty Events

Numerous reports in the 1999–2001 period documented a host of problems concerning the capability of the U.S. health system to cope with large numbers of casualties, whether from naturally occurring diseases or an act of terrorism.

- Hospitals and other primary care facilities lacked sufficient bed space, staff expertise, and communication capability to adequately respond to mass-casualty occurrences.[89] Indeed, the patient load produced by a "regular" influenza season in the late 1990s was enough to overtax the system.[90]
- Local officials expressed concerns that federal efforts to augment local capacity via the supply of emergency teams, resources, and medical supplies would not be timely or effective.[91]
- Almost two-thirds (64.5 percent) of the emergency medical physicians polled in the previously cited 1998 survey indicated that their ability to manage mass-casualty events was inadequate.[92]
- A 1999 IOM report cited shortcomings in pre-event planning and communications, decontamination procedures, mass-casualty triage, and countermeasure availability.[93]

The May 2000 TOPOFF exercise, which involved a simulated release of a bioweapon in Denver, Colorado, produced a situation in "which health care officials quickly found their medical facilities sinking under the patient load" and determined they would have needed an immediate, large-scale infusion of additional health care personnel to cope with the disaster.[94]

Deteriorating Disease Surveillance and Laboratory Capability

The overall disease surveillance system had been in decline since the 1950s, and reductions in public health laboratory personnel and training during the 1990s had significantly hindered the ability of health authorities to identify disease agents. In addition to the personnel cutbacks, the surveillance system suffered from considerable variations in state and local reporting requirements that, as of 2000, in some states allowed health-care providers to wait for up to ten days before reporting a communicable disease to state public health authorities. And the shortcomings in communication capabilities discussed above obviously impaired the speed and effectiveness of the disease surveillance system.[95]

More specifically, GAO reported to Congress in 1999 that "surveillance of and testing for important emerging infectious diseases are not comprehensive in all states" and "both [state] laboratory directors and epidemiologists were frustrated by the lack of integrated systems within CDC and the lack of integrated systems linking them with other public and private surveillance partners."[96]

The summary for the 2000 IOM workshop on emerging infections reported that a number of states did not have a state epidemiologist and "the responsibility of daily disease surveillance is often sporadic and inadequate." With regard to laboratory services, it noted a lack of standardized data elements that "can impair the ability of the private sector to report back to the state epidemiology officer and challenges the reporting systems of the state health laboratory." Furthermore, it found the categorical grant programs that provided much of the funding for laboratory services did not allow some states to monitor disease trends.[97]

Other lab-related concerns centered on safety and security issues. Standards on best practices and contamination procedures had long existed in order to reduce the possibility of accidental release of pathogens, and in 1999 CDC issued guidelines that sought to address the security of laboratory facilities against intentional attempts to remove dangerous biological agents. However, there was general consensus that these measures were not fully adequate, and further steps would be required, including improved monitoring of labs and lab personnel, and expanded tracking of biological agent transfers between laboratories.[98]

Unready Vaccines and Other Countermeasures

A number of long-term factors had combined, by the turn of the twenty-first century, to limit the U.S. capacity for vaccine production. The rapid declines in the incidence of infectious disease among most segments of the population had made Americans less disposed to subject themselves (or their children) to the risk, albeit slight, of adverse reactions from vaccines, thus reducing the "market" for these medicines. In addition, the overall funding constraints in public health programs meant that many states cut back on their support for vaccination programs. Increasing concentration in the pharmaceutical industry reduced the potential sources of supply, and the long lead times (ten to fifteen years) and high research and development costs ($300 million to $500 million) typical of vaccine development further limited the nation's vaccine production capacity.[99]

Certain specific developments in the period immediately prior to 2001 also hampered the readiness of vaccines and other countermeasures for infectious diseases, including those caused by acts of bioterrorism.

Prior to 2001, as part of cost cutting, many hospitals had switched to "just-in-time" stocking of medicines (including vaccines) and retained sufficient supplies for only two to three days of regular patient loads. Thus, they were increasingly reliant for "surge capacity" on the national pharmaceutical stockpile managed by CDC. However, a large portion of that stockpile consisted of antibiotics rather than vaccines because of limited supplies and other problems with the latter. For example, the anthrax vaccine existed in limited quantities, had to be administered as a series of shots over an eighteen-month period to be fully effective, and was found to be potentially ineffective against certain strains of anthrax. Furthermore, the only firm that was making the vaccine ceased production in December 1999 because of financial difficulties.[100]

And, though CDC committed to delivering supplies from the national stockpile to the affected locality within twelve hours of a request, local officials expressed concern about the time and resources that would be required in order for them to adequately prepare and distribute these supplies during an emergency.[101]

Another of the key findings from the Dark Winter simulation was "the lack of sufficient vaccine or drugs to prevent the spread of disease severely limited management options . . . Smallpox vaccine shortages significantly affected the response available to contain the epidemic, as well as the ability of American political leaders to offer reassurance to the American people."[102]

Antiquated and Conflicting Legal Authorities

Primary legal authority for public health matters rests with state governments, though a federal role has long been recognized as well. For example, the ability to impose and enforce quarantines is generally regarded as an exercise of a state's police powers, but under the power granted to the federal government by the Constitution's commerce clause, the Public Health Service Act authorizes the Secretary of HHS to take action "to prevent the introduction, transmission, or spread of communicable diseases from foreign countries into the states or possessions [of the United States], or from one state or possession into any other state or possession." The covered communicable diseases are defined by Executive Order of the President.[103]

A 1999 analysis of "infectious disease law" in the United States found that such statutes were often overlapping, contradictory, and not in keeping with either contemporary best medical practices or Constitutional safeguards for individual rights. Few states were deemed to have created "a uniform legal basis" for disease control.[104] Moreover, substantial uncertainties existed with respect to federal versus state authority in this area, as highlighted by Dark Winter:

Federal and state priorities may be unclear, differ, or conflict; authorities may be uncertain and constitutional issues may arise. In Dark Winter, tensions rapidly developed between state and federal authorities in several contexts. State leaders wanted control of decisions regarding the imposition of disease-containment measures (e.g., mandatory vs. voluntary isolation and vaccination), the closure of state borders to all traffic and transportation, and when or whether to close airports. Federal officials argued that such issues were best decided on a national basis to ensure consistency and to give the President maximum control of military and public-safety assets.[105]

Insufficient Funding

The evolution of American health care in the twentieth century, in which personal medical care gained in effectiveness, attention, and resources, was accompanied by chronic underfunding of the public health sector,[106] which played a significant role in the various deficiencies in the pre-9/01 U.S. public health system.

By 1960, total national spending for governmental public health activities[107] totaled $417 million, which represented just 1.5 percent of all health care expenditures in the United States. Over the next forty years, the resources devoted to public health slowly increased in terms of both overall amount and as a percentage of total health care spending (see Table 3.1). This was accomplished primarily as a result of relatively large increases at the state and local levels beginning around 1980, with federal public health expenditures representing the same share (0.4 percent) of total health spending in 2000 as in 1960.[108]

According to most pre-2001 analyses of the U.S. public health system, though, the modest, largely state and local-driven increases in public health spending did little to remedy the long-standing shortcomings in the national system.

In requesting the CDC status report on the U.S. public health infrastructure, the U.S. Senate Appropriations Committee observed in September 1999 that "There continues to be insufficient capital funding by private and public sources of hospitals, laboratories, clinics, information networks, and other necessary elements to the provision of public health services."[109] A number of independent studies found that the U.S. public health system had "worsened significantly" over the last quarter of the twentieth century because of "fiscal neglect."[110]

Uncertain Performance

Though the foregoing makes clear that a number of analyses of the public health system were performed prior to September 2001, there was little in the way of comprehensive assessment or performance measurement.[111] One

TABLE 3.1
U.S. Public Health Expenditures, 1960–2000 (in $ millions)

Expenditure Source	1960	1970	1980	1990	2000
Total national health expenditures	27,534	74,895	253,916	714,019	1,353,593
Federal public health expenditures	102	594	1,235	2,258	5,071
As percent of total national health expenditures	0.4	0.8	0.5	0.3	0.4
State/local public health expenditures	315	799	5,199	17,701	38,318
As percent of total national health expenditures	1.1	1.1	2.0	2.5	2.8

Source: Centers for Medicare & Medicaid Services, Office of the Actuary, National Health Statistics Group, *National Health Expenditures By Type of Service and Source of Funds: Calendar Years 2006–1960* (Washington, DC, 2008).

of the limited number of such attempts were field tests conducted in three states by CDC in 2000. These tests found that the three state public health departments delivered 40, 51, and 56 percent of what were deemed to be "essential" public health services, whereas the local health agencies in the states received scores of 62, 55, and 53 percent respectively. In addition, two independent nationwide surveys in the 1990s concluded that just one-third of the American public was being effectively served by the public health system.

After recounting these and other system assessments, the 2001 CDC status report termed the results "troubling" and observed, "Both the vigilance to anticipate and identify threats and the capacity to respond quickly are lacking in too many health departments."[112]

CHAPTER 4

Response to the Anthrax Attacks: Criminal Investigation

The anthrax attacks occurred when the country was still attempting to cope with the impact of the terrorist hijackings of September 11. With the exception of the Florida outlier, the same metropolitan areas—New York City and Washington, DC—bore the brunt of the assaults. And many of the same institutions, especially the FBI, the U.S. Congress, and high-level officials at the White House, were charged with spearheading the response.

In comparison to the situation with respect to 9/11, the federal government's reaction to the anthrax attacks was somewhat slower to unfold, and received far fewer resources. It was made up of three principal components: the criminal investigation, headed up by the FBI and Justice Department; the public health response, coordinated by the U.S. Department of Health and Human Services (HHS) and the U.S. Centers for Disease Control and Prevention (CDC); and the policy response, led by the Congress and officials at HHS and the White House Office of Homeland Security (later to become the Department of Homeland Security).

EARLY STAGES

Prior to 2001, both criminal and public health investigators had very limited experience in dealing with the inhalational form of anthrax, which was responsible for all of the fatalities in the 2001 attacks. Most of the information they did possess was based on the 1979 accidental release of anthrax spores from a Soviet bioweapons facility in Sverdlovsk, Russia and on eighteen occupational exposures in the United States over the course of the twentieth century. The mortality rate for the U.S. cases was 89 percent, but most of these occurred prior to the development of antibiotics and thus were felt to be of limited relevance to the 2001 cases. Initial data from the Sverdlovsk incident suggested a similarly high rate, but later analysis placed the level at around 40 percent.[1]

Together with the Sverdlovsk and occupational exposure data, animal testing had led researchers to believe that inhalation of a substantial number of anthrax spores was required for a fatal exposure. It was estimated that those who inhaled 8,000 to 10,000 spores had a 50 percent chance of developing a lethal infection.[2] (By December 2001, both of these previous conclusions were called into serious question with respect to the anthrax letters. It was found that far fewer spores were necessary to produce a potentially life-threatening infection, but the mortality rate for those who did become infected was much lower than had been indicated in the U.S. results or in the earlier reports from Sverdlovsk.)[3]

The first case in Florida was initially treated as a public health investigation, though even then law-enforcement authorities were brought in because of the rarity of naturally occurring inhalational anthrax, the known possibility of anthrax use as a biological weapon, and the heightened concern about terrorism in the wake of 9/11. Once the second instance of inhalational anthrax was discovered, which made it clear that the incidents were the result of an intentional act, a criminal investigation led by the FBI was initiated. Among other consequences, this meant that the subsequent discoveries of the anthrax-bearing letters in New York and Washington were treated as crime scenes, with the public health role limited to consequence management and the provision of technical assistance to the FBI and other law enforcement agencies.[4]

In the aftermath of the discovery of the anthrax letters, the FBI's investigation, called "Amerithrax," was frequently called into question. Some felt that the Bureau, which was at that time simultaneously probing the 9/11 hijackings,[5] had not been sufficiently diligent in pursuing potential leads in the anthrax case. Partly in response, Attorney General John Ashcroft and FBI Director Robert Mueller held a press conference on October 16, 2001 at which they defended the ongoing investigation and announced the arrest of a man for perpetrating an anthrax hoax in Connecticut.[6]

At the press conference, Mueller highlighted the challenge posed by such hoaxes.

> Since October 1, the FBI has responded to more than 2,300 incidents or suspected incidents involving anthrax or other dangerous agents. And as all of you know, an overwhelming majority of those incidents have been false alarms or practical jokes . . . Every threat is taken seriously. Every threat receives a full response. We have no choice but to assume that each reported instance is an actual bio-threat.[7]

Though the FBI was clearly in charge of all aspects of the criminal investigation, Director of the White House Office of Homeland Security,

Tom Ridge, emerged early on as the primary public spokesman on the status of the investigation. One of the first official characterizations of the anthrax used in the 2001 attacks was provided by Ridge at an October 19, 2001 press conference at which he announced that the spores found in the letters to the *Enquirer*, NBC News and Senator Daschle were "indistinguishable" from each other, and thus came from the same strain, or family, of anthrax. He added, "The tests have shown that these strains have not been 'weaponized.' " When asked to elaborate, Ridge said,

The term [weaponize] as I think people have been using it, it relates to some kind of a reduction in size and then coating with another substance that makes it easier to release with less energy. And so far as they've been able to detect with all of the tests they've run, and they continue to run tests, there [are] no results that would suggest that it has been "weaponized." That's not necessarily a scientific term or a medical term.[8]

At another press briefing three days later, Director Ridge indicated that, other than it being an act of terrorism, few conclusions had been reached with respect to the likely perpetrator or perpetrators.

Well, whether it's—they are a group of isolated attacks or a collective attack, I mean, we just view these individuals, whether they be foreign or domestic, who work either in concert with one another or independently, as terrorists.[9]

Questions about the sophistication of the anthrax employed in the attacks and the implied expertise and resources necessary for its production were (and still are) key to efforts to determine the identity of the perpetrator, or perpetrators. Thus, at Director Ridge's regular homeland security briefings—during which the anthrax case was almost always the primary component—he began to face more and more questions about what was being discovered about the anthrax that had been recovered from the letters. On October 22, 2001 he was asked whether he was "reconsidering" his comment about "weaponized" anthrax, in view of the additional cases that had just come to light. Ridge replied, "I don't think 'weaponize' is a medical term or necessarily helpful . . . I think it adds more confusion to our discussion than clarity. And so all I can tell you today is the information I have available today . . . The strains are the same and I have no additional information to give you."[10]

For the October 25, 2001 press conference, Director Ridge was accompanied by Major General John Parker, Commanding General of the U.S. Army Medical Research and Material Command. General Parker's command included the United States Army Medical Research Institute of Infectious Diseases (USAMRIID), which had been given the anthrax letters for testing by the FBI because of its experience in dealing with biological weapons in general and anthrax in particular. They spoke in somewhat greater detail on the subject of the composition of the anthrax spores. They reported that the letters were all from the same strain, which they identified as the Ames strain.[11] The spores in the Daschle letter were more highly concentrated, purer, and smaller than those in the letter to the *New York Post*, and thus more dangerous, although it was stressed that the anthrax in the *Post* letter itself was very potent, with "densely packed . . . highly concentrated" spores. (There was an insufficient amount of recoverable material to allow similar analysis of the anthrax found in the Florida and NBC News cases.) However, neither Ridge nor Parker was willing to speculate what this additional information portended about the perpetrator.

Question: Given the nature of the powder, especially that was sent in the letter to Senator Daschle, what can you and the others say about where this was produced, how it was produced, and ultimately by whom—domestically or foreign?

Ridge: Tests may give us the answers to some or all of those questions, as well as investigations being conducted by the FBI and the Department of Justice. The tests now give us very specific characteristics, but the tests may or may not lead us to the source.

Question: At this point are you able to say at any level, preliminarily or otherwise, that this is the kind of anthrax that could have been produced by an individual or several individuals here in the United States? Or is this the kind of stuff that could only be produced by a foreign nation?

Ridge: I believe further testing will give us the range. It will either expand it or contract it. But right now there are other, I believe, chemical tests and other tests in a series of tests that have to be conducted. I mean, one of the challenges we have with trying to give you as much information as we have as quickly as we get it, and give America this information, is that the properties of this anthrax and our ability to describe its characteristics really depend on the ability for us to conduct several tests—some simultaneously, some in different parts of the world, some one after the other. I will tell you that one set of tests often generates a recommendation that another set of tests [be performed]. So we just—the testing is incomplete, and we can't give you the answers to that question yet, if ever . . .

Question: Doesn't the very fact that, as General Parker said, this is free and floaty anthrax that was sent to Senator Daschle, aerosolized, show that it is a very sophisticated operation that produced it, not a grad student in a basement, and that the knowledge of how to do that would be limited to a very narrow circle of persons, some state actors and some people with access to American secrets?

Ridge: I'm not prepared to tell you what level of competency, accessibility to equipment, and other training either an individual or an institution needs in order to develop this level of anthrax.[12]

General Parker was questioned at the October 29, 2001 press briefing about the presence of bentonite or other additives that would make the anthrax spores "more easily aerosolized" and thus more lethal.

Question: What can you tell us about the possible presence of bentonite or aluminum silicon in the sample of anthrax that was discovered in Senator Daschle's office?

Parker: There seems to be a lot of questions about bentonite. I'm not sure where they're coming from or their importance. But if you ask what is bentonite, it's a volcanic clay. And one of its principal ingredients is aluminum... And we have subjected the *New York Post* sample and the Daschle sample to very high energy x-ray studies, and I will say to you that we see no aluminum presence in the sample. And, therefore, if you go back to the definition... we can say that there is no bentonite in the *New York Post* sample or the Daschle sample.

Question: Does that suggest then that there was no additive, there's been nothing... added to the spores to make them more easily aerosolized?

Parker: We do know that we found silica in the samples. Now, we don't know what that motive would be, or why it would be there, or anything. And that led us to be absolutely sure that there was no aluminum in the sample because the combination of a silicate, plus aluminum, is sort of the major ingredients of bentonite.[13]

The question of what additives, if any, were used to enhance the lethality of the anthrax spores was part of the debate on whether the attacks were sponsored by a foreign government or organization. In particular, it was believed that the presence of bentonite would suggest Iraqi involvement because that mineral was believed to be the preferred coating in Iraq's bioweapons program.[14]

General Parker's statement that "silica" had been found in the anthrax samples, along with a similar report in the Armed Forces Institute of Pathology (AFIP) newsletter, led many at the time, and for some time thereafter, to assume that this was the additive or coating that both allowed the anthrax in the letters to avoid degradation during its transit through the postal system and yielded spores small enough to penetrate deeply into the victims' lungs thereby enhancing its lethality.[15]

In fact, what USAMRIID scientists had discovered in the anthrax samples was not the compound silicon dioxide (silica) but rather the element silicon, which is not an effective coating agent. Though the public perception was that silica was used—implying a high level of sophistication in the manufacture of the anthrax employed in the 2001 attacks—according to a molecular biologist who was consulted in the Amerithrax probe, "I don't know of anybody with spore expertise who actually worked on the stuff who said the spores were coated." He further indicated the FBI never publicly claimed the spores were coated with silica and had in fact provided classified briefings to members of Congress in which it was clearly stated that the evidence indicated the spores were not coated.[16] This disconnect between what was known to researchers and what was reported publicly helped fuel a number of controversies about the criminal investigation that have persisted up to the present.

COMPETING THEORIES

Though little was being communicated publicly, the FBI was beginning to develop some more definitive theories about the case. For example, on November 7, 2001 New York FBI agent Barry Mawn was quoted as saying that the anthrax used in the attacks had originated in the United States and the attacker was likely a single individual rather than a group.[17] At this point, the FBI turned to a tactic that had ultimately helped it to identify the so-called Unabomber[18] after a 17-year search: a public release of certain information about the case in hope of reaching individuals who might be able to connect that evidence to a possible suspect.[19]

Thus, on November 9, 2001 the FBI released its "Amerithrax Press Briefing," which provided the Bureau's "Linguistic/Behavioral Analysis," derived from its investigation of the recovered letters sent to Tom Brokaw, the *New York Post* and Senator Daschle. The assessment concluded, "It is highly probable, bordering on certainty, that all three letters were authored by the same person." And, "Based on the selection of Anthrax as the 'weapon' of choice," the behavioral profile indicated the perpetrator likely was an adult male with a scientific background or a strong interest in science, had access to anthrax, and knew how to refine it, was familiar with the Trenton/Princeton, New Jersey area, was nonconfrontational socially, may harbor long-term grudges, and preferred solitude. Finally, he probably chose his victims deliberately.[20]

Shortly after the November 9 release a representative of the FBI Academy's Behavioral Analysis Unit expressed optimism that "before long we'll have some real good information, and the investigation will lead us to the person who is responsible for this." He indicated that he and his colleagues believed the perpetrator was a single individual acting alone with no direct connection to either the 9/11 terrorists or to any foreign government. Furthermore, they calculated that the anthrax used in the attacks might have been produced with as little as $2,500 worth of lab equipment.[21]

The FBI evaluation was greeted by considerable skepticism, in part because it was noted that the profile of the anthrax assailant was similar to the one developed for the Unabomber, which turned out to have been at some variance with the individual ultimately arrested and convicted. Others believed the Bureau had not adequately considered the possible involvement of foreign terrorists, including those connected to the 9/11 hijackings.[22]

After 9/11, it was discovered that United Airlines Flight 93 hijacker Ahmad al Haznawi had been treated by a physician in Ft. Lauderdale, Florida for a wound on his leg, which was covered by a dry, blackish scab. An independent review of the available evidence by the Johns Hopkins University Center for Civilian Biodefense Studies (undertaken at the request of an unidentified FBI agent not directly involved in the case) concluded that cutaneous anthrax was "the most probable and coherent interpretation" of al Haznawi's lesion. A FBI representative replied, "Exhaustive testing did not support that anthrax was present anywhere the hijackers had been," and other experts questioned whether some descriptions of al Haznawi's wound as a gash, and its location on the lower leg were consistent with cutaneous anthrax. The Johns Hopkins researchers, however, remained concerned that the Bureau was not taking this evidence seriously enough, and that the reported symptoms were "specific" to instances of cutaneous anthrax and "should be treated with high suspicion."[23]

Another assessment of the anthrax perpetrator appeared on November 12, just three days after the FBI's version. It was authored by Barbara Rosenberg, a biochemist then working for the Federation of American Scientists (FAS). Her analysis, which was similar to the FBI's in several respects, opined that the perpetrator of the anthrax attacks was an American scientist, with access to, or knowledge of how to produce, "weaponized" anthrax. In an updated assessment the following month, Rosenberg wrote that the federal government had "undoubtedly known for some time that the anthrax terrorism was an inside job."[24]

Following the October 2001 discovery of the anthrax-laden letter addressed to Senator Daschle, mail received by the Congress and several other federal agencies in Washington, DC was confiscated by the FBI and ultimately placed in 280 55-gallon drums for further processing and analysis. In mid-October CDC Director Dr. Jeffrey Koplan had expressed his belief that the pattern of the anthrax infections discovered thus far indicated that another anthrax letter had been processed by the postal system but not yet discovered. On November 16, 2001, investigators going through the confiscated mail discovered a letter addressed to Senator Patrick Leahy (D-VT), which had the same postmark date (October 9, 2001) and location (Trenton, New Jersey) as the Daschle letter with handwriting very similar to that on the Daschle letter. It was pulled aside and sent to USAMRIID for further testing.[25]

Because of concerns, not made public at the time, that much of the anthrax material in the Daschle letter had been consumed in destructive testing that had yielded limited information, the FBI held a series of meetings in late 2001 and early 2002 to, in the words of acting assistant director of the FBI's Washington field office, Joseph Persichini, "develop a comprehensive analytical scheme for evaluating and analyzing the anthrax evidence."[26]

Testing of the Leahy letter by USAMRIID began on December 5, 2001 and over the next few weeks it was announced that the anthrax it contained was the same type of highly concentrated, powdered anthrax present in the Daschle letter, and the message on the paper inside was identical to that in the Daschle letter. The news media reported the tests indicated that the anthrax spores in the letters to both Senators matched those produced over the preceding ten years by the U.S. Army's Dugway Proving Ground in Utah. Together with the previous information, this led to growing speculation that the perpetrator had to be one of a relatively small number of individuals with specialized technical expertise and access to U.S. defense labs, such as USAMRIID and Dugway.[27]

At a hearing of the House International Relations Committee in early December 2001, the former head of the UN biological weapons inspection program in Iraq, Richard Spertzel, testified that he believed the FBI theory about a lone perpetrator was "a lot of hokum" because of the quality of the spores involved in the attacks. Furthermore, he told the Committee that if the attacks proved to be state sponsored, Iraq was the most likely culprit because of its experience with aerosolizing techniques.

Appearing at the same hearing, former Soviet bioweapons researcher Ken Alibek disputed Spertzel's contention about the level of expertise that would have been required to produce the anthrax used in the September/October 2001 letters, stating that his preliminary conclusion was that those who produced it were "not very highly trained professionals."[28]

In January, 2002, Homeland Security Director Ridge told reporters that although the investigation had initially focused on the possibility of "external terrorists," currently, the "primary direction of the investigation is turned inward" toward domestic suspects.[29] Later that month another Rosenberg update indicated, "By now the FBI must have a good idea of who the perpetrator is," adding a much more specific profile describing him as follows:

- Insider in U.S. biodefense, doctoral degree in a relevant branch of biology.
- Works for a CIA contractor in Washington, DC area.
- Worked in USAMRIID laboratory in the past, in some capacity, and has access now.
- Knows Bill Patrick [who had run the U.S. bioweapons program] and has probably learned a thing or two about weaponization from him, informally.
- Has had a dispute with a government agency.
- Has been questioned by the FBI.

Rosenberg's hypothesis was based in part on the identification of the Ames strain as the type of anthrax used in the attacks, as well as the reports on the "weapons-grade" quality of the spores in the Daschle letter. It was then thought that the Ames strain had been distributed to no more than twenty labs, all in the United States except for two in Great Britain. Thus, Rosenberg believed the characteristics of the anthrax used in the Daschle letter pointed to the former U.S. bioweapons program and those who had been a part of it.[30]

Around the time of this Rosenberg update, the FBI agent in charge of the Amerithrax investigation, Van Harp, wrote a letter that was sent to the 30,000 members of the American Society for Microbiology. The letter stated

A review of the information to date in this matter leads investigators to believe that a single person is most likely responsible for these mailings. This person is experienced working in a laboratory . . . I would like to appeal to the talented men and women of the American Society for Microbiology to assist the FBI in identifying the person who mailed these letters. It is very likely that one or more of you know this individual.

The letter reiterated most of the characteristics described in the Bureau's November profile, reminded readers of the $2.5 million reward being offered for information leading to the arrest and conviction of anyone responsible for the anthrax attacks and indicated the perpetrator was likely not involved in the 9/11 plot but rather used the hijackings as a cover to hide his own plan and motives.[31]

In a February 5, 2002 commentary, Rosenberg wrote, "For more than three months now the FBI has known that the perpetrator of the anthrax attacks is American. This conclusion must have been based on the per- petrator's evident connection to the US [U.S.] biodefense program." After recounting a number of hoax anthrax letters, which reportedly had many similarities to the letters used in the actual attacks, and which she believed "map out an itinerary of the perpetrator(s) and indicate certain connections, which taken together must single out the perpetrator from the other likely suspects," she continued,

This evidence permits a more refined estimate of the perpetrator's motives. He must be angry at some biodefense agency or component, and he is driven to demonstrate, in a spectacular way his capabilities and the government's inability to respond. He is cocksure that he can get away with it. Does he know something that he believes to be sufficiently damaging to the United States to make him untouchable by the FBI?[32]

Rosenberg continued to work on, and update, her analysis, including her February speech in Princeton, New Jersey where she indicated her belief that the FBI was then focusing on a single suspect but was delaying an arrest because of fears of adverse publicity. In June 2002, she was asked to present her analysis to the staff of the U.S. Senate Judiciary Committee, with representatives of the FBI also invited to attend. When asked whether she knew who the individual was, Rosenberg indicated that she did not. She was contacted by the FBI the day after the staff briefing, and later told a reporter, "[The FBI] agents knew very well from the beginning who and what I had in mind. Trying to make me verbalize it was a form of intimidation."[33]

David Tell of *The Weekly Standard* had a very different take on the anthrax investigation. In an April 2002 column, he criticized both the FBI profile and Rosenberg's analysis, especially in their mutual conclusion that the perpetrator was most likely an American. Taking specific aim at the question of additives, and who their presence might implicate, Tell wrote:

> It has been widely reported, but never confirmed, that American scientists eventually settled on silica [as a chemical additive that would keep anthrax spores "floaty"]. It has been just as widely reported, and more or less confirmed, that the Soviet and Iraqi biowarfare programs each at some point used a substance called bentonite, instead... Based on this result [the discovery of trace amounts of silica but no sign of aluminum, an element basic to the most common form of bentonite], government investigators have concluded, according to the *Washington Post*, that "it is unlikely that the spores were originally produced in the former Soviet Union or Iraq." On the same basis, and getting similarly ahead of herself, Barbara Hatch Rosenberg has decided the spores were prepared by a rogue or sanctioned U.S. laboratory worker. But the fundamental chemistry involved here cannot sustain such certainty. Silica, or silicon dioxide, is simple quartz or sand, the most abundant solid material on earth. "Bentonite" is the generic term for a class of natural or processed clays derived from volcanic ash, all of which are themselves mineral compounds of silica — and not all of which necessarily contain aluminum. In other words: Trace amounts of silica in an anthrax powder are consistent with the presence of bentonite. And the absence of aluminum from that powder is not enough to exculpate any foreign germ-warfare factory thought to have used bentonite in the past.[34]

As of the spring of 2002, the FBI had conducted over 5,000 interviews, including over 500 at laboratories in the United States and abroad. Investigators then believed that the technical sophistication revealed by the purity and potency of the anthrax contained in the letters mailed to Senators Daschle and Leahy indicated the processing would have to have taken place in one of approximately two dozen laboratories. However, no particular suspects had yet been identified.[35]

THE INVESTIGATION OF STEVEN HATFILL AND LATER DEVELOPMENTS

The case took a dramatic turn on June 25, 2002 when the FBI interviewed Steven J. Hatfill at its regional office in Frederick, Maryland, and, with his consent, searched his nearby apartment. Though the Bureau indicated to the news media that Hatfill was not a "suspect," his background matched in several respects the FBI and Rosenberg profiles of the anthrax perpetrator. Among other things, he had worked for two years at USAMRIID, had commissioned a study on the use of mail to transmit anthrax as an employee of the Scientific Applications International Corporation (SAIC), and had displayed considerable professional interest in biological warfare and defense. Furthermore, he had been in London during November 2001 when a second "anthrax" letter—this time a hoax—had been mailed from there to the office of Senator Daschle.[36]

Hatfill's apartment was searched a second time on August 1, 2002, this time as the result of a search warrant. Though still indicating that Hatfill was not a suspect, both the FBI and Attorney General John Ashcroft now named him as one of approximately thirty "persons of interest." He was the only one named publicly as well as the only one apparently to receive sustained attention by the Bureau.

Hatfill called a press conference on August 11, 2002 at which he maintained his complete innocence, and held another on August 25 when he stated, "I know nothing about the anthrax attack...I had nothing to do with this terrible crime." He also produced timesheets indicating that on the dates the anthrax letters had been mailed from Princeton, New Jersey (September 17–18, 2001, and October 8–9, 2001) he was working overtime at the SAIC office in McLean, Virginia.[37]

The day after the August 1, 2002 search of his apartment, Hatfill was placed on thirty-day administrative leave from his new job as an instructor in counterterrorism at Louisiana State University, and was terminated at the end of that period. Hatfill contends this was a direct result of intervention by the FBI. In this same period, FBI agents travelled to the Princeton neighborhood where the Daschle and Leahy letters had been mailed and asked individuals there if they recognized a photo of Hatfill.[38]

At the end of August 2002, Hatfill provided blood and fingerprint samples to the FBI, and his Frederick apartment, which he had by that time vacated, was searched again in early September 2002. In spite of this apparent focus on a single individual, government sources continued to maintain that Hatfill was not a suspect, and that there were still some twenty to thirty persons of interest to the Amerithrax investigation.[39]

The apparent lack of progress in the investigation of Hatfill led to increasing skepticism of the FBI's approach. An October 28, 2002 article in the *Washington Post*, entitled "FBI's Theory On Anthrax Is Doubted," began:

A significant number of scientists and biological warfare experts are expressing skepticism about the FBI's view that a single disgruntled American scientist prepared the spores and mailed the deadly anthrax letters that killed five people last year. These sources say that making a weaponized aerosol of such sophistication and virulence would require scientific knowledge, technical competence, access to expensive equipment and safety know-how that are probably beyond the capabilities of a lone individual.

Among other things, the article cited the following assertions made by the experts interviewed for the story.

- The size (reported to be 1.5 to 3 microns in diameter) and concentration (one trillion spores per gram) of the anthrax in the Daschle letter was said to be fifty times finer than anything produced in the former U.S. bioweapons program and ten times finer than anything developed by the Soviets.
- Contrary to some earlier reports, Iraq had developed, or was developing, silica as a biological weapons dispersant and "UN and U.S. intelligence documents reviewed by *The Post* show that Iraq had bought all the essential equipment and ingredients needed to weaponize anthrax bacteria with silica to a grade consistent with the Daschle and Leahy letters... That Iraq had the wherewithal to make the anthrax letters does not mean it is the guilty party. Still, the FBI's early dismissal of the possibility may have prematurely closed a legitimate line of inquiry."
- The most likely way to produce anthrax with the reported characteristics of that in the Daschle and Leahy letters was said to be mixing the anthrax spores with the silica additive in a "spray dryer," which implied the need for equipment costing at least several hundred thousand dollars, experience in working with such "aerosols," and access to relatively large quantities of anthrax on which to practice the process.
- On the other hand, the total amount of anthrax in the letters (said to be 1.5 grams or less in each letter) was well within "laboratory quantities" allowed to be retained by research laboratories under the Biological Weapons Convention, and thus it is possible the attacker could have stolen the anthrax from a biodefense research or training program.[40]

Toward the end of 2002, the FBI was informed by a former Hatfill associate that he had once spoken about how someone seeking to dispose of materials contaminated with anthrax might utilize a body of water for that purpose. The Bureau began investigation of a series of ponds in the Frederick, Maryland area as a result. Searchers recovered a box that could have been employed as a scientific "glove-box" for the handling of dangerous material from one pond that was subsequently (in June 2003) drained and searched more thoroughly. However, no traces of anthrax were discovered.[41]

In late August of 2003, Hatfill filed suit in federal court against Attorney General Ashcroft and the FBI seeking unspecified monetary damages, and a declaration that these officials had violated his Constitutional rights by preventing him from earning a living, retaliating against him after he tried to clear his name in the anthrax investigation, and improperly disclosing information from his FBI file.[42]

When the examination of the Maryland pond was completed, the Amerithrax probe entered its next phase, which was characterized by a lower public profile, steadily diminishing investigative resources and limited apparent progress.

During 2005, it was reported that FBI agents were trying to pinpoint the laboratory that produced the anthrax used in the 2001 attacks by matching gene sequences. Though nothing conclusive had been determined, researchers were said to be particularly interested in such facilities as USAMRIID, Louisiana State University, and Dugway Proving Ground. However, some skeptics noted that even if a match could be found, inadequacies in record-keeping at the labs might preclude determination of who had access to the anthrax material, and when, at the identified lab.[43]

The August 2006 publication of an article by Douglas J. Beecher, a researcher in the FBI's hazardous materials unit, finally shed some public light on the Bureau's findings with respect to the anthrax letters, and in particular the Leahy letter.[44] In what was mostly a discussion of the methodology employed in investigating the contents of the Leahy letter, Beecher included one paragraph that spoke about some of the most fundamental issues raised in the Amerithrax investigation.

Individuals familiar with the compositions of the powders in the letters have indicated that they were comprised simply of spores purified to different extents. However, a widely circulated misconception is that the spores were produced using additives and sophisticated engineering supposedly akin to military weapon production. This idea is usually the basis for implying the powders were inordinately dangerous compared to spores alone. The persistent credence given to this impression fosters erroneous preconceptions, which may misguide research and preparedness efforts and generally detract from the magnitude of hazards posed by simple spore preparations.[45]

This represented the Bureau's first public comment on the composition of the anthrax material, but many questioned the fact that it came in a relatively unknown scientific journal, *Applied and Environmental Microbiology*, and that Beecher provided no source for the key assertion concerning the question of additives, nor any other information to back up the claim. Furthermore, the FBI declined to make Beecher available for interviews. However, several researchers who were allowed to view scanning electron micrographs of the anthrax spores from the Daschle letter in early 2002 came forward after the Beecher article to support his point by indicating that, while the spores were remarkably "pure," they saw no evidence of milling or of any use of silica or any other additive.[46]

As of the September 2006 five-year anniversary of the start of the anthrax attacks, the Amerithrax Task Force had conducted 9,100 interviews, obtained over 6,000 grand jury subpoenas and performed 67 searches. The number of FBI special agents assigned to the investigation had dropped (from 35) to 17, and the number of postal inspectors had fallen (from 15) to 10.[47]

Though the investigation of Steven Hatfill had produced no solid evidence linking him to the attacks, the primary focus had remained on a domestic perpetrator or perpetrators. However, increased scientific understanding of the anthrax used in the attacks reportedly led the FBI to consider a much broader list of potential suspects. For example, in addition to the information contained in the Beecher article, authorities had discovered that the Ames strain was far more widely distributed than first thought, with a former Soviet bioweapons researcher commenting, "Ames was available in the Soviet Union. It could have come from anywhere in the world."[48]

The anthrax probe took a dramatic turn in late July 2008 when USAM-RIID microbiologist Bruce E. Ivins apparently committed suicide just before he was to be charged for the crimes. Ivins, who had been notified by the FBI of the impending charges, was a lead researcher on anthrax vaccines and had been called upon by the Bureau to assist in the analysis of a sample of the anthrax used in the attacks.[49] In 2005, newly developed techniques for determining the genetic composition of specific anthrax strains led to the identification of the unique sub-strain used in the 2001 anthrax letters, which was traced to Ivins, who had created it in his Fort Detrick lab in 1997. While other researchers had access to this material, the FBI indicated that its investigation had ultimately ruled them all out, and one of the federal prosecutors announced, "Based upon the totality of the evidence we had gathered against him, we are confident that Dr. Ivins was the only person responsible for these attacks."[50]

Government authorities acknowledged that much of the evidence was circumstantial, including Ivins' work record, which documented a much higher level of late night work during August-October 2001, and the tracing of the envelopes used in the attacks to post offices in Virginia and Maryland, including one in Frederick, Maryland near Ft. Detrick. Furthermore, investigators were not able to conclusively place Ivins in the Princeton area on the days when the anthrax letters were mailed, and had been unable to match his handwriting with the writing in the anthrax envelopes and letters.[51]

LAW ENFORCEMENT AND PUBLIC HEALTH COORDINATION

The 2001 anthrax attacks posed unprecedented challenges in the coordination of simultaneous law-enforcement and public health investigations. Though there had been many previous occasions where such joint investigations had been conducted, the 2001 incidents were unique in several respects.

"Close collaboration" was required "because of the immediate and ongoing threat to public safety," and unlike most previous situations, the circumstances on this occasion did not clearly dictate which component should take priority. For example, most previous terrorist incidents had involved explosives, with the FBI and other law-enforcement entities taking the lead and public health agencies playing a supportive role in ensuring safe working conditions for the criminal investigators and assessing the health consequences of the explosion. On the other hand, when an infectious disease outbreak occurred from natural causes, the primacy of the public health role was clearly recognized.

Part of the difficulty encountered in coordination efforts during late 2001 resulted from the differences in the nature of the work, and in the approach, experiences, and training of law-enforcement and public health officials. For instance, "while the public health investigator's aim is to collect data that will withstand the scrutiny of subject matter experts and the global scientific community, with the ultimate goal of developing effective control measures, the law enforcement investigator's goal is gathering evidence that will meet constitutional standards and withstand legal challenges to obtain a conviction."[52]

Among the other factors that inhibited effective coordination between law-enforcement and public health authorities during the anthrax attacks were the lack of experience in working closely together, the involvement of multiple jurisdictions, the lack of security clearances and secure communication systems within public health agencies, and the unfamiliarity of most public health officials "with the principles of maintaining the chain of custody of specimens submitted for microbiologic testing so that laboratory results could be used for criminal prosecution."[53]

The most serious problem arising from all of these factors was in the flow of necessary information between the criminal and public health investigations. Officials acknowledged a communication problem between the FBI and CDC at the outset of the investigations, with a mutual reluctance to share information.[54]

According to later reports from local public health officials, as the inquiries proceeded, some local health agencies indicated the criminal investigation "sometimes hindered their ability to obtain information they needed to conduct their public health response." More specifically, these officials stated that "if they had received more detailed information earlier about the nature of the anthrax spores in the envelopes, it might have affected how their agencies were responding," and a state laboratory director reported that the requirements of the criminal investigation constrained his ability to communicate laboratory results to other public health officials.[55]

Many of these concerns centered on the transmission of information from the USAMRIID's investigation of the anthrax spores from the Daschle letter. The following timeline, as shown in Table 4.1, is based on information obtained by GAO in 2004 from the relevant federal agencies.

By late October 2002, accounts of communication difficulties between the FBI and CDC were appearing in the news media and Office of Homeland Security Director Ridge convened a meeting at the White House on

TABLE 4.1
Timeline of USAMRIID Information Disclosure, Fall 2001.

Date(s)	Event
10/15/2001	USAMRIID communicates the initial results of its analysis of the Daschle letter to the FBI and CDC.
10/16/2001– 10/17/2001	USAMRIID conducts additional analysis of the Daschle letter and communicates its generalized findings to the FBI, CDC, and selected other agencies, but not to the Postal Service.
10/18/2001	USAMRIID continues its analysis of the anthrax in the Daschle letter.
10/19/2001	FBI personnel are briefed by USAMRIID on, among other things, its findings that some of the anthrax particles in the Daschle letter were as small as one micron in diameter. Staff from CDC and the Postal Service are not present at the briefing.
10/21/2001	USAMRIID faxes to the FBI a more detailed report on its analysis of the Daschle letter.
10/22/2001	The FBI receives a hand-delivered copy of the 10/21/2001 report. According to FBI officials, the CDC liaison is briefed on the results of the 10/21/2001 USAMRIID report, but CDC's liaison said he was not briefed until later.
10/23/2001	The HHS Secretary is briefed on the results of the USAMRIID analysis of the Daschle letter. The Postal Service participates in discussions with USAMRIID about test results from the Daschle letter. The FBI learns that an envelope similar to the ones used in the anthrax mailings had pores up to 50 microns in size.
10/24/2001	According to the CDC liaison, he is informed of the results of the USAMRIID 10/21/2001 report on its analysis of the Daschle letter.

Sources:
"Timeline of Key Events, Fall 2001," in Government Accountability Office (GAO), *U.S. Postal Service: Better Guidance Is Needed to Ensure an Appropriate Response to Anthrax Contamination*, GAO-04-239 (Washington, DC, September 9, 2004), pp. 70–72; and GAO, *U.S. Postal Service*, p. 25.

October 24, 2002 to address the problem. In particular, HHS officials were complaining that the FBI had not shared information about the "potency" of the anthrax spores in the Daschle letter, information that might have led to a faster, more effective response to the contamination of the Brentwood postal facility.[56]

Ridge was questioned about these reports and the White House meeting at his October 25 press briefing.

Question: There have been reports recently of tensions between the FBI, CDC and other federal agencies over the sharing of information, or full disclosure of information, on the quality of the anthrax in the Daschle letter. Could you address that please? And also, could you tell us a little more about the meeting last night at the White House?

Ridge: Yes. First of all, you know that as Director of Homeland Security, I interact with these agencies on a daily basis. And I would tell you from day one, there has been collaboration and coordination, and every day it continues to accelerate as the circumstances of the threat bring people and people closer together...There have been new relationships that have developed. And I thought it was important to have the meeting last night not just with the principals, but with the scientists that we're all relying upon, in order to consolidate whatever information we have, and to see if we can further accelerate the process of answering the questions that America seeks from the administration.[57]

Communication difficulties between law-enforcement and public health officials also appear to have impaired governmental communications to the general public during the anthrax attacks. Part of the problem was the provision of what proved to be misleading information, for example about the nature and composition of the anthrax spores. One federal official later indicated, "Those judgments were premature and frankly wrong," resulting in part from the fact that the primary governmental spokespersons were not scientists and "the nuances [of the laboratory findings] got lost [in the information provided to the public]."[58]

Other officials expressed concerns that limitations placed by the criminal investigation on information disclosure impaired the ability of health officials to help the general public understand the risks involved and that "fear in the community could have been reduced if they had been able to release more information to the media and the public."[59]

CHAPTER 5

The Public Health Response to the Anthrax Attacks

While the criminal investigation was proceeding, the public health system was facing its own challenges in coping with the anthrax attacks of 2001, including diagnosing and testing for additional exposures, treating confirmed or suspected infections, and preventing their spread, decontaminating affected locations, and communicating the necessary information to other government officials and to the general public.

DIAGNOSIS, SURVEILLANCE, AND TESTING

The first challenge for public health authorities in the fall of 2001, as indeed is always the case with infectious disease (whether naturally occurring or intentional), was in recognizing the first case.

By 2001 naturally occurring anthrax was exceedingly rare in the United States and there was virtually no experience in the public health system in dealing with anthrax as a biological weapon. Under these circumstances, and given the well-known inadequacies in public health preparedness, it was not surprising that less than 30 percent of emergency room physicians polled in a 1998 survey indicated they were adequately prepared to recognize the clinical signs of an act of bioterrorism.[1] Thus it is also not surprising that when the anthrax attacks of 2001 began, awareness of the nature and extent of the attack was slow to develop.

The first wave of anthrax-infested letters was mailed on or about September 18, 2001 from somewhere in the Trenton–Princeton, New Jersey area to national media outlets in New York City and South Florida. Subsequent research revealed that at least nine individuals were exposed to and developed anthrax between September 22 and October 1, 2001, but it was not until October 4 that the first confirmed[2] case was recognized and reported.[3]

That first case was Robert Stevens of Lantana, Florida whose situation was brought to the attention of Dr. Larry Bush on October 2, 2001. By that time, Stevens was seriously ill. With a background in infectious diseases and microbiology, Dr. Bush presciently interpreted the Stevens lab results as indicative of anthrax, and initiated a series of contacts that culminated in the confirmation of Robert Stevens' inhalational anthrax two days later.[4]

Upon that determination the public health system—in this instance, led by the U.S. Centers for Disease Control and Prevention (CDC), the Florida Department of Health, and the Palm Beach County Department of Public Health—launched an epidemiological investigation "to determine the extent and source of the event, develop control strategies, and protect potentially exposed persons."

The investigation involved visual inspection and specimen taking at places the victim was known to have been over the previous sixty days (including his home and his workplace at the AMI building in Boca Raton, Florida), review of hospital intensive care unit records in Palm Beach County, Florida (where both Lantana and Boca Raton are located) and parts of North Carolina recently visited by Stevens, laboratory testing where appropriate, and alerts to local medical examiners and requests that state health laboratory directors send any suspicious culture samples to the Florida Department of Health.[5]

Speculation that the Stevens case was an isolated one arising from natural causes was disproved by preliminary results from the investigation at AMI. On October 7, 2001, CDC reported that anthrax had been found in one environmental sample taken in the building and in a nasal swab from one AMI employee, and the Palm Beach County public health department closed the AMI facility.[6]

Two of the 1,076 cultures obtained from nasal swabs of individuals potentially exposed to anthrax in the AMI building tested positive: one from Ernesto Blanco (who was finally confirmed with inhalational anthrax on October 15) and the other from the AMI worker who had recalled opening the suspicious September 25, 2001 letter that had released a powdery substance, but who apparently never developed an infection. Six potential cases of workplace exposure were reported to the public health authorities by medical providers, but only one of these (once again Blanco) was found to be infected with anthrax.

The possibility that the anthrax had been disseminated via the postal system was strongly suggested by the fact that both of the workers who had tested positive were extensively involved with processing mail, as well as by the environmental testing that occurred from October 8 through 10, 2001, which found the highest concentration of positive results (by far) for the presence of anthrax in the mailroom and associated locations.

However, all of the thirty-one nasal cultures from postal workers at two local post offices that serviced the AMI building were negative for anthrax, and the expanded surveillance for potential cases of anthrax among all Palm Beach County postal workers that was begun on October 25 found no anthrax exposure among any of the 3,263 workers.[7]

The second individual to be confirmed with anthrax, Erin O'Connor of NBC News in New York, was initially diagnosed by her physician (on October 1) as suffering from a spider bite and treated with antibiotics. After the Stevens case was reported, the doctor informed New York City public health authorities that he was treating O'Connor as a possible anthrax victim. Their initial testing did indicate cutaneous anthrax, which was confirmed by CDC on October 12.

The confirmation of an anthrax case in New York and the recovery later that same day of the letter that was the likely source of the exposure (the September 18, 2001 letter to Tom Brokaw) verified the conjecture about the means of attack but also indicated that it had not been confined to the AMI site in Florida.[8]

The New York City health department had been on heightened alert since the September 11 aircraft hijackings, and, after consultation with CDC, began to test workers in the NBC building and those who had visited there between September 19 and 25, 2001. Over 1,300 nasal swabs were ultimately obtained, and only one suspected case of cutaneous anthrax was identified (an NBC intern who had handled the Brokaw letter). Environmental samples also revealed significant anthrax contamination within the building.

By October 19, 2001, three more cases of cutaneous anthrax had been confirmed, each involving a different news media outlet in New York City: an infant who had visited the ABC News office (October 15), CBS News assistant Claire Fletcher (October 18), and *New York Post* employee Johanna Huden (October 19). By this time, over 1,200 nasal swab tests had been administered at these three additional sites, and environmental testing was underway,[9] and though two other cases would eventually surface (a *New York Post* mail handler on October 22 as a suspect case of cutaneous anthrax and another *New York Post* employee on October 28 with a confirmed case of cutaneous anthrax),[10] the scope of the New York attack was coming into focus.

The third location of targets of the anthrax letters became known on October 15 when the letter to Senator Daschle was opened in his office. Because of the widespread media attention that had been given to the Florida and New York cases, and also because of Congress' ongoing focus on terrorism after September 11, the event was quickly recognized as a potential act of bioterrorism. Diagnostic, environmental testing, and treatment operations were begun at once in the affected area, and none of the individuals exposed on Capitol Hill ultimately developed an anthrax infection.[11]

Though the national public health system was now thoroughly alerted to the seriousness of the anthrax attacks, a crucial piece of information was still not recognized. As bioterrorism experts Drs. Tara O'Toole, Thomas Ingelseby, and Donald Henderson wrote in 2002,

> Before the 2001 mailings, it was not anticipated that powdered anthrax contained in sealed, unopened envelopes would pose a danger to individuals handling such material. During this crisis, public health recommendations regarding postexposure antibiotic prophylaxis and vaccination as well as the risk of acquiring anthrax through environmental exposure were based on information that evolved as events unfolded... There was no information available that showed *Bacillus anthracis* spores of "weapons grade" quality could leak out of the edges of envelopes or through the pores of envelopes. When it became clear that the first case of anthrax in Florida was likely caused by a *B anthracis*-contaminated letter that had been opened, evaluation of the postal workers who might have handled or processed the unopened letter showed no illness. When anthrax cases were discovered in New York City, each was believed linked to the handling of an opened letter containing anthrax spores... Judgments based, in part, on these facts were then revised when illness was first discovered in persons handling or processing unopened letters.[12]

In fact, research in the spring of 2001 by the Ottawa-Carleton First Responders Group in Ontario, Canada had revealed that large amounts of finely powdered, simulated anthrax spores leaked out of unopened envelopes. The research, which was undertaken in response to the recent receipt of an anthrax hoax letter in a Canadian government office in Ottawa, found "contamination was present on the desk, papers, file folders, and pen prior to opening the envelope (contamination was concentrated at the corners of the envelope where it was leaking out)... Potentially contaminated persons are not limited to those in direct contact with the envelope and/or its contents."[13]

Representatives of the Federal Emergency Management Agency (FEMA) and the U.S. military were briefed on the Canadian research in mid-May and they subsequently shared the information with the Environmental Protection Agency (EPA), the FBI, the Secret Service, the U.S. Capitol Hill Police, and the U.S. Public Health Service, but apparently not with the CDC because the individuals receiving the data either assumed or were told that the latter had already been made aware of the findings.

After the anthrax attacks began, one of the Canadian researchers involved in the tests attempted to share the results with CDC officials by e-mailing a brief description of the Ottawa results along with a longer report on another Canadian anthrax study to the head of CDC's Laboratory Response Network. However, since the attached note did not highlight its potential importance, and the CDC official was then being inundated with "hundreds" of messages each day, the e-mail was not noticed at the time, and CDC did not become aware of the Canadian findings until November 2001.

Whereas CDC officials later indicated that earlier knowledge of the Canadian research would have been helpful, it was unclear whether such test data would have materially altered the agency's recommendations, given the actual field observations from Florida and New York City.[14]

The first discoveries of exposure via unopened mail involved postal workers Richard Morgano of the Hamilton processing center and Teresa Heller who was based in West Trenton. Morgano is thought to have developed an anthrax infection on September 26, 2001, with disease onset occurring two days later for Heller. Heller went to see her doctor on October 1, having developed a scab on her wrist that had turned black. She was given antibiotics to treat what was thought to be an insect bite, but was also referred to an orthopedic surgeon because the infection appeared to have reached to a bone. By October 3, when she went to see the surgeon, her condition had worsened, with a fever, so he had her admitted to the hospital. She improved and was discharged on October 5, 2001.

Meanwhile, Morgano had developed two lesions on his arm, and went to a local hospital on September 26, where he was treated with antibiotics for a skin infection.

On October 13, the day after reports about Erin O'Connor's diagnosis with anthrax, Heller's doctor determined that she might have been exposed to the disease. The doctor contacted the orthopedic surgeon who had removed the damaged tissue earlier in the month, and he in turn forwarded a sample of it to the FBI for testing. The Bureau had also become aware of the Morgano case by that time, and asked Heller's doctor if she would examine him, which she did on the following day.

On October 18, laboratory testing provided positive confirmation of Heller's cutaneous anthrax, and though not conclusive, identified Morgano as a suspected victim of the same form of the disease. This information led to the closing of the Hamilton postal facility, and the initiation of the testing and treatment of workers there, as well as the environmental sampling of the premises. The following day, Patrick O'Donnell, who also worked at the Hamilton Center, was confirmed with cutaneous anthrax.[15]

As a result of the regional surveillance of hospital and other records carried out by health authorities in Maryland, Virginia, and the District of Columbia, the first potential case of anthrax exposure within the Brentwood postal facility in Washington, DC (Leroy Richmond) was identified on October 19, and on the following day, CDC and the District of Columbia (DC) Department of Health began their investigation of the Brentwood building, which revealed that sections of it were "heavily" contaminated with anthrax spores.

Additional cases of infected Brentwood workers became known on October 20, 21 (Thomas Morris, who died on that day), and 22, 2001

(Joseph Curseen who also died on the day his case was recognized). On October 21, the mail processing area on the first floor of the Brentwood facility was closed, and it was recommended that all those who had worked near Richmond's mail sorting area receive antimicrobial treatment. "Because of concern about the potential for unrecognized aerosol exposures among postal workers," this recommendation was expanded on October 22 to cover all workers and visitors to the nonpublic areas of the facility, and shortly thereafter was extended to encompass "all postal workers in the DC area directly served by [Brentwood] pending results of ongoing epidemiologic[al] and environmental investigation."[16]

At Homeland Security Director Tom Ridge's October 22 press conference, a question was asked, "Can anthrax be transmitted through the covers of letters or the envelopes, not the inside?" Mitch Cohen of CDC responded, "Much of what we have determined has been from the previous investigations. This is really a new phenomena. At first, we had no evidence that any of the mail handlers were at risk, so this phenomena of first having skin disease in New Jersey and now having inhalational disease is an evolution. Now, how it is actually occurring isn't clear, and that is part of our epidemiologic[al] investigation is to try to track down what are those kinds of exposures and try to eliminate them so that we can make things safer." Another question focused on the difference in public health responses on Capitol Hill compared to the Brentwood situation.

Question: Why did the CDC decide it was not necessary to err on the side of caution and test workers at Brentwood, when the employees on Capitol Hill were immediately tested? And who is responsible—do you take personal responsibility for what seems to be this lapse?

Ridge: I think I will let CDC speak to this, but they obviously proceeded aggressively on the Hill in response to that threat. Again, there was a little difference; they knew they had a hot spot and they had identified it. It took a while to learn that they had a problem at Brentwood—remember, they worked that line back. But I will let CDC give you the answer to that question.

Cohen: As was pointed out, there is risk in prophylaxis when it is not necessary. One of our basic goals is to identify who is at risk. Previous investigations in Florida and New York did not identify that the postal workers were at risk. So this was, again, evolving. And so now, they are clearly identified as having the component of risk. So the effort is to identify risk and to intervene by using prophylaxis to prevent disease, but not to use drugs that may be unnecessary, which could cause further problems.[17]

Four more anthrax infections were confirmed over the next few days: State Department mail processor David Hose (who had likely been exposed to anthrax in the letter to Senator Leahy that was recovered on November 16) on October 25; Hamilton mail processor Norma Wallace on October 28;

Hamilton mail processor Jyotsna Patel on October 29; and Hamilton book-keeper Linda Burch also on October 29. Thus, by that date, twenty cases of anthrax had been either confirmed or were strongly suspected, and three of the victims had died (Stevens, Morris, and Curseen).

The still evolving awareness of the public health system was illustrated on that same date, at another of Director Ridge's press briefings. A question was asked about the possible cross-contamination of letters, and whether mail delivered to people's home addresses, particularly in the Washington, DC area, might be contaminated. Dr. Pat Meehan, Director of Emergency Services at CDC, replied.

> We think—we believe strongly that people that live—the individuals who receive mail in the Washington, DC area are at extremely—are essentially at no risk of inhalation anthrax. They are not in a situation where they're going to be agitating letters that have spores. If there's a remote possibility that a letter has a few spores on it, because it was in the Brentwood facility at the same time, those people may have a very, very small risk of cutaneous type anthrax. But it's important to remember that we're doing very aggressive surveillance and case finding, working with Maryland, Virginia, and Washington, DC, and have seen no cases of this so far.[18]

The very next day, lab results confirmed that New York City hospital worker Kathy Nguyen had inhalational anthrax, which led to her death on October 31. The fifth and final fatality from the anthrax attacks (and the twenty-second confirmed or suspected case), Ottillie Lundgren of Oxford, Connecticut, died from inhalational anthrax on November 21. With no definitive links to any known sources of anthrax exposure, cross-contamination of their mail has been cited as the possible source.[19]

Over 120,000 specimens were tested for anthrax during October and November of 2001.[20] *B. anthracis* was obtained from the four recovered letters (addressed to Tom Brokaw, *New York Post*, Senator Daschle, and Senator Leahy), from seventeen clinical specimens collected from patients, and from 106 environmental samples. All of these samples were found to be "indistinguishable" from a molecular standpoint.

In addition to the anthrax contamination confirmed at the sites where anthrax-bearing letters were opened (AMI building in Florida; the offices of NBC News, the *New York Post*, ABC News, and CBS News, all in New York; Sen. Daschle's office in Washington), environmental testing discovered anthrax traces at the following places: Trenton Mail Processing and Distribution Center in Hamilton, New Jersey (through which all of the recovered letters had passed), the Morgan Central Postal Facility in New York City (which handled the letters to Brokaw and the *New York Post*), at least five other New Jersey postal facilities associated with the Hamilton Center, at least six postal facilities "along the path of mail delivered to AMI," the Brentwood Mail Processing and Distribution Center in Washington, DC, and at least twenty-five other government or postal facilities affiliated with Brentwood (including the State Department mail facility in Winchester, Virginia).[21]

Of the twenty-two cases of anthrax identified between October 2 and November 20, 2001, eleven were confirmed as inhalational anthrax, seven were confirmed as cutaneous anthrax, and four were ultimately listed as suspected cases of cutaneous anthrax. Investigators later determined that eleven of the cases (Huden, O'Connor, Morgano, Blanco, Heller, the NBC News intern, the infant exposed at ABC, Stevens, Fletcher, and the two other *New York Post* employees) were associated with the initial September 18 attack letters, while eight (O'Donnell, Wallace, Patel, Richmond, Morris, Curseen, the other Brentwood mail worker, and Hose) were traceable to the October 9 letters. The remaining three cases (Burch, Nguyen, and Lundgren) could not be definitively associated with either grouping.[22]

The National Anthrax Epidemiologic Investigation Team summarized the differences in the two attack clusters:

We found that case-patients associated with the September 18 envelopes were more likely to have been exposed at news media facilities than at postal facilities compared with patients associated with the October 9 envelopes. Cases associated with the October 9 envelopes were more likely to be inhalational anthrax than those associated with the September 18 envelopes. These findings suggest that the October 9 mailing was associated with more severe illness and with the development of illness following exposures along the path of the mail.[23]

The Investigation Team also commented on other key epidemiological lessons learned from the 2001 attacks, first concerning the dangers associated with unopened envelopes containing anthrax spores.

No prior experience with mailed *B. anthracis*-positive, powder-containing envelopes is described in published reports; previous descriptions of aerosolized *B. anthracis* spores indicated the risk for re-aerosolization or resuspension of spores was low. Previous preventive strategies for presumed *B. anthracis* exposures now appear inadequate in light of recent findings. Before this incident, antimicrobial prophylaxis was recommended only for direct exposures to the envelopes, and limited decontamination was suggested only for the immediate site of envelope opening.[24]

In addition, they reported that, "contamination found at postal processing facilities off the direct mail path of implicated envelopes indicates that cross-contamination of mail occurred," though the evidence indicated that the risk of such exposure was "extremely low:" of the 85 million pieces of mail processed at postal facilities in New Jersey and Washington, DC just after the October 9 anthrax letters, only two cases of anthrax infection (Nguyen and Lundgren) that may have resulted from such cross-contamination were found. However, the investigation team warned,

> Although the risk for B. anthracis infection from cross-contaminated mail may be low, investigations of future bioterrorist attacks with B. anthracis-positive powders should consider the potential role of secondarily contaminated items in transmission of disease. An attack using a greater number of spore-containing envelopes would likely lead to many more cases due to cross-contaminated mail.[25]

TREATMENT AND PREVENTION

As of 2001, the medical consensus recommended the use of oral penicillin in cases of cutaneous anthrax (based on its historical efficacy in treating the disease), whereas ciprofloxacin (or Cipro), administered intravenously, was the preferred treatment for inhalation anthrax because of its effectiveness against a larger variety of anthrax strains in animal studies. However, if the strain in a case of inhalational anthrax was shown to be susceptible to either penicillin or doxycycline, that would be the preferred treatment in order to prevent the development of drug resistance to Cipro.[26]

Before the diagnosis of inhalation anthrax in the case of Robert Stevens, the first nine victims of the anthrax attacks of 2001 (all likely exposed to anthrax contained in the original September 2001 attack mailings) went unrecognized for the disease. Thus, the initial treatment of these individuals was based on the diagnoses and prescriptions of their medical providers. The seven who were ultimately identified with confirmed or suspected cutaneous anthrax were all initially diagnosed with either cellulitis or some other form of skin infection, or with spider bites. With the exception of the infant who became infected while visiting the ABC office, the others were all treated initially with antibiotics (including Cipro in the case of Erin O'Connor) and ultimately recovered. The infant was diagnosed with a spider bite and initially treated with an antihistamine.[27] When his condition continued to worsen, the diagnosis was changed to cellulitis and he was treated with amoxicillin. Further deterioration led to his admission to the hospital, where he was switched over to ampicillin and, after cutaneous anthrax was confirmed (October 15), to ciprofloxacin, which led to gradual improvement and subsequent recovery.[28]

Of the two initial inhalational anthrax cases, Robert Stevens was diagnosed with meningitis when he checked into the hospital on October 2, 2001 and received antibiotic treatment with cefotaxime and vancomycin. His diagnosis was changed to inhalational anthrax on October 4 and he died the next day. Ernesto Blanco was originally diagnosed with pneumonia on October 1 and treated with antibiotics (azithromycin, cefotaxime).

However, his condition continued to worsen, until he was put on Cipro after the Stevens anthrax diagnosis was confirmed.[29]

The second wave of anthrax cases involved seven postal workers from the Hamilton and Brentwood processing centers, likely exposed to the October 9 anthrax letters, who contracted an infection between October 14 and 16. All of these occurred after reporting of the Florida and New York City attacks, and were simultaneous with the opening and recovery of the Daschle letter. Yet, as discussed above, there was not yet awareness of the threat of anthrax escaping from unopened envelopes, and thus no recognition that postal workers were at risk.

Thus, like the first group of cases, those who developed symptoms and sought medical advice prior to such recognition were dependent on the judgment and treatments prescribed by their own medical providers. Patrick O'Donnell (the only one of the seven to have the cutaneous form of anthrax) was treated with antibiotics for a skin infection on October 16, and he subsequently recovered, as did Jyotsna Patel, who was diagnosed with bronchitis on the same day but treated with a type of antibiotic related to Cipro (levofloxacin), and subsequently treated with Cipro. Both Norma Wallace (on October 17) and Thomas Morris (on October 18) were initially diagnosed with viral infections and told to take Tylenol.[30]

Recognition of the potential for anthrax exposure at postal facilities emerged on October 19, when Leroy Richmond and Norma Wallace were hospitalized with suspected inhalational anthrax and put on Cipro. Both subsequently recovered. Another Brentwood postal worker was hospitalized the following day, with the same diagnosis, prescription, and outcome as Richmond and Wallace.[31]

Joseph Curseen went to Southern Maryland Hospital on October 21, but this facility had not received the alerts sent out to many area hospitals about the two other Brentwood workers who had been hospitalized with suspected inhalational anthrax. Curseen was diagnosed with dehydration and gastroenteritis. Also on October 21, Thomas Morris was hospitalized as a suspected victim of inhalational anthrax and placed on antimicrobial treatment but he died later that same day. Curseen was admitted to the hospital on October 22 with suspected inhalational anthrax; he received antimicrobial medicines but succumbed to the disease shortly thereafter.[32]

The final six cases of confirmed or suspected anthrax were dispersed in time (with disease onset occurring between October 17 and November 14), and do not fit neatly into any overall classification. Two were *New York Post* employees almost certainly exposed to the September 18 letter sent to the *Post*, which was not recovered until October 19. Both were infected with cutaneous anthrax (one confirmed and one suspected) and both survived. Hamilton bookkeeper Linda Burch, whose exposure could never be authoritatively determined, was also diagnosed as having cutaneous anthrax, and she, too, recovered.[33]

State Department mail annex worker David Hose (who likely was exposed to the Leahy letter when it was temporarily misdirected to the facility in which he worked) went to an emergency room on October 24, 2001. Though the attending physician doubted Hose had anthrax, he nonetheless provided the patient with Cipro and had him tested. The next day, the diagnosis was confirmed as a case of inhalational anthrax and Hose was admitted to the hospital. He survived.

Suffering from chest pains and shortness of breath, New York hospital supply worker Kathy Nguyen went to the emergency department at Lenox Hill Hospital in New York City on October 28, and was presumptively diagnosed with congestive heart failure and treated with nitrates. She was also given the antibiotic levofloxacin to treat possible pneumonia and inhalational anthrax and was admitted to the intensive care unit. As her condition continued to deteriorate, additional antibiotics (rifampin, clindamycin) were added to the treatment, but with little effect. She was confirmed as suffering from inhalational anthrax on October 30, and Cipro was substituted for the levofloxacin. She died the following day.[34]

Retiree Ottillie Lundgren was taken to her local hospital suffering from fatigue and shortness of breath on November 16. Given her age (94) and pre-existing conditions (chronic obstructive pulmonary disease, hypertension, and chronic renal insufficiency), the initial diagnosis was viral syndrome and dehydration, treated with intravenous hydration. However, the following day tests revealed a bacteriological infection, and she was started on a series of antibiotics, including Cipro. Her condition continued to deteriorate, however, as suspicions grew that she may have been suffering from anthrax. On November 20, laboratory testing confirmed that she had inhalational anthrax, and she died on November 21.[35]

Based on previous experience and medical guidance, in the 2001 anthrax attacks, antimicrobial treatment was initially recommended for those thought to be at risk for inhalational anthrax based on their presence at a facility where an inhalational case had occurred (such as the AMI building in Florida), or their exposure to an air space known to be contaminated with aerosolized *B. anthracis* from an opened letter (such as the Hart Building in Washington, DC). As understanding of the threat evolved, a third category was added for those who came into contact with facilities along the path of a contaminated letter where aerosolization might have occurred and where environmental samples tested positive for anthrax. Under this guidance, and including instances of self-initiated treatment, an estimated 32,000 individuals began antimicrobial treatment in response to the anthrax attacks of 2001; 10,300 of these were recommended to receive the full sixty-day course of such treatment. After the twenty-two cases described above, no additional anthrax infection was reported, including from any of the sites where anthrax contamination was detected.

The National Anthrax Epidemiologic Investigation Team observed,

> The fulminant systemic illness associated with the October mailing to U.S. senators differed greatly from the less severe cutaneous cases in media company employees in New York City, suggesting that substantial illness and death likely might have occurred among senate staff after implicated envelopes were opened. Exposure to *B. anthracis* spores from processing unopened envelopes at the Hamilton and Brentwood postal facilities went unrecognized until after the implicated envelope was opened at the Hart Senate Office Building. Administration of postexposure chemoprophylaxis likely prevented further cases in postal workers and almost certainly averted disease in senate staff . . . Our findings suggest that prompt use of antimicrobial prophylaxis following suspected bioterrorist attacks can prevent disease.[36]

Subsequent laboratory testing revealed that all of the anthrax specimens recovered from the 2001 attacks were susceptible to a wide array of antibiotics, including penicillin, amoxicillin, ciprofloxacin, doxycycline, chloramphenicol, clindamycin, tetracycline, rifampin, clarithromycin, and vancomycin. They were found to be somewhat susceptible to azithromycin, erythromycin, and ceftriaxone.[37]

Previous experience, including animal testing, led researchers to conclude that anthrax would not be spread by patient-to-patient transmission, and thus certain communicable disease strategies (such as the use of high-efficiency air filter masks and other measures to limit exposure to the air around a patient) were not deemed necessary in response to the 2001 attacks. No evidence has emerged to indicate that any patient-to-patient transmission occurred during these attacks.[38]

The medical consensus prior to the September–October 2001 anthrax letters had recommended that those exposed to anthrax in a biological weapons attack be given the U.S. anthrax vaccine (anthrax absorbed vaccine, or AVA), in conjunction with sixty-day antibiotic treatment, "to provide optimal protection to those exposed." For a variety of reasons, especially the limited availability of the vaccine supply, such vaccination was not initially undertaken in the fall of 2001. However, in December 2001, the Department of Health and Human Services (HHS) announced that it would offer AVA vaccination to the 10,000 individuals still on antibiotics because of presumed high risk of exposure to anthrax. Because the vaccine had not been cleared by the Food and Drug Administration (FDA) for postexposure usage, participants were required to sign a consent form indicating they understood the potential risk, and only 130 of those eligible ultimately decided to receive the vaccine.[39]

The two primary methods employed in late 2001 to prevent the spread of anthrax were the closing of locations where anthrax had been detected, and the precautionary irradiation of mail addressed to federal government locations in Washington, DC.

After the death of Robert Stevens from inhalational anthrax and the recovery of anthrax spores from environmental sampling in the facility, the Palm Beach County Department of Public Health ordered the AMI building in Boca Raton, Florida to be closed on October 7.[40] On October 12, the NBC "Nightly News" studio in New York City was closed by the New York City health department after the confirmation of NBC employee Erin O'Connor's cutaneous anthrax and the discovery of the anthrax-contaminated letter to Tom Brokaw.[41]

Shortly after the opening of the October 9 letter on October 15, the office of Senator Tom Daschle in the Hart Building in Washington, DC was vacated by order of the U.S. Capitol Police.[42] In all, twenty-six buildings in the area around the U.S. Capitol building were tested, and anthrax was found in seven: the Hart Senate Office Building and the Longworth House Office Building (both closed on October 17); the Ford House Office Building and the Dirksen Senate Office Building (closed on October 20); the Russell Senate Office Building (closed initially on October 20 and then again on November 17); and the Supreme Court Building and the P Street Mail Warehouse, which were never closed.[43]

The Postal Service had actually developed guidelines in 1999 for responding to the increasing number of suspicious incidents involving "mail allegedly containing anthrax," which called on postal managers to minimize the possibility of exposure by isolating the suspicious mail and promptly evacuating the affected facility. However, since it covered only instances where the suspicious letter was discovered within a post office, it was deemed inapplicable to the circumstances in the 2001 anthrax attacks, and the Postal Service relied on the advice of public health agencies in making decisions about closing facilities linked to those attacks.[44]

Based on what was then thought to be the limited risk of anthrax contamination from unopened, sealed letters, and on the absence of reported illness among the Florida and New York City postal workers who had handled or processed the unopened anthrax letters, CDC and other public health authorities initially believed that the health risk at postal facilities was minimal. Furthermore, they felt even that limited risk was for cutaneous anthrax, which was readily treatable. Thus, until anthrax infection was confirmed in postal employees, CDC advised the Postal Service that the postal facilities that had processed the contaminated letters did not have to be closed. Postal authorities later reported that without such a public health recommendation, they kept the facilities open because of the post-9/11 psychological importance of continuing mail delivery, and the negative economic consequences of shutting down even a part of the U.S. mail system.[45]

When the diagnoses of Teresa Heller and Richard Morgano became known on October 18, CDC did not initially recommend that the entire Hamilton Center be closed since both cases involved cutaneous anthrax, but it did concur with the subsequent recommendation by the New Jersey

Department of Health and Senior Services to close the facility for environmental testing. The Postal Service complied, and the Hamilton Center was closed that day.[46]

With regard to the Brentwood Center, the Postal Service had arranged for a local hazardous materials response contractor to conduct environmental tests at the facility once it was learned that a U.S. Senate mailroom served by Brentwood had tested positive for anthrax on October 17. The initial results from those tests, which were conducted on October 18 with the results available later that day, were negative. On October 20, CDC and the DC Department of Health began their investigation at Brentwood that ultimately revealed heavy anthrax contamination there. The first floor of the Brentwood Center was closed on October 21, after CDC confirmed inhalational anthrax in Leroy Richmond and Thomas Morris died, and the entire facility was shuttered on the next day when Joseph Curseen died.[47]

Environmental testing also found anthrax contamination at twenty-one other postal facilities that were not closed, including the processing and distribution centers in West Palm Beach (associated with the AMI letter delivery), New York City (the Morgan facility associated with the deliveries of the NBC and *New York Post* letters), and Wallingford, Connecticut (possibly linked to the anthrax exposure of Ottillie Lundgren), "based on the advice of public health officials who indicated that postal employees [there] were at minimal risk . . . [because] by the time environmental testing revealed contamination, the typical incubation period for inhalational anthrax (less than 2 weeks) had already passed."[48]

After the discovery of the Daschle letter the United States Postal Service decided to "sanitize" all mail destined for all federal government offices in the Washington, DC metropolitan area (zip codes 20200–20599) by having such mail sealed into secure containers and then shipped to subcontractors in Lima, Ohio, and Bridgeport, New Jersey where it was sterilized by irradiation. (By February 2002, the Postal Service reported that virtually all of the undelivered mail from October 2001 had been processed and delivered.)[49]

Decontamination

Over sixty locations were contaminated by exposure, both direct and secondary, to the anthrax letters of 2001, including government buildings, postal facilities, media offices, and residences.[50] The most heavily contaminated large buildings included the AMI building, the Hart Senate Office Building, and the USPS Processing and Distribution Centers in Hamilton, New Jersey, New York City (the Morgan Center), and Washington, DC (the Brentwood Center). While there was limited experience in ameliorating anthrax contamination in military and civilian research facilities, little was known about what to do in situations like those presented by the 2001 anthrax attacks, where the contaminated locations were widely dispersed and in close proximity to the general public.[51] Guidance from CDC issued in February of 1999 indicated that the area in direct contact with a possible source of anthrax, such as a contaminated letter, should be treated with a bleach solution, though a subsequent communication from the agency acknowledged that the effectiveness of such a procedure was "questionable."[52]

The U.S. Capitol Hill complex was the first of the major affected areas to be decontaminated. Over fifty organizations became involved in what proved to be a $27 million effort for removing literally "trillions" of anthrax spores from the seven contaminated buildings and preparing those buildings for reoccupation. No single entity was in overall charge, however, which resulted in different standards being applied as to when each building could be reoccupied and "likely added to the uncertainties, costs, and length of time that buildings were closed." After the contaminated area in each was sterilized, six of the seven federal facilities were reoccupied before the end of 2001 (including the P Street warehouse and Supreme Court buildings that had never been completely closed).[53]

The most seriously contaminated of the Capitol Hill facilities, the Hart Building, was also the first of the large contaminated buildings to be subjected to comprehensive decontamination. While it was initially thought that the entire building might need to be sterilized, eventually, the decision was made to take samples from throughout the facility and to concentrate decontamination efforts in those sections found to have anthrax spores present. Eventually, 100,000 cubic feet of the Hart Building were sealed off for fumigation with chlorine dioxide. The process was completed in January 2002 and the building was reopened on January 22.[54]

Postal authorities faced even greater challenges in cleaning up their facilities, which were larger and far more widely distributed than in the case of the Capitol Hill buildings. As previously noted, a total of twenty-three postal facilities were found to have traces of anthrax. For all but two of these, decontamination involved only a temporary shutdown or isolation of the impacted area for decontamination while work continued at other locations within the building.[55]

The two exceptions were the most highly contaminated of the mail centers. The Brentwood Center in Washington, DC (renamed as the Joseph Curseen Jr. and Thomas Morris Jr. Processing and Distribution Center in memory of the two Brentwood workers who died from the anthrax attacks) was decontaminated (using the same process employed for the Hart Building), renovated, and then reopened on December 22, 2003. The second was the Trenton Center in Hamilton, New Jersey, where the cleanup (once again employing the same chlorine dioxide gas fumigation technique used for the Hart and Brentwood buildings) was completed and the facility reopened on March 14, 2005.[56]

Total costs for the Postal Service's decontamination efforts have proven difficult to pin down, but a March 2004 report by the United States Postal

Service (USPS) office of Inspector General identified $275.3 million in contracts (as of November 14, 2003) for decontamination, cleanup, and renovation of the Brentwood and Hamilton facilities.[57]

The first site where anthrax presence was detected, the AMI building in Boca Raton, Florida, was the last to be reopened. Initial decontamination was completed in July 2004 at a cost of well under $5 million,[58] but follow-up work was required in July 2005 and November 2006, before the Palm Beach County Public Health Department lifted its quarantine order on February 12, 2007.[59]

Communications

The Centers for Disease Control and Prevention had traditionally been the national "go to" center in providing information during infectious disease outbreaks. However, a number of factors complicated its performance of that role in the anthrax crisis of 2001. First of all, at the time of the attacks the agency lacked a thorough compilation of the relevant scientific literature on anthrax and of outside experts who could be consulted about the disease. In addition, for dissemination of important information to the public health community, CDC was initially reliant on its Health Alert Network (HAN), which did not then reach most local public health agencies, and the *Morbidity and Mortality Weekly Report* (*MMWR*), which, as the name indicates, was published on a weekly basis. And its internal process for clearing such information prior to external release was somewhat cumbersome and time consuming.[60]

A further complicating factor in public health communications in the early fall of 2001 was the tighter control that HHS headquarters had exercised over CDC's external communications since earlier that year. Designed to better align CDC pronouncements with the policy preferences of the new Bush administration as well as to address some perceived shortcomings in CDC management, that control was strengthened further after the 9/11 terrorist hijackings, with the activation of the Federal Response Plan that placed the White House and relevant cabinet officials (including HHS Secretary Thompson) in charge of all federal terrorism-related communications to the public and news media.[61]

As part of its initial reaction to the request for help from Florida health officials in the Robert Stevens case, CDC sent a single media relations specialist to South Florida in early October to assist the Palm Beach County health department respond to media inquiries. With Stevens' death on October 5 and the discovery of additional anthrax cases in Florida and then in New York City over the next week, public and media interest "exploded" and CDC's small media-relations staff was hard-pressed to keep up. One journalist who was covering the story for a national publication reported that the CDC personnel were "harassed and overwhelmed" at the time, and many other reporters experienced considerable difficulty in getting a response to their inquiries about unfolding events.[62]

The problem was compounded by the fact that in the period between October 4 and October 18, 2001, CDC did not assign additional staff to deal with the massive increase in media requests (which totaled over 2,500 during that interval), nor did it hold any press conferences or telephone briefings for reporters. Much of this was the result of the Bush administration's attempt to centralize federal communications in the aftermath of 9/11 and "to speak with one voice."[63]

A 2003 *Century Foundation* report on communications during the anthrax attacks summarized the situation as of late October 2001.

A behind-the-scenes struggle was developing between government agencies, which held a near monopoly on information about the attacks, and journalists clamoring for access to what government scientists and investigators knew. This situation came to light about three weeks into the crisis, when prominent journalists began venting their frustrations in print: usually helpful press officers were stonewalling, government scientific experts were not being made available for interviews, and public officials were generally failing to make accurate health information available fast enough.[64]

One of those negative press accounts was provided by Dana Milbank of the *Washington Post*, who wrote, "As public worry about anthrax attacks increases, Bush administration officials and congressional leaders have been responding with inconsistent and, at times, incorrect information about the incidents. The government has been slow in the release of some information, and, some critics have said, there has been no single reliable source of information."[65]

The October 15 discovery of the anthrax letter to Senator Daschle further ratcheted up national attention, with press calls to CDC doubling, to up to 500 per day, and HHS headquarters fielding a similar number. At this point, the HHS leadership started to let CDC officials communicate more directly with the news media in order to improve the media's (and the public's) understanding of the medical dimensions of the crisis. In response, CDC increased the size of its staff assigned to handle anthrax-related media inquiries, and began to provide more frequent reports to keep the media and the public better informed on the evolving situation.[66]

The new, more proactive federal communication strategy was in evidence by October 18. On that day, new White House Office of Homeland Security Director Tom Ridge, who was supposed to unify the federal government's public message,[67] led the major press briefing that also included HHS Secretary Thompson, FBI Director Robert Mueller, Surgeon General David Satcher, Postmaster General Jack Potter, and CDC representative Mitch Cohen. The primary message of this session was summed up by the surgeon general.

Americans should be reassured in knowing that we are responding quickly and effectively to cases of anthrax exposure and presumed exposure throughout the country. We are delivering the appropriate medications to those who need it, and we are erring on the side of caution in making health care available to those who may have been exposed to anthrax spores.

Director Ridge pointed out that, as of that time, only five or possibly six people had tested positive for anthrax out of the "thousands and thousands" who had been tested.[68]

On the same day, CDC issued a press release on the latest developments in the epidemiological investigation, made available a videotaped statement by Dr. Koplan, director of the CDC, that provided general information about CDC's role and the relative risks of anthrax exposure, and conducted a conference call with reporters (led by the agency's Dr. Julie Gerberding) to provide information and respond to questions.[69]

Over the next three days, the gradual discoveries of anthrax exposures in postal workers and the closure of postal facilities in Hamilton, New Jersey, and Washington, DC produced a public debate about the nature of the anthrax spores in the Daschle letter compared to the earlier Florida and New York letters, the validity of CDC's assumption that anthrax contamination was unlikely from inside sealed envelopes, and the apparent difference in treatment offered the Brentwood postal workers in Washington, DC compared to Congressional staff members.[70]

The Centers for Disease Control and Prevention experienced difficulties in providing public responses to these concerns. For one thing, agency officials later acknowledged that they were not successful in communicating the significant degree of uncertainty involved in their understanding of, and guidance on how to respond to, the anthrax attacks. As an October 2003 GAO report put it, "Although the [CDC] messages were based on the best available information, they were subject to change when new facts became known" and CDC was ineffective in preparing the public for the reality that as "new information is learned, recommendations about who is at risk and how people should be treated may change."[71] This was clearly the case with respect to CDC's evolving understanding of the threat to postal workers from unopened anthrax letters.

In addition, because the FBI had immediately assumed jurisdiction of the Daschle letter as part of the criminal investigation, and had sent the same and the anthrax spores recovered with it to the United States Army Medical Research Institute of Infectious Diseases (USAMRIID) for analysis, CDC officials were not well positioned to provide clarification or inform the ongoing debate about the characteristics of the spores contained in that letter.[72]

The deaths of Brentwood mail workers Thomas Morris and Joseph Curseen (on October 21 and 22, 2001 respectively) raised serious questions about the federal government's handling of the situation in general and CDC's guidance with respect to the risk to, and proper treatment of, postal workers in particular.[73]

At his October 25 press conference Homeland Security Director Ridge emphasized that the latest test results indicated the anthrax in the Daschle letter was "more dangerous" than in the Florida or New York cases because the spores were smaller and more concentrated.[74] Meanwhile, leading national public health authorities, including Surgeon General Satcher and Dr. Koplan, were made available to respond to "tough questions from reporters about the anthrax situation."[75]

The reporting of Kathy Nguyen's inhalational anthrax on October 30 led to another surge of media interest and public anxiety, this time fed by concerns that anthrax infections could be spread by mail that merely came into contact with contaminated letters or postal equipment, potentially meaning that anyone receiving mail at home could be at risk. In order to stem the rising worries, CDC's telebriefings by Dr. Gerberding for reporters were instituted on a daily basis, and media appearances by Satcher, Koplan, and Anthony Fauci, who was head of the National Institute of Allergy and Infectious Diseases and had become increasingly active as an administration spokesman on the health dimensions of the anthrax situation, were stepped up.[76]

There was one more fatality (Ottillie Lundgren on November 21), but no additional confirmations of anthrax exposure. Therefore, much of the remaining public health communications challenge involved provision of treatment guidance to those who were at greatest risk of having been exposed to the bacteria, who, for the most part, were mail workers.

The September 2004 GAO report, *U.S. Postal Service: Better Guidance Is Needed to Ensure an Appropriate Response to Anthrax Contamination*, summarized the problems in communications to postal employees during the anthrax crisis.

The Postal Service communicated information to affected postal employees about the health risks posed by, and the extent of anthrax contamination . . . but problems with the accuracy, clarity and timeliness of the information provided led employees to question the information they received. Problems with accuracy occurred because the early health risk information public health officials provided was based on their existing knowledge and experience that proved to be far more uncertain than the officials initially recognized and which resulted in underestimating the health risks to postal employees. Problems with clarity occurred because information on the medical response to anthrax contamination changed as knowledge evolved . . . Problems with the accuracy and clarity of information were exacerbated by (1) postal employees' perceptions of unequal treatment between the responses to anthrax contamination on Capitol Hill and at postal facilities and (2) longstanding distrust of postal management.[77]

The particular challenges for public health communications at the end of 2001 included explaining why:

- CDC switched the recommended "drug of choice" for treatment from Cipro to doxycycline on October 18;[78]
- CDC was advising individuals who were about to complete the originally indicated sixty-day course of antibiotics to consider extending their treatment for forty more days;[79] and
- individuals who wished to receive the postexposure vaccine offered by CDC in late December had to agree to a number of paperwork and monitoring requirements, since the vaccine had not been formally approved for such use by the FDA.

In each case, postal workers were particularly suspicious because of the above-mentioned problems, and fewer individuals than might have been anticipated took advantage of this belated, but better-informed guidance.[80]

ASSESSMENTS OF THE PUBLIC HEALTH RESPONSE

The public health system's performance in the anthrax crisis of late 2001 must be viewed in the context of the circumstances within which it occurred. The terrorist hijackings of September 11 were still very fresh in the national consciousness, and the focus of governmental attention, including public health agencies, was on how to respond and cope with those events. Furthermore, though increased attention had recently been directed toward preparing for a bioterrorist incident, the means (anthrax disseminated through the mail) and scope (multiple, near-simultaneous disease outbreaks caused intentionally) were "virtually unknown" to the public health community and represented an unprecedented challenge.[81]

The response by the public health system to the anthrax attacks did display certain strengths, including CDC support for state and local health authorities, timely deployments from the Strategic National Stockpile, a generally rapid and coordinated response by the state and local public health agencies most directly involved, and, in spite of a number of shortcomings, evidently effective communication with the general public about the nature and extent of the anthrax threat.

As the anthrax crisis unfolded CDC was able to mobilize as many as 2,000 of its 8,500 employees to work on the anthrax cases, and instituted round-the-clock (24 × 7) operations to keep up with the demanding work load. In all, more than 350 CDC personnel were expeditiously dispatched to the impacted areas in South Florida, New York City, New Jersey, the Washington, DC area, and Connecticut, and the agency provided aid as requested to other localities. For example, between October 8 and the end of the month, CDC's emergency response center received 8,860 phone inquiries coming from all fifty states, plus the District of Columbia, Guam, Puerto Rico, and twenty-two other nations.[82]

In addition, CDC was able to quickly increase its laboratory capacity to deal with the urgent need for lab analysis of specimens of suspected anthrax[83] by expanding secure laboratory space so that the diagnosis and typing of anthrax specimens could be done simultaneously, creating a new lab in less than 72 hours to process environmental samples, and instituting a new integrated data management system to coordinate all of the anthrax-related lab results from all participating facilities within and outside the CDC.[84]

In the field and back at headquarters in Atlanta, GA, CDC personnel performed all of the following tasks in support of the agency's traditional mission of assisting the local response to a disease outbreak:

- Assessing the health of those who might have been exposed to anthrax;
- performing laboratory work to confirm the presence of *Bacillus anthracis* in those thought to have been exposed to anthrax;
- advising on treatment for those at risk;
- performing autopsies; and
- leading the epidemiologic investigation to ascertain the cause and path of the disease.[85]

The Strategic National Stockpile program quickly "delivered antimicrobial medications for postexposure prophylaxis and provided for the transportation of anthrax vaccine, clinical and environmental samples, and CDC personnel, including epidemiologists, laboratory scientists, pathologists, and special teams of researchers."[86]

State and local public health officials interviewed by GAO reported that the speed and coordination of their reaction to the 2001 anthrax attacks had been assisted by existing emergency response plans (most of which included provision for coordination with law enforcement and other emergency response entities), training exercises (including both table-top and full-scale drills), and experience with previous health emergencies (including anthrax and other hoaxes).[87]

Another strength in the public health response to the events of late 2001 was in what was perceived to be generally effective communication between the various health and other local and state emergency response agencies. This was facilitated in large part because channels for such communication between the public health agencies and the other emergency responders (including law enforcement, emergency management, and hazardous materials agencies) had been established prior to the anthrax incidents, and could be built upon to address the increased demands at that time (for example, via the institution of regular conference calls between the agencies).[88]

Lastly, in spite of the many problems with and criticisms of the government's communications with the general public, two public opinion surveys taken during the height of the crisis in October 2001 suggest that, at least in some respects, federal authorities, especially public health authorities, were able to convey accurate and necessary information to a majority of the American people. For example, though a mid-October *Washington Post–ABC News* poll found that 54 percent of Americans worried that they or someone they knew might become an anthrax victim, an even larger majority (85 percent) expressed satisfaction with the way the government was handling the situation, and 70 percent were confident that it could deal effectively with any large-scale biological or chemical attack.[89]

More importantly, a nationwide survey conducted by the Harvard School of Public Health between October 24 and 28, 2001 found that 75 percent were aware that anthrax is not contagious, 78 percent recognized that inhalational anthrax is more deadly than the skin (cutaneous) form of the disease, and fully 87 percent realized there are effective medical treatments available for those exposed to anthrax. Furthermore, among the overall population, respondents were largely on target with their own risk assessment, which rated their chance of contracting anthrax (14 percent felt it was very or somewhat likely they or a close relative would contract anthrax during the next twelve months) as much lower than catching the flu (73 percent), being injured in a fall (50 percent), or being hurt in a car accident (41 percent). (For those who either were themselves or had a family member who was a postal worker, however, the perceived risk of anthrax jumped to 32 percent.) And the widespread anxiety observed in the *Post*–ABC poll just two weeks before had subsided considerably, with 25 percent indicating they were very or somewhat worried about getting anthrax through the mail at home or work (though the figure again spiked among postal worker families to 56 percent). The director of the Harvard survey surmised that federal authorities had done a better job of communicating with the general public than many critics had alleged (though clearly there was a failure to address the concerns of postal workers and their families, the portion of the population most affected by the anthrax attacks). Another interpretation credited reporters, rather than government officials, with conveying the necessary information to the public.[90]

Whatever its successes, as a 2003 GAO report noted, "The [public health] response has been characterized by several public officials, academics, and other commentators as problematic and an indication that the country was unprepared for a bioterrorist event."[91] Not surprisingly, many of its long-standing problems hampered the public health system's performance in the 2001 crisis.

The continued fragmentation of the public health system was evident in one of the main problems cited by the National Anthrax Epidemiologic Investigation Team.

The detection of anthrax cases involved numerous local, state, and federal public health and law enforcement officials. Because of the widely distributed activities of various investigators and the need to act quickly in identifying potential exposure sources, data collection instruments were not uniform. Collation of information across sites was limited to a select set of demographic, exposure, and risk factor data elements . . . Environmental sampling of potentially contaminated facilities used different testing methods; because less sensitive testing methods were used, certain sites may have underrepresented the degree of contamination.[92]

The role of coordinating the fragmented federal public health response fell largely to CDC, which, as agency officials later acknowledged, the agency was not fully prepared to handle. Because of this unpreparedness, CDC was forced to employ a number of ad hoc arrangements, such as the creation of an emergency response center in an auditorium while the situation was still unfolding.[93] Bioterrorism expert Tara O'Toole was particularly critical of shortcomings in this area, stating, "I think the CDC [performance] was terrible. The official response was a national security travesty . . . We have numerous separate public health departments in the United States. They are mainly unconnected to each other, and most are not prepared for any sort of bioattack."[94]

Workforce inadequacies were also on display in the public health response to the anthrax attacks. O'Toole commented, "I think there were a lot of mistakes, a lot of missed connections, a lot of misjudgments. I think what we see reflected is the total disengagement of the medical community from any biopreparedness planning or exercises to date . . . Doctors haven't seen anthrax, they haven't seen smallpox, they don't know what to look for. They don't know how to diagnose it."[95] The 2003 GAO report noted shortages of trained personnel necessitated that state and local public health agencies had to borrow workers from other parts of their organizations, from CDC, or from elsewhere to meet the suddenly increased demands for disease surveillance, laboratory testing, environmental investigation, staffing of emergency hotlines, and other duties. Furthermore, some of these borrowed workers lacked proper training for their new assignments and had to be trained as the incidents were ongoing.[96]

Shortages of appropriately trained personnel were also present at CDC itself, especially with respect to environmental microbiology.[97] Such limitations were cited as one of the major reasons why CDC was unable to conduct comprehensive follow-ups with survivors of the anthrax attacks.[98]

In addition to the generally recognized shortcomings in public health communications technology, the 2001 events disclosed the additional problem of interoperability: "Fire and rescue personnel, law enforcement officers, and public health officials soon found that their communication systems and operating protocols did not function well across organizational disciplines and jurisdictions."[99]

The long-standing capacity problems within the public health sector were also brought into sharp relief in late 2001. State and local public health officials later reported that their resources were seriously strained by the anthrax attacks and "they might not have been able to manage if the crisis had lasted longer." In addition, some of the clinical laboratories in the affected areas "were not prepared in terms of equipment, supplies, or available laboratory protocols to test for anthrax, and most of them were unprepared for and overwhelmed by the large number of environmental samples they received for testing."[100]

The most frequently expressed criticism of the public health response to the anthrax letters of September–October 2001, however, was directed at the communications effort. Part of this was with regard to internal contacts within the public health system itself. For example, state and local health authorities reported difficulties in providing timely information to hospitals and physicians on the proper diagnosis and treatment of anthrax. Among the reasons for this were the wide variety of communication capabilities among health providers, especially individual physicians who did not have a hospital-based practice, and insufficiencies in the contact information possessed by the state and local health agencies.[101]

Problems were experienced by CDC in processing the very large amount of incoming information it received from many sources about the anthrax incidents, and then quickly producing guidance based on that information to the other components of the public health system. As a GAO report put it, "CDC's efforts to manage all of this incoming information and associated internal communication problems were complicated by its concurrent responsibility for coordinating the day-to-day activities involved in the federal public health response to the unfolding incidents."[102]

The other communication problem was in the provision of information externally to the news media and general public. Dr. Julie Gerberding of CDC acknowledged some shortcomings on CDC's part, but sought to place these difficulties in the context within which the agency was then operating.

> Our communications capacity was not the strength of this organization, to say the least. We did field hundreds of phone calls during the peak times of this investigation and provided a great deal of information to those who needed it most, including critical partners in the investigation. Immediately after the attack in New York and Washington, DC, there was almost no communication from CDC because we were operating under federal emergency response management plans. But as the investigation unfolded, we were allowed to carefully communicate a limited amount of information. Later, it became clear that more information from CDC was desperately needed, but by then we were in a reactive phase where we were trying to catch up with information needs.[103]

In addition to the problems produced by the unprecedented and rapidly evolving nature of the anthrax attacks, CDC experienced considerable difficulty in conveying the uncertainties within its guidance and other communications about exposure risks and treatments in a manner that was comprehensible to the media and public.[104]

Dr. Thomas Inglesby, then of the Johns Hopkins Center for Civilian Biodefense Strategies, applauded CDC's initial communication efforts with respect to the Stevens case in Florida, but felt that "after the early days, the CDC did not respond well. They didn't get information out quickly, and often they did not get accurate information out at all."[105]

The communication failures were reflected in some of the results of the aforementioned October 2001 Harvard School of Public Health opinion poll, which found that, though CDC's Director Dr. Koplan fared best, none of the key federal officials who were involved in the communications response to the anthrax attacks were "trusted by the majority of the public as a source of reliable information."[106] The percentage of respondents who expressed "a great deal" or "quite a lot" of trust in the various officials were as follows:

CDC Director Jeff Koplan	48 percent
U.S. Surgeon General David Satcher	44 percent
HHS Secretary Tommy Thompson	38 percent
FBI Director Robert Mueller	33 percent
Homeland Security Director Tom Ridge	33 percent[107]

The consequences of all of this were summed up in a 2003 report by the Partnership for Public Service: "The government lost several rounds in the battle for [public] confidence during the anthrax threat. Confusing and contradictory communications to the public fueled widespread anxiety."[108]

Finally, operating in much the same manner as the failure of "imagination" observed by the 9/11 Commission with respect to overall U.S. counterterrorism efforts prior to the September 11 attacks,[109] the mind-set of public health system officials also impeded the response to the anthrax attacks.

Prior experience of CDC in responding to naturally occurring diseases led to a belief that initial clues in the epidemiological investigation would provide reliable information on the means and sources of exposure, though as demonstrated by the events of 2001, such assumptions do not necessarily apply in acts of bioterrorism "where the perpetrator can vary the mode and source of exposure." In congressional testimony from July 2002, a CDC official stated, "[CDC] clearly did not know what we did not know last October and that is the cardinal sin that resulted in deaths."[110]

CHAPTER 6

Public Policy Response to Bioterrorism, SARS, and Avian Flu

Policy makers in the Congress and the executive branch also reacted to the emergency created by the September–October 2001 anthrax letters. One important policy change that affected the federal response to the anthrax attacks was the establishment of the White House Office of Homeland Security by Executive Order on October 8, 2001. This step, which occurred prior to full awareness of the scope of the anthrax crisis, was taken more in light of the 9/11 terrorist hijackings but several parts of the directive did articulate a role for the new office in responding to acts of bioterrorism by calling on it to coordinate:

- Development of monitoring protocols and equipment for use in detecting the release of biological, chemical, and radiological hazards.
- National efforts to ensure public health preparedness for a terrorist attack, including reviewing vaccination policies and reviewing the adequacy of and, if necessary, increasing vaccine and pharmaceutical stockpiles and hospital capacity.
- Efforts to prevent unauthorized access to, development of, and unlawful importation into the United States of, chemical, biological, radiological, nuclear, explosive, or other related materials that have the potential to be used in terrorist attacks.
- Containment and removal of biological, chemical, radiological, explosive, or other hazardous materials in the event of a terrorist threat or attack involving such hazards and coordinate efforts to mitigate the effects of such an attack.

However, given that the Office of Homeland Security was just staffing up as the anthrax situation unfolded, it played little role in any of these areas.[1]

There was one field in which the newly established Office was to have a significant impact on the federal response in late 2001: communications. The formal responsibility was outlined in Section 3(i) on Public Affairs.

> The Office, subject to the direction of the White House Office of Communications, shall coordinate the strategy of the executive branch for communicating with the public in the event of a terrorist threat or attack within the United States. The Office shall also coordinate the development of programs for educating the public about the nature of terrorist threats and appropriate precautions and responses.

In the event, though, the principal effect of this communications role was in the emergence of the first Director of the Office, Tom Ridge, as a primary spokesman for the federal government about key developments in the crucial period from mid to late October 2001.[2]

Another preliminary administrative response was the creation of a bioterrorism advisory committee in the office of the Secretary of Health and Human Services.[3] This entity, which was to be headed by Dr. Donald A. Henderson, was rapidly subsumed by the establishment of the Health and Human Services (HHS) Office of Public Health Preparedness, also headed by Dr. Henderson, on November 1.[4] As was the case with the White House Office of Homeland Security, these new entities were not organized sufficiently to play a major part during the anthrax crisis and its immediate aftermath, and were in any case superseded by policy developments during 2002.

And as the anthrax crisis was unfolding, Secretary of Health and Human Services Tommy Thompson called for the creation of a multilateral group composed of countries "fighting bioterrorism" that would serve as a forum for information sharing and coordination. This was followed by the formation of the Global Health Security Initiative (GHSI), which held its first ministerial meeting on November 7, 2001 in Ottawa, Canada, attended by senior health officials representing Canada, the European Union, France, Germany, Italy, Japan, Mexico, the United Kingdom, the United States, and the World Health Organization (WHO). Initially, the group focused on the threats of biological, chemical, and radio-nuclear terrorism, but in December 2002 it expanded its scope to include pandemic influenza.[5]

LEGISLATIVE RESPONSE, 2001–2002

The reaction in Congress to the anthrax attacks in some respects followed the pattern seen in the case of 9/11, with the enactment of ad hoc appropriation measures to provide additional resources to address the shortcomings revealed by the attacks and major legislation to revamp and expand federal counterterrorism efforts.[6]

In one important respect, however, the policy response to the two attacks was very different. In November 2002, legislation (PL 107-306) was enacted that created the National Commission on Terrorist Attacks Upon the United States (the 9/11 Commission) to "examine and report upon the facts and causes relating to the terrorist attacks of September 11, 2001; ... make a full and complete accounting of the circumstances surrounding the attacks, and the extent of the U.S. preparedness for, and immediate response to, the attacks; and investigate and report to the President and Congress on its findings, conclusions, and recommendations for corrective measures that can be taken to prevent acts of terrorism." The Commission issued its Final Report in July 2004, which made a number of policy recommendations with respect to intelligence, foreign policy, transportation, and border security and other areas, and these suggestions have helped to frame the issues and influence relevant legislation (including PL 108-458, the Intelligence Reform and Terrorism Prevention Act of 2004, and PL 110-53, Implementing the 9/11 Commission Act of 2007) since then.[7] No comparable mechanism was established with respect to the anthrax attacks.

The first significant post-attack actions taken by the Congress to address bioterrorism preparedness were in the January 2002 adoption of the FY 2002 Labor, Health and Human Services and Education Appropriations bill (PL 107-116), which included $242.9 million in emergency funds for public health preparedness, and the FY 2002 Department of Defense Appropriations bill (PL 107-117), which contained an amendment that provided HHS with a total of $2.5 billion for bioterrorism-related activities. The major programs funded by these combined sums included

- CDC State and Local Capacity grants $940 million
- CDC National Pharmaceutical Stockpile $645 million
- CDC Smallpox Vaccine $512 million
- NIH Research $198 million
- HHS Recovery Activities $150 million
- CDC Capacity $142 million
- HRSA Hospital Preparedness and Infrastructure $135 million[8]

Funding for federal bioterrorism preparedness and response programs for FY 2003 was provided through a series of short-term "continuing resolutions," before a final appropriations measure for the fiscal year was enacted in February 2003. Under that measure (PL 108-7), total funding for bioterrorism-related activities within the Department of HHS was increased from $3.062 billion in FY 2002 to $4.34 billion.[9] Centers for Disease Control and Prevention (CDC) state and local capacity grants were maintained at $940 million, whereas Health Resources and Services Administration (HRSA) Hospital Preparedness and Infrastructure grants were boosted to $518 million. The other area to receive a substantial increase was the bioterror-related program within the National Institutes of Health, which obtained $3.83 billion, up almost $1.5 billion compared to the FY 2002 total.[10]

In recognition of the central role played by state governments in public health matters, in late 2001 the Center for Law and the Public's Health at Georgetown and Johns Hopkins Universities released the Model State Emergency Health Powers Act. This "Model Act" was designed to provide a blueprint for state legislation to "grant public health powers to state and local public health authorities to ensure a strong, effective, and timely planning, prevention, and response mechanism to public health emergencies (including bioterrorism) while also respecting individual rights." (As of June 2005, thirty-seven states and the District of Columbia had enacted laws derived in whole or in part from the Model Act.)[11] Some observers expressed concerns that the model statute was "largely silent" on the federal role and did not "clearly establish the nature and scope of federal assistance."[12]

The principal congressional response to the anthrax attacks was the enactment in June 2002 of the Public Health Security and Bioterrorism Preparedness and Response Act (PL 107-188), which is often cited as "the Bioterrorism Act." The new law amended the Public Health Service Act by adding a new section on "National Preparedness for Bioterrorism and Other Public Health Emergencies," which required HHS to "further develop and implement a coordinated strategy, building upon the core public health capabilities ... for carrying out health-related activities to prepare for and respond effectively to" such emergencies.[13]

At the center of the strategy was a National Preparedness Plan that was to further the objectives of

1) providing effective assistance to state and local governments in the event of bioterrorism or other public health emergency;
2) ensuring that state and local governments have appropriate capacity to detect and respond effectively to such emergencies;
3) developing and maintaining medical countermeasures (such as drugs, vaccines, and other biological products, medical devices, and other supplies) against biological agents and toxins that may be involved in such emergencies;
4) ensuring coordination and minimizing duplication of federal, state, and local planning, preparedness, and response activities, including during the investigation of a suspicious disease outbreak or other potential public health emergency; and
5) enhancing the readiness of hospitals and other health care facilities to respond effectively to such emergencies.

The particular state and local capacities to be supported were identified as public health surveillance and reporting, laboratory readiness, "properly trained and equipped emergency response, public health, and medical personnel," health and safety protection of first responders, coordination capabilities for provision of health services during emergencies, and effective communications systems.[14]

The primary means for improving the capacities and readiness of state and local public health entities were the existing CDC grant program for state and local capacity, which was reauthorized with a new funding formula that for the first time provided a base amount to ensure that every state and U.S. territory receive some assistance (the previous program awarded all grants on a competitive basis), and the newly funded program for Hospital Preparedness and Infrastructure, which was assigned to HRSA and directed to help prepare hospitals, clinics, and other health care facilities to respond to bioterrorism and other mass-casualty events.[15]

The provisions of the Bioterrorism Act covered many other areas as well. It established the position of HHS Assistant Secretary for Public Health Emergency Preparedness, augmented CDC facility security and preparedness activities, expanded the National Pharmaceutical Stockpile of drugs for emergency usage and renamed it the Strategic National Stockpile, provided for the registration and regulation of facilities in possession of particularly dangerous biological agents and toxins, and included measures to promote the protection of U.S. food, drug, and water supplies.[16]

Concerns about communications were addressed in Section 104, which created an advisory committee to make recommendations to HHS "on appropriate ways to communicate public health information regarding bioterrorism and other public health emergencies to the public," recommended the establishment of a federal Internet site on bioterrorism, mandated a study of public health agency communication systems, and directed HHS to "develop a strategy for effectively communicating information" about public health emergencies, including bioterrorism.[17]

In implementing PL 107-188, HHS, CDC, and HRSA established guidance for the state and local public health entities seeking grants in the form of "Critical Benchmarks," which laid out requirements for the grantees and were "intended to balance state autonomy and disparate levels of preparedness with an obligation to assure responsible use of federal resources and adequate preparedness nationwide." For example, one of the CDC benchmarks for FY 2002 was a requirement for grantees to "assess current epidemiologic[al] capacity and prepare a timeline for providing at least one epidemiologist for each metropolitan area with a population greater than 500,000."

For CDC, the benchmarks covered the areas of preparedness planning and readiness assessment, surveillance epidemiology capacity, laboratory capacity, communications and information technology, public information and communication, and education and training. For HRSA, the identified requirements were for governance and administration, regional surge capacity planning, emergency medical services, linkages to public health departments, education and preparedness training, and terrorism preparedness exercises. Six areas were identified as "cross-cutting benchmarks" that required coordination between both funding programs: incident management, Joint Advisory Committees for CDC/HRSA Cooperative Agreements, laboratory connectivity, laboratory data standards, jointly funded health department/hospital activities, and pandemic influenza preparedness.[18]

In November 2002, the Homeland Security Act was signed into law (PL 107-296). This legislation created the Department of Homeland Security (DHS) by combining the White House Office of Homeland Security with twenty-two other federal agencies, and assigned it the lead role in coordinating domestic preparedness for and response to terrorist acts.[19]

As originally proposed by the White House, the new department would have assumed responsibility for a number of programs managed by HHS, including the select agent registration and enforcement program, the Office of the Assistant Secretary for Public Health Emergency Preparedness (which housed the Office of Emergency Preparedness, the National Disaster Medical System, and the Metropolitan Medical Response System), and the Strategic National Stockpile.[20]

The final version of the legislation transferred only the National Disaster Medical System, the Metropolitan Medical Response System, and partial responsibility for the Strategic National Stockpile to DHS. It also delineated the new department's role in coordinating (in collaboration with HHS) priority setting and planning for a variety of public health-related activities, including biodefense research and delivery of health services to areas affected by emergencies.[21]

The Homeland Security Act also contained a provision that required the DHS Under Secretary for Emergency Preparedness and Response to develop a national incident management system, and to consolidate existing federal disaster response plans, including those for public health emergencies, into a single national response plan. Homeland Security Presidential Directive 5 (HSPD-5), which was issued by President Bush on February 28, 2003, sought to implement this provision by requiring DHS to develop and implement a National Incident Management System (NIMS) to facilitate unified command during emergencies by creating common principles and terminology, and a National Response Plan (NRP) to supersede the existing Federal Response Plan and improve upon it by clearly designating federal agency roles as lead or support, depending on the type of emergency.[22]

As public health authorities were trying to assimilate their new resources and responsibilities provided by policy makers in 2001 and 2002, their attention was dramatically refocused back to naturally occurring infectious disease by two serious outbreaks of "newly emerging" infections in 2003.

SEVERE ACUTE RESPIRATORY SYNDROME (SARS)

On February 11, 2003 the WHO was notified by the Chinese Ministry of Health that 305 individuals (five of whom had died) had contracted a heretofore unknown acute respiratory syndrome in the southern Chinese province of Guandong between November 2002 and February 9, 2003. Over the next few weeks, the disease spread (apparently by human travelers) to Vietnam and Hong Kong, and on March 12, 2003 WHO issued a global alert about the outbreak and initiated international surveillance for the disease. Shortly thereafter, outbreaks were reported in Singapore, Taiwan, and Toronto, Canada—all traceable to individuals who had recently visited China.

On March 15, 2003, CDC issued a preliminary description of the new disease —"a respiratory illness of unknown etiology with onset since February 1, 2003, and the following criteria: documented temperature >100.4°F; one or more symptoms of respiratory illness (e.g., cough, shortness of breath, difficulty breathing, or radiographic findings of pneumonia or acute respiratory distress syndrome); close contact within ten days of onset of symptoms with a person under investigation for or suspected of having SARS or travel within ten days of onset of symptoms to an area with documented transmission of SARS as defined by the World Health Organization." It also began enhanced domestic surveillance for SARS, and issued a travel advisory recommending that those planning nonessential travel to Hong Kong, Guandong, or Hanoi consider postponing their trip. On the following day, the agency started advising passengers arriving on direct flights from these three areas to seek medical attention if they began to display symptoms of respiratory illness.[23]

Ultimately, it was determined that SARS was caused by a newly identified virus (SARS-associated coronavirus, SARS CoV), making it the first "severe and readily transmissible disease of the 21st century." Between November 2002 and July 2003, approximately 8,100 probable SARS cases were identified, which resulted in 774 deaths in twenty-six countries, the vast majority of which were in the western Pacific region. By July 2003, WHO determined that "human-to-human transmission of the virus had been broken," and thus the disease had been contained.[24] In late April 2004, an additional nine cases of SARS (one fatal) were reported in China, all apparently linked to a research laboratory in Bejing that was known to be conducting research on SARS coronavirus.[25] No further cases have been reported.[26]

Though no fatalities occurred in the United States, serious concerns arose about the potential dangers of newly emergent infectious diseases capable of rapidly spreading because of global transportation networks. Congressional investigations during mid-2003 found a number of worrisome shortcomings exposed by the national response to SARS.

- Concerns were raised about under what circumstances and under whose authority quarantines or other means of isolation would be imposed at the country's ports and airports.
- Some local health authorities reported a lack of supplies for testing for infectious diseases, and of procedures for expedited transmission of samples to CDC headquarters on weekends.
- A number of local health departments were found to be using "passive" disease surveillance systems, which, in the words of GAO, "may be inadequate to identify a rapidly spreading outbreak in its earliest and most manageable stages."
- Though acknowledging that recent improvements had ameliorated the problem somewhat (CDC's laboratory response network had grown from eighty in 2001 to 120 by late 2003), New York City's health commissioner termed inadequate laboratory capacity as "the first and most urgent [problem] . . . at the national, many state, and certainly our local and many other local levels."
- The New York health commissioner also identified shortcomings in hospital preparedness, including in "building additional airborne isolation rooms, stockpiling and maintaining inventory for a three-day supply of pharmaceuticals, conducting internal tabletop drills, and increasing security at hospitals."[27]

AVIAN INFLUENZA

Most influenza viruses are confined to a single species, but occasionally one will cross over to cause infection in another species. In 1997 a certain type of avian influenza (designated H5N1[28]), which had first been detected in Guandong, China in 1996 among geese, spread to humans and killed six of eighteen infected persons in Hong Kong. That particular H5N1 virus was eradicated at the time by the culling of all domestic poultry in Hong Kong, but other versions of H5N1 continued to exist and evolve, and in late 2002 the virus reemerged and killed large numbers of wild and domestic waterfowl in Hong Kong nature parks. In February 2003, the new type of H5N1 spread to humans in Hong Kong, resulting in two infections, one of which proved fatal. This new form of the virus was the precursor of the so-called Z genotype, which has become the dominant form of the disease that spread "in an unprecedented fashion" throughout Southeast Asia, and then elsewhere, beginning in December 2003.[29]

CDC summed up the serious public health implications of the emergence of the H5N1 virus.

The highly pathogenic avian influenza A (H5N1) [animal outbreak] in Asia, Europe, the Near East, and Africa is not expected to diminish significantly in the short term. It is likely that H5N1 virus infections among domestic poultry have become endemic in certain areas and that sporadic human infections

resulting from direct contact with infected poultry and/or wild birds will continue to occur. So far, the spread of H5N1 virus from person-to-person has
been very rare, limited and unsustained. However this [animal outbreak] continues to pose an important public health threat. There is little pre-existing
natural immunity to H5N1 virus infection in the human population. If H5N1
viruses gain the ability for efficient and sustained transmission among humans,
an influenza pandemic could result with potentially high rates of illness and
death worldwide.[30]

As of mid-August 2007, WHO reported 321 cases of H5N1 avian flu
infection among humans since 2003, resulting in 194 fatalities. Indonesia
(104 cases, 83 deaths) and Vietnam (95 cases, 42 deaths) accounted for the
majority of both cases and deaths. No cases had been reported in the United
States as of that time.[31]

During 2003, bioterrorism preparedness remained a central concern of
the federal government, with the new structures and resources provided
by the 2002 policy initiatives going into effect even as the investigation
of the anthrax attacks continued to make little progress in identifying the
perpetrator or perpetrators. But the emergence of SARS at the beginning
of the year and the reemergence of avian flu at year's end began to refocus
policy attention on the broader field of infectious disease control. Over the
ensuing years, efforts to address both of these closely related, but—in terms
of policy priorities—sometimes competitive, objectives occupied the ongoing
attention of policy makers.

PANDEMIC PLANNING

The World Health Organization issued its first influenza pandemic plan
in 1999, but this was significantly revised and expanded in 2005 to address
"the possibility of a prolonged existence of an influenza virus of pandemic
potential, such as the H5N1 influenza virus subtype in poultry flocks in Asia,
which has persisted from 2003 onward[s]."[32]

Recognizing "the responsibility for management of the national risk of
pandemic influenza rests with the relevant national authorities," the WHO
document provided objectives for WHO and individual nations in the areas of planning and coordination, situation monitoring and assessment,
prevention and containment, health system response, and communications.
Recommended actions in each of these categories were identified for the six
phases of a pandemic, as redefined in the new plan.

Interpandemic Period

Phase 1. No new influenza virus subtypes have been detected in humans.
An influenza virus subtype that has caused human infection may be present

in animals. If present in animals, the risk of human infection or disease is considered to be low.

Phase 2. No new influenza virus subtypes have been detected in humans. However, a circulating animal influenza virus subtype poses a substantial risk of human disease.

Pandemic Alert Period

Phase 3. Human infection(s) with a new subtype, but no human-to-human spread, or at most rare instances of spread to a close contact.

Phase 4. Small cluster(s) with limited human-to-human transmission but spread is highly localized, suggesting that the virus is not well adapted to humans.

Phase 5. Larger cluster(s) but human-to-human spread still localized, suggesting that the virus is becoming increasingly better adapted to humans, but may not yet be fully transmissible (substantial pandemic risk).

Pandemic Period

Phase 6. Pandemic: Increased and sustained transmission in general population.[33]

The year 2005 also witnessed the revision and significant expansion of WHO's International Health Regulations (IHR). The World Health Organization's Director General Dr. Margaret Chan explained the objectives of the changes.

The IHR (2005) expand the focus of collective defence from just a few "quarantinable" diseases to include any emergency with international repercussions for health, including outbreaks of emerging and epidemiologic-prone diseases, outbreaks of food-borne diseases, natural disasters, and chemical or radionuclear events, whether accidental or caused deliberately. In a significant departure from the past, IHR (2005) move away from a focus on passive barriers at borders, airports, and seaports to a strategy of proactive risk management. This strategy aims to detect an event early and stop it at its source—before it has a chance to become an international threat.[34]

The primary means of accomplishing these ambitions was to be through the identification of core capacities that member nations would need to meet in order to be able to adequately detect, assess, and report the covered diseases and other events. However, "Rather than take to task violators, the new Regulations aim to strengthen collaboration on a global scale by seeking to improve capacity and demonstrate to countries that compliance is in their best interests."[35]

In the United States, the National Response Plan (NRP) continued to serve as the blueprint for how the federal government was to react to major domestic disasters, including pandemics. As revised in December 2004, the

NRP designated the Department of Homeland Security as the lead for coordinating the implementation of the plan, including with respect to all federal influenza pandemic operations and resources. Furthermore, all subsequent federal, state, and local disaster plans were to be consistent with the NRP and its professed all-hazards approach.[36]

On November 1, 2005 President Bush issued the "National Strategy for Pandemic Influenza," with the objectives of, "(1) stopping, slowing or otherwise limiting the spread of a pandemic to the United States; (2) limiting the domestic spread of a pandemic, and mitigating disease, suffering, and death; and (3) sustaining infrastructure and mitigating impact to the economy and the functioning of society."

The strategy was an outline of general principles and objectives in planning, communications, vaccine and antiviral production and distribution, research and development, disease reporting and surveillance, and response and containment. It also set forth broadly defined roles and responsibilities for federal, state, local, and international authorities, as well as for the private sector and individuals. On the federal side, HHS was designated as the lead for the medical response, with the Department of Agriculture given primary responsibility for veterinary response, the State Department for International Activities, and the Department of Homeland Security for "overall domestic incident management and federal coordination."[37]

The administration plan was accompanied by an appropriations request of $7.1 billion in emergency spending, consisting of $6.242 billion for purchase and stockpiling of vaccines and antiviral drugs, and for development of new vaccine technologies; $644 million for federal, state, and local preparedness activities; and $259 million for enhanced domestic and international planning and surveillance activities.[38]

As a follow-up to the National Strategy, an Implementation Plan was issued by the White House in May 2006. It outlined over 300 actions that would be undertaken to ensure "that our efforts and resources will be brought to bear in a coordinated manner against this [pandemic] threat."[39]

A December progress report indicated that most of the actions that were to have been completed within six months had been finished. A few examples of the Implementation Plan's requirements and the reported progress are included in Table 6.1.[40]

In the same month the National Strategy for Pandemic Influenza was released, HHS issued its own Pandemic Influenza Plan. The department had unveiled a draft plan in August 2004, which had been criticized by some for lacking sufficient detail and for delegating certain key responsibilities (such as for vaccine rationing) to state authorities. The November 2005 DHS plan modified and updated the original by addressing some of the concerns raised about the previous version (for example by providing additional guidance on setting priorities for vaccine and antiviral drug distribution), integrating the recent changes made by WHO in refining its classification of pandemic

TABLE 6.1
Status of National Strategy for Pandemic Influenza Implementation Plan,
December 2006

Action	*Status*
DHS . . . shall be prepared to provide emergency response element training and exercise assistance upon request of state, local, and tribal communities and public health entities . . .	Complete. Our exercise and evaluation program provides direct support for State, local, and tribal exercises upon request. Exercises that address pandemic influenza response are eligible for funding support and vender assistance. Thus far, we have fulfilled 70 percent of submitted training requests.
HHS shall reduce the time between reporting of virologic laboratory data from state, local, tribal, and private sector partners and collation, analysis, and reporting to key stakeholders . . .	Complete. CDC has the ability to collate, analyze, and report results to stakeholders within seven days of receiving virologic data from State, local, and tribal partners.
HHS . . . shall develop and disseminate a risk communication strategy . . . updating it as required.	Complete. Overall [U. S. Government] risk communication principles are described in the "World Health Organization's Outbreak Communications Guidelines." This risk communications strategy is being applied in the development, testing, and distribution of message maps that are used to support public communications in the event of an emergency.
DHS shall develop a pandemic influenza tabletop exercise for state, local, and tribal law enforcement/public safety officials that they can conduct in concert with public health and medical partners, and ensure it is distributed nationwide.	Complete. A tabletop exercise template has been developed for use by public health authorities. We are continuing to work with federal partners to develop additional pandemic exercises for state, local, territorial, and tribal law-enforcement/public safety officials that can be conducted with broader participation and focus . . .

Source: PandemicFlu.gov, *National Strategy for Pandemic Influenza Implementation Plan: Summary of Progress, December 2006*, http://pandemicflu.gov/plan/federal/strategyimplementationplan.htm.

phases and in expanding somewhat the international role in infectious disease control, and conforming to the 2004 National Response Plan.[41]

As issued, the HHS Pandemic Influenza Plan contained a "Strategic Plan," which outlined federal public health and medical preparedness plans for pandemics, and described the roles of HHS and its components in those circumstances. The Assistant Secretary for Public Health Emergency Preparedness was designated as the coordinator for HHS pandemic response activities. The second part of the plan was "Public Health Guidance for State and Local Partners," which sought to provide guidelines in eleven key areas of pandemic preparedness and response: surveillance, laboratory diagnostics, health care planning, infection control, clinical procedures, vaccine distribution and use, antiviral drug distribution and use, community disease control and prevention, travel-related disease risk management, public health communications, and workforce support. Part three of the plan—still under development at that time—was to consist of the operational plans of the various HHS agencies, detailing their specific roles and responsibilities during pandemic outbreaks.[42]

The Influenza Pandemic Operation Plan (OPLAN) of CDC was released in December 2006. According to CDC, the document

> is designed to allow the planners at every level within CDC to gain insights into "what" actions need to be taken in preparing for an influenza pandemic. The "how" to carry out these actions is left for the Subject Matter Experts (SMEs) selected to review and take actions articulated in their plan. Only the SMEs have the scientific and technical expertise necessary to determine all the actions and steps necessary to successfully mitigate the deadly effects of an influenza pandemic. CDC's myriad of tasks in this OPLAN are simply a starting point for the tremendous effort needed for a successful response to the devastating global effects of a pandemic like the 1918–1919 pandemic.[43]

Among the major assumptions and provisions of the CDC plan were the following:

- State and local authorities would have initial responsibility for responding to a domestic pandemic.
- Under certain circumstances, regular CDC functions may be "significantly reduced or ceased in order to permit a 'surge' to accomplish CDC's essential pandemic functions."
- Once human-to-human transmission of the pandemic disease is confirmed within the United States, CDC will begin deployment of the Strategic National Stockpile's antivirals, with none retained in reserve.
- The primary objectives are "(1) early recognition and reporting of a human outbreak through the use of global and domestic disease surveillance resources; (2) rapid assistance with the necessary resources and actions to contain outbreaks and delay further spread of the disease; (3) when available, the adequate and successful provision of vaccine to provide prophylaxis to at risk populations; (4) the adequate and successful provision of antiviral medications to treat affected populations."[44]

Effective for FY 2005, states were required to submit to CDC their own pandemic influenza preparedness plans as a condition for receiving federal public health preparedness funds. CDC reported receiving plans from all of the states before the end of 2005.[45]

POLICY INITIATIVES, 2004–2006

During 2004, Congress modified and approved three administration proposals designed to improve emergency preparedness: the Cities Readiness Initiative (CRI), the Biosurveillance Initiative (BI), and Project BioShield. The first two of these were directed at both bioterrorism and naturally occurring infectious disease threats, whereas the BioShield effort was aimed primarily at bioterrorism.

The Cities Readiness Initiative provided federal funds directly to, initially, twenty-one major cities to enhance their ability to rapidly deliver vaccines and other countermeasures from the Strategic National Stockpile in emergencies. The program was intended to address what HHS believed were undue delays at the state level in planning and expending funds for this purpose. Its stated objectives included development of the cities' capacity to provide antibiotics from the Strategic National Stockpile to their residents within forty-eight hours of receipt of the drugs, and full integration of all of their emergency components (including Fire, Police, Emergency Medical Services, and health departments) into this process. Another element of CRI was the investigation of possible use of the postal service as a means of delivery of supplies from the Stockpile.[46]

The second program, the Biosurveillance Initiative (BI), involved the departments of HHS, Homeland Security, and Agriculture in gathering, integrating, and analyzing relevant health data from a variety of existing sources of information, including hospital laboratory reports, sales records for over-the-counter drugs, and environmental monitoring from various sources, such as DHS's BioWatch network composed of environmental sensors in certain American cities that are designed to detect possible releases of bioterrorism agents. The BI was to build upon CDC's existing BioSense program, which integrated public health data in order to "enhance detection, quantification, and localization of possible bioterrorism attacks and outbreaks ... [and to] support subsequent case identification, epidemiological investigation, response, medical consequence management and recovery operations."[47]

In July 2004, the Project BioShield Act was signed into law (PL 108-90). This legislation was conceived as a means of addressing the scarcity of effective vaccines and other medical countermeasures for use against potential bioterrorism threats due to a lack of a commercial market for such drugs. To accomplish this objective, the new law relaxed certain federal acquisition procedures for the development of bioterrorism-related countermeasures, and provided for expedited review of grants, contracts, and cooperative agreements for research on such countermeasures. It further guaranteed a federal government market for new, successfully developed countermeasures by authorizing HHS to purchase such products for the Strategic National Stockpile, and, under certain circumstances, also authorized HHS to permit emergency use of medical products not yet approved by the Food and Drug Administration (FDA). The Department of Homeland Security appropriations bill for FY 2004 advance-appropriated $5.593 billion to fund Project BioShield from FY 2004–2013.[48]

In 2005, CDC reorganized itself, resulting in the creation of separate coordinating offices for Global Health, and for Terrorism Preparedness and Emergency Response, and a coordinating center for Infectious Diseases (in addition to other centers for environmental health, health promotion and health information, and the National Institute for Occupational Safety and Health). The goal was "to improve the ability of CDC experts to share what they knew, to streamline the flow of information to top officials, and to improve the agency's ability to leverage the expertise of its partners." Although applauded as a necessary revision by some outside experts, the plan generated morale problems within the agency, documented by a 2005 employee survey that found two-thirds of CDC workers opposed the realignment.[49]

By the end of 2005, the sustained policy attention devoted to public health security had produced some real gains, yet a number of independent assessments found continuing deficiencies in the public health system. Among the most comprehensive of such evaluations was the annual analysis (started in 2003) of the nation's public health emergency response capabilities by the nonpartisan Trust for America's Health (TFAH). The group's 2004 report had pointed to significant progress in public health emergency planning, communication systems, and response preparedness, "dramatic" upgrades in public health laboratory capabilities, an improved flu vaccination program, and enhanced pandemic planning.[50]

The December 2005 TFAH study indicated, "While considerable progress has been achieved in improving America's health emergency preparedness, the nation is still not adequately prepared for the range of serious threats we face." With respect to federal preparedness, the report stated

> Four years after September 11, 2001, there is still little consensus about priorities and objectives for bioterrorism preparedness programs. Additionally, no formal, validated, or publicly available national performance measures for the tracking of federal bioterrorism funds are in place. There is also a lack of accountability on which to measure federal bioterrorism preparedness efforts.

In addition, TFAH polled twenty public health and bioterrorism experts about the current (2005) state of federal public health and bioterrorism preparedness (see Table 6.2). Though these experts acknowledged that real

TABLE 6.2
Federal Preparedness Grades, 2005

Subject	Grade	Subject	Grade
Strategic National Stockpile	C+	Leadership	D+
Influenza vaccine shortage of 2004	C	Agency coordination	D
HHS management of federal funds and programs	C−	Measurable goals and directions	D
Cities readiness initiative	C−	BioWatch	D
Pandemic flu planning	C−	Hurricane Katrina public health	D
BioSurveillance	C−	Smallpox vaccination initiative	D−

Source: Trust for America's Health (TFAH), "Ready or Not? Protecting the Public's Health from Diseases, Disasters, and Bioterrorism 2005, Executive Summary," (Washington, DC, December 2005), p. 6.

improvements had been made in a number of areas, they nonetheless provided a cumulative grade of D+ for these federal efforts, with scores ranging from a high of C+ to a low of D− for specific aspects of those activities.[51]

The TFAH annual assessments also examined state preparedness, noting that under the U.S. Constitution it is the states that have primary legal jurisdiction and responsibility. The 2005 report found that

- Only seven states and two cities were rated by CDC as adequately prepared to administer and distribute supplies from the Strategic National Stockpile during an emergency.
- Over one-fourth of the states lacked sufficient bioterrorism laboratory response capabilities.
- Nearly half of states did not use national standards to track disease outbreak information.
- In almost a third of states, hospitals were not sufficiently prepared to care for a surge of extra patients during an emergency.
- In over 40 percent of the states, hospitals lacked sufficient backup supplies of medical equipment to meet surge capacity needs
- In almost a third of states, hospitals had insufficient capacity to consistently and expeditiously consult with infection control experts.[52]

Two 2005 reports by GAO identified additional concerns about the preparedness of the nation's public health system to deal with bioterrorism, pandemic influenza, and other emergencies.

A March 2005 GAO survey of overall emergency preparedness highlighted questions about the adequacy of the newly established planning and priority-setting mechanisms (such as the DHS National Response Plan, and the CDC and HRSA Critical Benchmarks), as well as the sufficiency of Congressional oversight of the large number of recently created programs, regulatory authorities, and reorganizations.[53]

In its November 2005 report on pandemic flu preparedness, GAO pointed to specific potential difficulties in

- Defining the leadership roles of HHS and DHS during the various phases of a pandemic.
- Coordinating multi-state and federal declarations of emergency.
- Rapidly detecting the outbreak of pandemic flu, given the vagueness of the symptoms and limitations in surveillance and detection capabilities.
- Determining whether to institute and, if so, how to implement isolation and quarantine measures.[54]
- Rationing scarce vaccines and antiviral drugs.
- Producing sufficient influenza vaccines and antivirals.[55]

Problems were also noted in Project BioShield, which had made little apparent progress in accelerating the development of bioterrorism countermeasures, with, for example, its largest contract (for the development of the "next-generation" anthrax vaccine) ultimately being cancelled.[56]

At the end of August 2005 Hurricane Katrina devastated coastal areas of Louisiana and Mississippi, and resulted in the submergence of large portions of the city of New Orleans.[57] What was widely seen as an inadequate federal response in the first major test of the new National Response Plan[58] led to the enactment of the Post-Katrina Emergency Management Reform Act of 2006 (PL 109-295). Though the act was primarily concerned with making changes in the operation of the Federal Emergency Management Agency, it codified the position of DHS' chief medical officer, who was assigned "primary responsibility within the department for medical issues related to natural disasters, acts of terrorism, and other man-made disasters."[59]

In addition, in response to the concerns identified by GAO and others, the Congress considered a variety of bills in 2006 to reauthorize programs created by the Public Health Security and Bioterrorism Preparedness and Response Act of 2002, and to reform the Project BioShield Act of 2004. These efforts culminated in the enactment of the Pandemic and All-Hazards Preparedness Act of 2006, which was signed into law on December 19, 2006 (PL 109-417).[60]

The new law sought to clarify lines of authority for public health emergencies by explicitly identifying the secretary of HHS as the lead federal official responsible for the public health and medical response to all national emergencies. In addition, it renamed the existing position of Assistant Secretary for Public Health Emergency Preparedness as the Assistant Secretary for Preparedness and Response, and aimed to strengthen this office's ability to unify and coordinate public health and preparedness programs, in part by returning responsibility for the National Disaster Medical System back to HHS from DHS and assigning it to the Assistant Secretary for Preparedness and Response.[61]

The Pandemic and All-Hazards Preparedness Act also reauthorized HHS grant programs for state, local, and hospital public health and medical preparedness. In an attempt to improve the accountability and effectiveness of these funds, HHS was directed to develop and apply evidence-based benchmarks and performance standards to measure progress, and was authorized to withhold a portion of these awards from grantees that fail to meet requirements.[62]

The 2006 legislation addressed the perceived shortcomings in the BioShield program by creating the Biomedical Advanced Research and Development Authority (BARDA) within HHS to manage the effort to develop drugs and vaccines for potential public health emergencies, and authorizing $1.07 billion over three years for BARDA-directed research not funded through Project BioShield or the National Institutes of Health (NIH). BARDA was directed to partner with other governmental agencies, universities, research institutions, and the private sector in developing promising pandemic and biodefense vaccines and other drugs.[63]

Other key provisions of PL 109-417 included.

- A requirement that HHS take into account the needs of "at-risk individuals" (defined as children, pregnant women, senior citizens, and others with special needs) in managing its emergency preparedness programs.
- A new planning document, called the National Health Security Strategy (to be submitted to Congress in 2009 and every four years thereafter), which is to be consistent with the National Response Plan and contain preparedness goals for federal, state, and local governments in the areas of: (1) integration of response capabilities and systems; (2) capabilities for public health preparedness and response; (3) capabilities for medical preparedness and response; (4) provisions for at-risk individuals; (5) coordination of federal, state, local, and tribal planning, preparedness, and response activities; and (6) continuity of federal, state, local, and tribal operations in the event of a public health emergency.
- A new grant program for "Real-Time Disease Detection Improvement," authorized at $35 million for FY 2007.
- A requirement that, within two years of enactment, HHS establish a nationwide, interoperable, near real-time electronic public health surveillance network.
- A provision to enhance the public health workforce via creation of a demonstration project of loan repayments to recruit and train qualified public health workers.

- Language to potentially expand the country's emergency medical surge capacity by mandating a feasibility study of the use of mobile hospitals and alternative federal facilities for such purpose.
- A requirement that HHS develop core health and medical response curricula and training for public health emergency response, and an authorization for HHS to establish Centers for Public Health Excellence at accredited public health schools.[64]

FUNDING

A common theme in analyses of public health security prior to and during the anthrax attacks of 2001 was the inadequacy of the resources provided for the public health system. After those attacks, the overall level of federal funding increased dramatically, but questions persisted about whether or not this response was sufficient to the need.

Table 6.3 utilizes the broadest measure of public health spending: HHS's National Health Expenditures statistics. It demonstrates that federal public health expenditures rose by almost 75 percent between 2001 and 2006, though the increases were unevenly spread, with large gains in 2002 (especially), 2003 and 2005, but little or no growth in 2004 and 2006. The net result was that the proportion of total national health spending represented by federal public health expenditures went up only slightly and still accounted for just 0.5 percent of the total by 2006. State and local public health spending also showed considerable variation during this time, remaining virtually level from 2002 through 2004 and falling as a share of total health expenditures throughout the period.

These trends at the state level were also reflected in the Trust for America's Health annual assessments of public health readiness, which found that thirty-three states cut their public health budgets in FY 2003, though only six did so in FY 2005.[65]

Concerns about bioterrorism and, from 2004 onward, pandemic flu, clearly drove the increased federal funding. However, federal spending for bioterrorism peaked in FY 2005 and for pandemic flu reached its highest level in the following fiscal year as evident from Figure 6.1.

The somewhat uneven federal investment in public health security is made even clearer by breaking down that spending into categories (see Table 6.4).

The large upward spikes in federal spending in FY 2005 and 2006 were almost entirely due to the substantial infusion of funds for Project BioShield and the HHS pandemic flu program respectively that were not sustained in subsequent years. Leaving these programs aside, it is apparent that after fairly dramatic increases in the first years after 2001, federal funding leveled off in the later years. Indeed, in the case of public health infrastructure, spending has actually declined since FY 2005.

TABLE 6.3

U.S. Public Health Expenditures, 2001–2006 (in $ billions)

Expenditure source	2001	2002	2003	2004	2005	2006
Total national health expenditures	1,469.6	1,603.4	1,732.4	1,852.3	1,973.3	2,105.5
Federal public health expenditures	5.6	8.0	8.9	8.8	9.6	9.7
Percent change vs. previous year	9.6	44.0	11.3	−1.7	9.6	0.7
As percent of total national health expenditures	0.4	0.5	0.5	0.5	0.5	0.5
State/local public health expenditures	41.4	44.1	44.9	45.1	46.7	49.0
Percent change vs. previous year	8.1	6.6	1.7	0.6	3.4	5.0
As percent of total national health expenditures	2.8	2.8	2.6	2.4	2.4	2.3

Source: Centers for Medicare & Medicaid Services, Office of the Actuary, *National Health Expenditures by Type of Service and Source of Funds: Calendar Years 2006–1960* (Washington, DC, 2008).

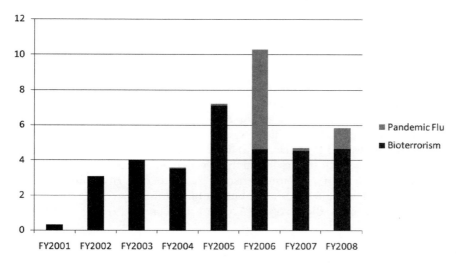

Figure 6.1 Federal Spending on Bioterrorism and Pandemic Flu, Departments of Health and Human Services and Homeland Security, FY 2001–2008 (in $ billions). *Sources*: HHS, *FY 2003 Budget in Brief*, pp. 104–105; HHS, *FY 2004 Budget in Brief*, pp. 93–94; HHS, *FY 2005 Budget in Brief*, pp. 105–106; HHS, *FY 2006 Budget in Brief*, p. 113; HHS, *FY 2007 Budget in Brief*, pp. 99, 101, 104; HHS, *FY 2008 Budget in Brief*, pp. 105, 109; DHS, *FY 2004 Budget in Brief*, p. 94; DHS, *FY 2005 Budget in Brief*, pp. 8, 47; DHS, *FY 2006 Budget in Brief*. p. 5; DHS, *FY 2007 Budget in Brief*, p. 116; DHS, *FY 2008 Budget in Brief*, pp. 86, 92.

BIOTERRORISM PREPAREDNESS AND PUBLIC HEALTH SECURITY: A ZERO-SUM GAME?

In the immediate aftermath of the fall 2001 anthrax attacks, considerable policy attention, and public resources were devoted to improving U.S. preparedness to deal with bioterrorism. Yet concerns about the overall status of the public health system continued, with many policy makers recalling the December 2000 admonitions of the Advisory Panel to Assess Domestic Response Capabilities for Terrorism Involving Weapons of Mass Destruction.

> Fundamental to our consideration is the premise that the nation must have a robust public health system. But that system, and additional resources required to improve it, should follow the multipurpose approach . . . Combating terrorism is a compelling reason for such efforts but should not be the exclusive impetus. Strengthening the public health infrastructure to deal with accidental chemical injuries, emerging infectious diseases, and a pandemic outbreak of

any kind should be the fundamental goal. Such efforts will expand the capability for decontamination, mass-trauma cases, and other surge requirements to deal with terrorism mass-casualty incidents.[66]

Though generally noting that the increased resources provided after the anthrax attacks had "infused public health departments... with the tools and capabilities needed to conduct 'core' business—computers to collect and analyze data, surveillance systems to detect unusual disease activity, and cell phones and Internet connectivity to report and alert other essential personnel,"[67] several studies found that the expanded federal efforts in 2001 and 2002 in the name of bioterrorism were not necessarily translating into gains in the development of a "robust public health system." One analysis of the impact of the Bioterrorism Act, and the increased resources it helped produce, concluded:

> As a result of that act, state health departments received a total of nearly $1 billion along with federal guidelines designated to improve state and local public health preparedness. However, biodefense preparedness funds were awarded concomitant with staggering state deficits and budget cuts, and many traditional public health programs were closed... Consequently, despite new bioterrorism funding, the process of federal funds in and state funds out netted public health departments a zero-sum game, often losing more human assets than they have acquired.[68]

Another survey found evidence "that bioterrorism preparedness funding in some locales may in fact be jeopardizing other public health functions," citing the following as among the examples:

- In California, "reassignments of staff to accomplish [bioterrorism] preparedness functions, coupled with pre-existing workforce shortages and county-level cuts in public health budgets, are compromising other public health functions."
- CDC's emphasis on syndromic surveillance (which attempts to identify the source of disease outbreaks prior to affected individuals seeking medical treatment by looking for "clusters of symptoms," and is thus of particular relevance in anticipating bioterror-caused outbreaks) was seen by a number of localities, including Pittsburgh, as a too costly alternative (the New York City system, which is the prototype, costs approximately $1.5 million a year) to simpler, far less expensive systems for disease monitoring.
- The federal smallpox vaccination program for certain first responders "diverted time and resources from other public health activities while yielding disappointing results in terms of the number of frontline responders who were vaccinated."[69]

TABLE 6.4
Public Health Security Budget, Selected Programs, FY 2001–2008 (in $ millions)

Program	FY 2001	FY 2002	FY 2003	FY 2004	FY 2005	FY 2006	FY 2007	FY 2008
Public Health Infrastructure								
CDC state/local capacity grants	67	940	939	918	919	823	824	698
Hospital preparedness grants	0	135	514	515	487	474	474	414
HHS bioterror training/curriculum development	0	0	28	28	28	21	21	0
CDC capacity, security, facilities (bioterrorism related)	25	188	177	151	140	137	137	137
CDC buildings, facilities (non-bioterrorism related)*	175	296	286	260	270	158	134	20
CDC public health research/improvement*	112	148	153	262	278	295	220	221
National Health Services Corps*	127	145	171	170	131	125	126	116
HRSA health professions programs/nurse loans*	360	388	421	387	403	295	295	115
NIH facilities/physical security	0	92	743	0	149	30	25	0
FDA physical security	2	13	7	7	7	7	7	7
Other HHS public health security	0	8	20	23	23	23	23	68
Sub-total	868	2,353	3,459	2,721	2,835	2,388	2,286	1,796
Bioterrorism Vaccines and Drug Countermeasures								
Strategic National Stockpile	51	645	398	398	467	524	491	581
Project Bioshield	–	–	–	885	2,508	0	0	0
CDC smallpox vaccine	0	512	100	0	0	0	0	0
CDC anthrax vaccine research	18	18	18	18	18	14	14	0
NIH anthrax vaccine procurement	0	0	123	0	0	0	0	0
FDA vaccine/drugs/diagnostics	6	46	53	53	57	57	55	57
Sub-total	75	1,221	692	1,354	3,050	595	560	638

(Continued)

TABLE 6.4
(Continued)

Pandemic Flu and Infectious Disease Control								
CDC infectious disease control*	407	428	436	501	543	592	514	573
HHS Pandemic Influenza	0	0	0	50	99	5,620	164	1,192
DHS Pandemic Influenza	–	–	–	0	0	47	0	0
Sub-total	**407**	**428**	**436**	**551**	**642**	**6,259**	**678**	**1,765**
Biodefense Research								
NIH biodefense research	53	198	687	1,629	1,548	1,604	1,610	1,628
HHS advanced R&D	30	5	5	5	5	54	54	189
Sub-total	**83**	**203**	**692**	**1,634**	**1,553**	**1,658**	**1,664**	**1,817**
Biosurveillance and Detection								
CDC biosurveillance initiative	–	–	–	22	79	78	78	88
DHS biosurveillance initiative	–	–	–	0	11	14	8	11
DHS biological countermeasures	–	–	–	455	398	380	350	314
Sub-total	**–**	**–**	**–**	**477**	**488**	**472**	**436**	**413**
Medical Emergency Preparedness and Response								
National Disaster Medical System	7	33	34	34	34	47	47	53
Metropolitan Medical Response System	17	22	50	50	30	30	33	0
HHS preparedness and response	33	44	79	36	36	36	36	95
DHS Chief Medical Officer	–	–	–	–	–	2	5	16
Sub-total	**57**	**99**	**163**	**120**	**100**	**115**	**121**	**164**
GRAND TOTAL	**1,490**	**4,304**	**5,442**	**6,857**	**8,668**	**11,487**	**5,745**	**6,593**

*Programs not classified as bioterrorism- related in HHS budgets.

Notes:

1. Amounts for FY 2001–2006 are actual expenditures, for FY 2007 are appropriated level, and for FY 2008 are President's budget request.

2. "Other HHS public health security" includes Commissioned Corps, health-care provider credentialing, security coordination and improvement, cyber security, and Medical Reserve Corps.

3. "Project BioShield" amounts reflect appropriations limitations placed on advance appropriations authority of $5.593 billion provided in FY 2004 DHS appropriations bill to fund Project BioShield for FY 2004–2013.

4. "HHS Pandemic Influenza" amount for FY 2006 includes $30 million transferred to United States Agency for International Development (USAID).

5. "DHS biological countermeasures" include BioWatch and National Biodefense Analysis and Countermeasures program. FY 2008 amount includes chemical countermeasures, which were combined into this account by DHS.

6. "HHS preparedness and response" includes preparedness and emergency operations, BioShield management, international early warning surveillance, and media/public information campaign.

Sources: Department of Health and Human Services

2003 *Budget in Brief,* pp. 19, 31, 104–105
2004 *Budget in Brief,* pp. 14, 24, 93–94
2005 *Budget in Brief,* pp. 16, 26, 105–106
2006 *Budget in Brief,* pp. 16, 28, 113
2007 *Budget in Brief,* pp. 20, 28, 99, 104
2008 *Budget in Brief,* pp. 19, 27, 103, 105, 109

Department of Homeland Security

    FY 2005 *Budget in Brief,* pp. 8, 47
    FY 2006 *Budget in Brief,* p. 5
    FY 2007 *Budget in Brief,* p. 116
    FY 2008 *Budget in Brief,* pp. 86, 92, 107

U.S. House of Representatives

    H. Report 109-241, pp. 78, 99–100
    H. Report 109-699, pp. 191–192, 194

Further attempts in 2004 and 2005 to validate such concerns about the use of the additional federal resources to supplant lost state funding rather than to boost the overall public health effort were inconclusive,[70] but increased state public health spending after FY 2004 somewhat alleviated these worries.[71]

CHAPTER 7

Current Status of Public Health Security

The anthrax attacks of 2001 and the rising concerns about a reemerging threat from naturally occurring infectious diseases (especially pandemic influenza) in the years immediately following led to major increases in federal funding (which grew from less than $1.5 billion in FY 2001 to an average of over $7.0 billion a year in the FY 2002–2007 period) and attention (with a series of executive branch directives and plans and congressional enactments) for public health security. At the same time, the basic structure of the public health system itself was not changed, with the initial response to disease outbreaks, whether natural or intentional, resting with private and local health providers (physicians, clinics, emergency rooms) and most authority for public health and medical preparedness residing in state governments. And, while federal funding went up dramatically, total state and local spending for all public health activities—which remained the primary funding source for such programs—remained fairly level throughout the period, averaging approximately $45 billion a year.

Six years after the anthrax letters were mailed, though there are some significant differences in the details, a general consensus exists, among both governmental and independent assessments, about the net result of post-2001 developments on public health security.

These [additional] resources and the efforts of many state and local officials made a positive difference in preparedness planning, training, and exercising; building necessary stockpiles of vaccines and other medical supplies; building laboratory and surveillance capacity; vaccinating at-risk populations; and building surge capacity in hospitals. The pace of progress varies across the country, however, and across the board, much more needs to be done . . . Our nation is not ready to respond to large-scale health emergencies. Our local, state, and federal governments are not fully prepared to protect citizens from disease outbreaks, natural disasters, or acts of bioterrorism. The result is that Americans remain unnecessarily vulnerable to these threats.

■ *Trust for America's Health, September 2007*[1]

We continue to make progress in the preparedness arena, but the combined capacity of federal, state, and local public health partners is not yet where it should be.

■ *Dr. Julie L. Gerberding, CDC Director, March 2007*[2]

Six years after anthrax was mailed to members of the U.S. Congress and to media organizations, the immediacy and potentially strategic significance of the bioweapons threat is not widely appreciated, nor is the country prepared to cope with the consequences of major bioattacks. This is the case in spite of the extensive efforts to improve U.S. biodefense capabilities.

■ *Dr. Tara O'Toole, Center for Biosecurity Director, October 2007*[3]

Such sentiments appear to be widely shared among the population as a whole. In an October 2007 national poll, 68 percent expressed the belief that their community was not prepared to respond to a bioterrorism attack and a similar proportion (66 percent) indicated that the country as a whole was not prepared to cope with a pandemic flu outbreak.[4]

On a more favorable note, whatever the shortcomings in current efforts, the American public continues to express considerable confidence in the federal agencies most involved in public health security, especially the Centers for Disease Control and Prevention (CDC). In a January 2007 nationwide survey, 84 percent of those polled provided a positive (excellent or good) evaluation of CDC's job performance, marking the fifth consecutive time (the previous polls having been conducted in 2000, 2001, 2003, and 2005) that the organization received the highest rating of any of the agencies included in the surveys. The National Institutes of Health (NIH, 78 percent positive) and the Federal Bureau of Investigation (FBI) with 74 percent positive rating ranked third and fourth, respectively, whereas the Food and Drug Administration (FDA) with 62 percent and the Department of Homeland Security (56 percent) trailed somewhat behind, though both still obtained mostly affirmative grades.[5]

ANTHRAX PREPAREDNESS

One measure of the changes that have occurred in public health security preparedness since 2001 is to hone in on what has been done to improve defenses against the agent employed in the attacks that precipitated much of the subsequent governmental response.

While no apparent breakthroughs have occurred (as of late 2007) in identifying and apprehending the person or persons responsible for the 2001 anthrax attacks, "much progress has been made [but] there is much left to do" in improving U.S. public health defenses against future such attacks.[6]

At the fifth anniversary of the 2001 events, the Center for Biosecurity produced an assessment of accomplishments and remaining challenges in anthrax preparedness. The Center report highlighted the following areas of progress:

- The Strategic National Stockpile includes enough doxycycline and ciprofloxacin tablets to provide sixty-day courses of treatment for 40 million individuals, and 10 million doses of the AVA anthrax vaccine.[7]
- Significant improvements have been made in laboratory diagnostic tests for anthrax, allowing for faster, more accurate identification of anthrax from specimens submitted to the Laboratory Response Network (LRN).[8] (By the beginning of 2007, CDC was reporting "100 percent capability to confirm anthrax" in the LRN labs,[9] and forty-six states plus the District of Columbia indicated they had sufficient numbers of trained scientists to test for possible anthrax outbreaks, compared to thirty-six in 2004.[10])
- The increases in federal funding for state and local preparedness "have allowed health departments to hire epidemiologists, train staff, develop labs, purchase information technology, conduct planning activities, and support the salaries of state bioterrorism coordinators."
- CDC's implementation of the Health Alert Network and other electronic communications systems, combined with similar initiatives at the state level and in the private sector have enhanced the public health system's information sharing capacity (though "the extent to which this information actually reaches the majority of clinicians in a timely fashion is unclear").
- Much more basic and applied research on anthrax has been conducted, including investigations of "the microbiology of the organism, the pathogenesis of the disease, vaccines, antitoxins, diagnostics, sensing, and early detection technologies."
- There is greater awareness of the bioweapons threat in general and anthrax in particular among policy makers and public health officials, with a number of relevant education and training activities provided at all levels.[11]

The Center for Biosecurity report also pointed to the need for further improvements in the distribution of the medical supplies in the Strategic National Stockpile, treatment strategies and guidelines, and the speed and expense of diagnostic testing. In addition, the report observed that hospitals' capacity to cope with mass-casualty events "has not improved significantly over the past five years [and] a national strategy to vastly improve inpatient surge capacity must be implemented." Finally, the Center's evaluation called for further education of primary health-care providers, noting that "while most physicians have heard of anthrax, knowledge is spotty at best, and misconceptions abound."[12]

Shortly after the September 2006 Center for Biosecurity assessment, the Department of Health and Human Services (HHS) terminated its contract with the pharmaceutical manufacturer VaxGen, which was to deliver 75 million doses of "second generation" anthrax vaccine for the Strategic National Stockpile. The cancellation occurred after the FDA had placed a clinical hold on the product, and the company had failed to meet a series of critical project milestone dates.[13] The House Committee on Homeland Security sent a letter to HHS Secretary Michael Leavitt on September 10, 2007 expressing concerns about the pace at which HHS was proceeding in acquiring the kind of recombinant protective antigen (rPA) anthrax vaccine to have been produced by VaxGen, and an anthrax antitoxin capable of treating multiple-drug resistant anthrax. The letter noted that the latter was not now scheduled to be acquired until sometime between 2009 and 2013.[14] As Dr. Tara O'Toole testified to Congress in October 2007,

> It took another nine months [after canceling the VaxGen contract] to conclude a contract to acquire 18.75 million doses of the original, "first generation" anthrax vaccine. So instead of anticipating delivery of the second-generation anthrax vaccine next year, the country is starting over in its quest for such vaccine. We currently have enough vaccine in the stockpile to immunize about three million people—not enough to immunize a single city.[15]

A further Strategic National Stockpile-related problem was uncovered in October 2007 with a GAO report indicating that, beginning in 2008, approximately $100 million worth of anthrax vaccine in the stockpile will begin to expire, while HHS currently lacks an effective strategy to deal with the problem.[16]

The 2006 analysis of the Center for Biosecurity concluded, "While a great deal of money has been spent, and much has been accomplished . . . preparedness for anthrax remains very much a work in progress. Were another attack with *B. anthracis* to occur today, even one relatively modest in size, it is unlikely that all of the essential elements of effective medical response—vaccine, prophylactic antibiotics, and intensive care—would be available in sufficient quantity and time to avert illness on a large scale."[17]

ORGANIZATION

As noted previously, the highly fragmented organization of the U.S. public health system that existed prior to 2001 has continued largely unchanged since then. "Ongoing problems resulting from this diffused structure" cited in the 2007 annual report on public health preparedness by the Trust for America's Health (TFAH) echoed concerns expressed about the pre-2001 system.

- Lack of clear roles for the various state, local, and federal agencies.
- Differing responsibilities and capacities among the some 3,000 local health departments.
- Limited coordination among the levels of government, including determination of how federal assets would be deployed to states and localities, and across jurisdictions, such as sharing assets and resources among states.
- No minimum standards, guidelines, or recommendations for capacity levels or services required of state and local health departments. This results in major differences in services and competencies across state and local levels.
- Lack of funding flexibility and comprehensiveness due to a federal funding structure that is largely based on categorical or program grants. These often-restrictive grants also lack a system of accountability.
- Ineffective and random capacity to coordinate with nongovernmental organizations, community groups, and the private sector.[18]

Under such circumstances, it has been recognized that "national leadership and action are essential to ensure disaster and emergency threats are well-assessed and standards for preparedness are set."[19] In the wake of the anthrax attacks and the looming possibility of an influenza pandemic, the federal government has undertaken a number of initiatives aimed at strengthening federal leadership and coordination capabilities, including: the Public Health Security and Bioterrorism Preparedness and Response Act of 2002, which directed HHS to "develop and implement a coordinated strategy" to improve the public health system's capacity for responding to emergencies; the Homeland Security Act of 2002, which created the Department of Homeland Security and gave it the lead in responding to terrorist acts, including bioterrorism and other disasters; and the Pandemic and All-Hazards Preparedness Act of 2006, which specifically designated the Secretary of HHS as the lead federal official for directing the public health and medical response to all national emergencies.

While offering new possibilities for coordination of federal counterterrorism and emergency preparedness efforts, the introduction of the new Department of Homeland Security (DHS) has also posed additional organizational challenges for public health security. Dr. Tara O'Toole of the Center for Biosecurity testified in March 2007 that "Responsibility and accountability for medical preparedness and response during large-scale catastrophes within HHS and DHS are unclear, and in both agencies these functions are grossly understaffed and underfunded... It would be desirable going forward to clarify the medical response authorities and responsibilities of DHS versus those of HHS."[20]

An August 2007 Government Accountability Office (GAO) report examined the National Strategy for Pandemic Influenza and its associated implementation plan, and found that

> The Strategy and Plan do not specify how the [federal] leadership roles and responsibilities would work in addressing the unique characteristics of a pandemic influenza, which could occur simultaneously in multiple locations and over a long period...The Strategy and Plan indicate that both the Secretary of Health and Human Services and the Secretary of Homeland Security will have leadership responsibilities that are consistent with the [National Response Plan]—the former for leading the federal medical response to a pandemic and the latter for overall domestic incident management and federal coordination. However, it is not clear how, in a pandemic, the Secretaries...would share leadership responsibilities in practice...Moreover, under recent legislation, the FEMA [Federal Emergency Management Agency] Administrator was designated the principal domestic emergency management advisor to the President, the [Homeland Security Council], and the Secretary of Homeland Security, adding further complexity to the leadership structure in the case of a pandemic.[21]

In addition to the issue of organizational arrangements, some independent observers have questioned whether the overall governmental effort has displayed sufficient leadership to meet the challenges of biodefense, with O'Toole stating, "The level of leadership attention—in both the executive and legislative branches, and at both the federal and state levels—has been inadequate."[22]

PLANNING

In reaction to the terrorist hijackings and anthrax letters of 2001, and the gaps they revealed in U.S. preparedness, a series of planning requirements, as displayed in Table 7.1, have been established for homeland security and public health security.

By the end of 2006, the federal government and all states had "plans on paper" for responding to both bioterrorism and pandemic flu, a vast improvement over the pre-2001 situation. Yet, serious questions remain about the extent to which the ever-expanding collection of plans and procedures has actually improved the coordination and execution of public health (and other homeland) security programs.

To be sure, crafting appropriate and effective planning documents has posed a daunting challenge for federal policy makers, who have been faced with a number of major obstacles, including constant shifts in organizational roles (especially the creation of DHS out of twenty-two separate federal agencies, each with its own institutional history and culture and some with major non-security responsibilities) and leadership personnel; the

TABLE 7.1
Post-2001 Key Homeland Security and Public Health Security Plans

Plan (responsible agency)	Description
National Preparedness Plan (HHS)	Required by Public Health Security and Bioterrorism Preparedness and Response Act of 2002. Designed to enhance federal, state, and local preparedness for bioterrorism or other public health emergencies.
National Response Plan (DHS)	Required by Homeland Security Presidential Directive 5 of Feb. 28, 2003. Superseded previous Federal Response Plan (which specified how federal government was to respond to terrorism and other national disasters) by providing clearer designations of federal agency roles as lead or support, depending on the type of emergency. Is to be replaced by the National Response Framework once the latter—which was presented for review in July 2007—is finalized.
WHO Global Influenza Preparedness Plan (WHO)	First issued by WHO in 1999, but revised and reissued in 2005. Establishes objectives for WHO and national health authorities for pandemic influenza planning, surveillance, prevention, response and communications.
National Strategy for Pandemic Influenza (HHS, DHS, USDA, State Department)	Established by Presidential announcement of Nov. 1, 2005. Sets out general principles, objectives, and roles for federal, state, and local authorities in planning, communications, countermeasures production and distribution, research and development, surveillance, response, and containment for pandemic flu outbreaks.
HHS Pandemic Influenza Plan (HHS)	Issued by HHS in November 2005. Outlines federal public health and medical preparedness plans for pandemics and describes roles of HHS and its agencies during such an occurrence.
State Influenza Preparedness and Response Plans (CDC, HHS)	HHS required states to submit pandemic flu plans to CDC by July 2005, with more detailed guidance provided by Nov. 2005 HHS Pandemic Influenza Plan, which suggested that effective state and local pandemic response plans should address such areas as surveillance, infection control and prevention, vaccine and antiviral distribution and use, communications, and workforce support.
National Infrastructure Protection Plan (DHS)	Required by Homeland Security Presidential Directive 7 of December 15, 2005. Seeks to provide a comprehensive and integrated plan for securing critical infrastructure by outlining national goals, milestones, and key initiatives necessary to achieve that objective.
Sector Specific Plans (DHS, various other agencies)	Required under National Infrastructure Protection Plan (NIPP). In implementing NIPP, DHS required federal

(Continued)

TABLE 7.1
(*Continued*)

Plan (responsible agency)	Description
	agencies designated as leads for each of seventeen infrastructure sectors to develop a Sector Specific Plan to establish means by which sector will identify, assess risks to prioritize and develop necessary protective measures for critical assets. (HHS is responsible for the public health and health-care Sector Specific Plan or SSP.)
National Strategy for Pandemic Influenza Implementation Plan (HHS, DHS, USDA, State Department)	Established by Presidential announcement of May 2006. Outlines over 300 specific actions to be taken in implementing the National Strategy.
National Health Security Strategy (HHS)	Required by Pandemic and All-Hazards Preparedness Act of 2006. To be submitted to Congress in 2009. Consistent with National Response Plan/Framework, is to set public health security preparedness goals for federal, state, and local governments.
CDC Influenza Pandemic Operation Plan (OPLAN) (CDC)	Issued by CDC in December 2006. Outlines what actions are to be taken by agency officials in preparing for an influenza pandemic, with an emphasis on early recognition, rapid assistance to impacted areas, and provision of vaccine and antivirals to at-risk or affected populations.

Sources:
1. U.S. House of Representatives, *Conference Report to Accompany HR 3448, Public Health Security and Bioterrorism Preparedness and Response Act of 2002*, H. Report 107-481, May 21, 2002.
2. Sarah A. Lister, Congressional Research Service, "An Overview of the U.S. Public Health System in the Context of Emergency Preparedness," RL31719, March 14, 2005.
3. GAO, *Department of Homeland Security: Progress Report on Implementation of Mission and Management Functions*, GAO-07-454, August 2007.
4. World Health Organization, *WHO Global Influenza Preparedness Plan*, 2005.
5. White House, *National Strategy for Pandemic Influenza*, November 2005.
6. Department of Health and Human Services, *Pandemic Influenza Plan*, November 2005.
7. Sarah A. Lister and Holly Stockdale, Congressional Research Service, "Pandemic Influenza: An Analysis of State Preparedness and Response Plans," RL34190, September 24, 2007.
8. GAO, *Critical Infrastructure: Sector Plans Complete and Sector Councils Evolving*, GAO-07-1075T, July 12, 2007.
9. White House, National Strategy for Pandemic Influenza Implementation Plan, May 2006.
10. Sarah A. Lister, Congressional Research Service, "The Pandemic and All-Hazards Preparedness Act (PL 109-417): Provisions and Changes to Preexisting Law," RL33589, January 25, 2007.
11. Centers for Disease Control and Prevention, CDC *Influenza Pandemic Operation* Plan (*OPLAN*), December 2006.

need to design an appropriate framework for encompassing the non-federal entities (state, local, private sectors) that represent a majority of the assets to be protected and of the capabilities to be employed in providing such protection; and the newly emerging discipline of security risk management, which is supposed to guide the planning process. With these constraints, it is not surprising that there have been a number of critical assessments of federal homeland security planning to date, including by, among others, the 9/11 Commission, its successor (the 9/11 Public Discourse Project), GAO, the Heritage Foundation, and the Center for Strategic and International Studies.[23]

Looking more specifically at the plans pertaining to public health security, the TFAH 2007 assessment of public health preparedness cited concerns about their "limited, non-systematic testing and exercising of emergency health plans, and inconsistent mechanisms for incorporating lessons learned into future planning." It also pointed to inadequacies in addressing the licensing and credentialing of emergency health-care volunteers and in communicating effectively with at-risk populations, including especially elderly and low-income minorities.[24]

Because of the security classification of major portions of the various DHS plans, publicly available evaluations of those plans are somewhat limited. An August 2007 GAO report to Congress concluded, "that DHS has generally not achieved this performance expectation [of establishing a single, all-hazards National Response Plan]. DHS issued . . . a limited post-Katrina revision in May 2006, but we and others have identified concerns with those revisions."[25]

Another GAO analysis from a month earlier provided mostly general assessments of several sector-specific plans required under the National Infrastructure Protection Plan (NIPP), including the one covering public health and health care.

Although the nine sector-specific plans GAO reviewed generally met NIPP requirements and DHS's sector-specific plan guidance, eight did not describe any incentives the sector would use to encourage owners to conduct voluntary risk assessments, as required by the NIPP. Most of the plans included the required elements of the NIPP risk management framework. However, the plans varied in how comprehensively they addressed not only their physical assets, systems, and functions, but also their human and cyber assets, systems, and functions, a requirement in the NIPP . . . Given the disparity in the plans, it is unclear the extent to which DHS will be able to use them to identify security gaps and critical interdependence across the sectors.[26]

The GAO report also considered the coordinating councils formed for each infrastructure sector, composed of governmental and private sector representatives, which "are envisioned as a primary point of contact for government to plan the entire range of infrastructure protection activities unique to the sector." GAO found considerable variation between the councils, including in their views as to the value of their sector plan and DHS' review and contribution to those plans. A particular problem was cited with respect to the health plan, reflective of the fragmentary nature of that sector.

> The public health and health care sector representative said that getting the numerous sector members to participate is a challenge, and the government representative noted that because of this, the first step in implementing the sector-specific plan is to increase awareness about the effort among sector members to encourage participation.[27]

The National Research Council's (NRC) Committee on Methodological Improvements to the Department of Homeland Security's Biological Agent Risk Analysis was established in order to review DHS' January 2006 Bioterrorism Risk Assessment. In its preliminary evaluation, the NRC committee indicated that the initial DHS risk assessment techniques are "a logical extension of previous risk analysis methods used for natural and technological hazards and engineering design. The implementation of the selected PRA [probabilistic risk assessment] framework appears, for the most part, to be consistent with well-accepted practice in other fields of risk analysis such as nuclear reactor safety and chemical safety."[28]

However, the committee went on to note,

> The DHS model requires a large amount of information, much of which is uncertain. This information includes the known properties of the pathogen, estimates of the propensities of terrorists to take different actions, and estimates of the reactions of the affected population and the timeliness and effectiveness of the government response...The major concern of the committee is that the current PRA event-tree paradigm does not fully support any of the components of risk analysis. It does not include consideration of the actions of an intelligent and reactive adversary, which is required for a complete risk analysis. It makes no provision for risk perception. It does not allow the exploration by decision makers of "what-if" questions, which is needed for risk management.[29]

More broadly, GAO found, "DHS's assessment efforts overall appear to be the early stages and substantial more work remains for DHS to more fully conduct assessments of chemical, biological, radiological, and nuclear threats."[30]

Compared to the DHS planning documents, considerably more information has been made public about the HHS preparedness plans, especially those concerning pandemic influenza. For example, in October 2007 testimony to Congress, HHS Assistant Secretary for Response and Preparedness

William C. Vanderwagen indicated over 80 percent of the approximately 200 action items assigned to HHS by the National Strategy for Pandemic Influenza Implementation Plan had been completed, and commented, "These gains are real and measurable, and they cover a broad range of preparedness, including enhancing our international laboratory networks, developing and releasing community-based measures to mitigate the effects of a pandemic, and expanding the Medical Reserve Corps program."[31]

The August 2007 GAO report gave a mixed evaluation on how well the National Strategy for Pandemic Influenza and the associated Implementation Plan address key elements of an effective national strategy.

> The Strategy and Plan represent an important first step in guiding the nation's preparedness and response activities, calling for a series of actions by federal agencies and expectations for states and communities, the private sector, global partners, and individuals. However, when viewed together, the Strategy and Plan do not fully address the six characteristics of an effective national strategy. Gaps and deficiencies in these documents are particularly troubling because they can affect the usefulness of the planning documents to those with key roles to play and affect their ability to effectively carry out their responsibilities.[32]

Specifically, GAO found the Strategy and Plan adequately addressed problem definition and risk assessment "by identifying the potential problems associated with a pandemic as well as potential threats, challenges, and vulnerabilities." Four other key characteristics were judged to be only partially addressed by the HHS documents.

- Clear purpose, scope, and methodology: Key stakeholders, such as state, local, and tribal governments, were not directly involved in developing actions and the performance measures that are to assess progress...
- Integration and implementation: The Strategy and Plan provide little detail about how the set of pandemic plans they propose, such as the individual agencies' pandemic plans, are to be integrated with other existing national strategies that are to provide an overall all-hazards framework...
- Goals, objectives, activities, and performance measures: [The] lack of a clear linkage between the performance measures and intended results makes it difficult to ascertain whether any progress beyond the completion of activities has in fact been made...
- Organizational roles, responsibilities, and coordination: The Strategy and Plan did not clarify how responsible officials will share leadership responsibilities.

Most negatively, the report indicated the National Strategy for Pandemic Influenza and its Implementation Plan did not address the crucial question of resources, investments, and risk management "because they do not discuss the financial resources and investments needed to implement the actions called for."[33] In this respect, planning for pandemic flu is similar to many other federal homeland security activities, for instance those in the field of transportation security.[34]

In a 2006 analysis, the Center for Biosecurity stated that the pandemic influenza implementation plan had "advanced the national pandemic planning efforts in a number of ways," citing in particular its more detailed assessment of the possible consequences of a pandemic flu outbreak, its provision of specific actions, performance measures, and timelines, and its description of the planned federal response to a pandemic. However, the Center also found shortcomings in a number of the plan's details.

- Inadequate goals for the timeline and target amounts for pandemic influenza vaccine.
- Inadequate funding.
- Insufficient attention to hospital preparedness.
- Unclear or inaccurate disease containment options (such as large-scale geographic quarantines).
- Insufficient support for provision of vaccine and antiviral supplies to low-income countries.
- Insufficient detail on how vaccination and antiviral distribution would be prioritized.
- Unclear assumptions about disease surveillance capabilities and situational awareness among policy makers.
- Insufficient attention to relevant animal health issues.[35]

Given the continuing central role of states in the public health security system, attention has also been focused on their plans for pandemic influenza preparedness. An independent review of forty-nine state plans published in September 2006 considered the contents of those plans in the areas of vaccination, surveillance and detection, and containment measures. In summary it found that all of the plans were generally consistent with the widely accepted vaccination priorities set forth by the Advisory Committee on Immunization Practices (ACIP), but most were reliant on passive surveillance methods (such as the National Sentinel Physician Surveillance system), with relatively few providing for the use of the more advanced real-time syndromic surveillance of patients with flu-like illnesses who seek care at clinics or emergency rooms. Finally, the authors of the analysis reported, "The various state plans are markedly heterogeneous in their personal contact-avoidance measures and prophylaxis. Most states outline pandemic influenza responses that do not include general and early encouragement of many specific personal avoidance steps, such as staying at home from work and keeping sick children at home."[36]

A year later, the Congressional Research Service performed another assessment of the state pandemic plans, this time including the District of Columbia as well as all fifty state plans.

The state pandemic flu plans analyzed here reflected their authorship by public health officials. Many of them addressed core public health functions such as surveillance or vaccine management, though specific aspects of these functions were addressed in varying degrees of depth. This suggests that challenges remain even in areas that are familiar to public health planners, such as: developing schemes to prioritize or ration limited medical assets; coordinating surveillance to optimize early detection and ongoing disease monitoring; and legal liability and civil rights issues associated with disease control measures. Fewer plans addressed leadership and coordination, or the continuity of non-health services, subjects which may be unfamiliar to public health planners, or which may exceed their authority. These elements may require stronger engagement by emergency management officials and others in planning.[37]

WORKFORCE READINESS AND EXERCISES

Many of the workforce problems cited in evaluations of the pre-2001 public health security system remain as challenges to current preparedness efforts.

According to a pair of 2007 surveys of local health departments conducted by the National Association of County and City Health Officials (NACCHO), the greatest need identified by these departments was for additional qualified staff. Almost two-thirds of the local health agencies that attempted to hire personnel for public health preparedness functions reported they were unable to recruit qualified candidates for these positions.[38] The 2006 TFAH report found "there is a growing public health professional and nursing workforce shortage," with forty states plus the District of Columbia experiencing a nursing shortage. The report also expressed concern about the limited efforts thus far to utilize volunteer medical workers in emergencies and the lack of policies to encourage health care workers to continue on the job in the event of a major infectious disease outbreak.[39]

In its first report on public health preparedness in February 2008, CDC noted that public health departments were experiencing difficulties in recruiting and retaining qualified epidemiologists, and thirty-one state public health laboratories were encountering problems in locating qualified laboratory scientists.[40]

Somewhat older data (from 2004) indicated that the average age of the public health workforce was over forty-six years, close to half of them would be eligible for retirement within the next few years, the job vacancy rate in public health systems was 20 percent, and the average annual turnover rate in those systems was 14 percent.[41]

The declines in federal funding for public health infrastructure beginning at mid-decade have had a discernible impact on workforce preparedness. For instance, almost a third (28 percent) of the local health departments responding to the 2007 NACCHO surveys reported they had reduced staff time devoted to preparedness because of cuts in FY 2006 federal funding, while 17 percent delayed or cancelled workforce training because of those cuts.[42] Summarizing the current situation, the 2007 TFAH preparedness survey reported, "The public health workforce is facing a shortage of crisis proportions that seriously threatens our nation's health... A workforce shortage could debilitate the system if a public health emergency were to occur."[43]

Emergency preparedness exercises are an important component in improving the readiness of the public health security workforce and its leadership. All fifty states, plus the District of Columbia, held some form of emergency preparedness drill involving state health officials and the state's National Guard Forces during 2007.[44] The Government Accountability Office's 2007 "progress report" on DHS indicated the department had developed a Homeland Security Exercise Evaluation Program that "provides standardized guidance and methodologies for scheduling, developing, executing, and evaluating emergency preparedness exercises." It further found that the program "generally achieved" the performance expectation that DHS "establish a program for conducting emergency preparedness exercises."[45]

However, translating the DHS exercise program standards into actual gains in readiness remains a work in progress. For example, DHS reported that in FY 2006, thirty-three of forty-eight federally funded exercises and just forty out of 110 state or locally funded exercises were compliant with the departmental guidelines. Furthermore, DHS has not evaluated how well regional or national exercises comport with the guidelines.[46]

Three major, multi-agency exercise scenarios involving bioweapons have been conducted since 2001.[47]

- TOPOFF 2 (Top Officials, the nation's premier terrorism preparedness exercises), from May 12 to 16, 2003, which simulated attacks by a fictitious foreign terrorist organization involving the detonation of a radiological weapon in Seattle, Washington and the release of pneumonic plague in several locations in the Chicago area. Top government officials from twenty-five federal, state, and local agencies, and the Canadian government participated.[48]
- Atlantic Storm, a privately sponsored tabletop exercise in January 2005, which depicted a series of bioterrorist attacks involving the release of the smallpox virus in a number of major transportation and commercial centers in Europe and North America. Participants represented the political leadership of Canada, the European Commission, France, Germany, Italy, the Netherlands, Poland, Sweden, the United Kingdom, the United States, and the World Health Organization (WHO).[49]
- TOPOFF 3, from April 4 to 8, 2005, which involved terrorist attacks using mustard gas in Connecticut and pneumonic plague in New Jersey. Again a number of federal, state, and local agencies were represented in the exercise.[50]

Among the key problems uncovered by these simulations were difficulties in the use of the Homeland Security threat advisory system (TOPOFF 2) and the inapplicability of certain federal disaster authorities, including the fact that the primary federal disaster law, the Stafford Act, did not explicitly cover biological incidents (TOPOFF 2 and TOPOFF 3). Other concerns identified by the exercises included uncertainties about the distribution policies for the Strategic National Stockpile and a lack of consistent information about those policies (TOPOFF 2), inadequacies in emergency communications systems (TOPOFF 2), hospital surge capacity (TOPOFF 2), and the capability of multilateral organizations—including the North Atlantic Treaty Organization (NATO), the European Union (EU), and WHO—to cope with the deliberate spread of infectious disease (Atlantic Storm), wide variations between countries in bioterror and pandemic response standards and capabilities (Atlantic Storm), inadequacies in international vaccine and antiviral supplies, information systems, and diagnostic technology (Atlantic Storm), insufficient communication of key information to the public (TOPOFF 3) and inadequate internal information-sharing systems and protocols (Atlantic Storm and TOPOFF 3).[51]

In addition to the problem areas, certain positive findings also emerged from the training exercises. TOPOFF 2 found that the designation of a DHS Principal Federal Official (PFO) was "well received and successfully integrated" into the local command structure and "facilitated and integrated communications and coordinated action planning."[52] Moreover, New Jersey public health officials reported that hospitals involved in the TOPOFF 3 drill were able to integrate the exercise-related activities "efficiently" into their normal operations.[53]

However, as former DHS Secretary Tom Ridge observed, in October 2007, "The challenge with TOPOFF is not the exercise itself. It's to move as quickly as possible to remedy . . . the problems that are uncovered." Ridge's comments were in response to the fact that over two and a half years after its occurrence, DHS had still not released the after-action report on TOPOFF 3. This also came after a 2005 DHS inspector general report had indicated that the department needed to do a better job of tracking lessons learned from its emergency exercises. In addition, the 2006 White House analysis of lessons learned from Hurricane Katrina pointedly observed, "The most recent Top Officials (TOPOFF) exercise in April 2005 revealed the federal government's lack of progress in addressing a number of preparedness deficiencies, many of which had been identified in previous exercises."[54]

While specific elements of pandemic response (such as distributions from the Strategic National Stockpile) have been used in training scenarios, no multisector, multi-jurisdictional pandemic influenza exercise has been conducted, nor has the new national leadership structure for response to such an outbreak been subjected to testing.[55]

Under the terms of the FY 2006 supplemental appropriations legislation that funded pandemic flu preparedness, states were required to conduct pandemic flu exercises in the fields of control of community gatherings (such as school closings), medical surge capacity, and mass vaccination/prophylaxis. A Congressional Research Service (CRS) report noted that, "While no doubt useful, these exercises will be carried out state-by-state, retaining a health-sector focus,"[56] thus repeating some of the problems noted above with respect to pandemic planning.

LABORATORY CAPACITY AND SURVEILLANCE SYSTEMS

Perhaps no element of public health security has experienced greater improvement since the anthrax attacks than laboratory capacity. By March 2007 CDC had increased the number of Laboratory Response Network labs from 91 in 2001 to 152, with coverage in all 50 states and 100 percent capability to confirm the presence of anthrax, tularemia, and plague. Also by that date, CDC had provided emergency response training to over 9,000 clinical laboratory workers.[57] Moreover, CDC developed a diagnostic test for H5N1 influenza that was approved by the FDA and delivered to the LRN labs by February 2006.[58]

The TFAH 2007 readiness report found that forty-three states were reporting sufficient biological agent testing capabilities (compared to just six in 2003) and forty-eight were indicating they are able to provide full-time coverage in analyzing laboratory samples during public health emergencies.[59]

As these figures reveal, though, some gaps in state laboratory capacity continue to exist, and other limitations in laboratory effectiveness that have been reported include shortages in reagents, which are the materials needed for biological agent testing,[60] and the fact that submission of specimens to the LRN for testing still requires the initial suspicion of the presence of the biological agent.[61]

In addition, long-standing concerns about lab safety and security have persisted, and with the number of U.S. facilities approved by the government to handle the most lethal substances having doubled (to 409) since 2004, the problem appears to be increasing. An October 2007 survey by the Associated Press reported over 100 missing shipments and lab accidents since 2003, with the largest number (thirty-six) occurring in the first two-thirds of 2007.

The mishaps include workers bitten or scratched by infected animals, skin cuts, needle sticks and more... [Confidential reports submitted to federal regulators] describe accidents involving anthrax, bird flu virus, monkeypox and plague-causing bacteria at 44 labs in 24 states.[62]

Gains have also been made in U.S. disease surveillance systems. It has been reported by CDC that "all state public health departments now receive and evaluate reports of urgent health threats 24/7/365," compared to just twelve that did so in 1999.[63] As of 2007, thirty-eight states (versus eighteen in 2004) plus the District of Columbia were compatible with CDC's National Electronic Disease Surveillance System (NEDSS) that allows for more integrated, accurate, and timely national disease reporting.[64] However, TFAH reported "Independent evaluations of public health IT systems find non-integrated, uncoordinated systems that are often duplicative, and problems with consistency of data."[65]

The difficulties inherent in these "non-integrated, uncoordinated systems" were highlighted in another analysis by TFAH.

> CDC coordinates and supports over 100 national surveillance systems that are implemented primarily by state and local health officials, and that are characterized by poor sharing of information among the systems and delays in reporting results to those who need the information in a timely fashion. Those systems are also characterized by inadequate funding making it difficult to protect the public's health.[66]

Another shortcoming in some current surveillance systems was called to attention in the February 2008 CDC preparedness analysis, which reported that sixteen states indicated they had no plans to electronically exchange health data with regional health-care provider networks.[67]

Given the overriding importance of prompt detection in mitigating the impact of infectious diseases of whatever source, the continuing absence of rapid, point-of-care diagnostic tests for biological weapon agents or any specific strain of influenza (including H5N1) is a significant shortcoming in current surveillance efforts.[68] (HHS failed to meet a June 2007 deadline for submission to Congress of a strategic plan on the development and implementation of "a near real-time electronic nationwide public health situational awareness capability network.")[69]

DHS' biosurveillance activities, particularly BioWatch, have also raised some controversy. As of mid-2007, the BioWatch program, which is a biological- and chemical aerosol-monitoring system designed to provide early warning of a biological (or chemical) attack, was deployed in thirty cities across the country. The Government Accountability Office reported that, as of that time, though progress had been made, DHS had not "generally achieved [the] performance expectation [of coordinating deployment of nuclear, biological, chemical and radiological detection capabilities]."[70]

At the end of 2007, the BioWatch program began limited deployment of a new sensor device, called the Autonomous Pathogen Detection System, in New York and other cities. Unlike the older sensors that have to be manually serviced once a day with the collected samples taken to a laboratory for analysis, the new system is designed to operate automatically and to immediately transmit results to authorities. However, DHS officials have expressed concerns about the reliability and affordability of the new devices, and are already beginning pilot testing of alternatives.[71]

The Center for Biosecurity has raised a number of questions about the effectiveness of BioWatch.

> The initial proposal [for BioWatch] was... based on erroneous assumptions about the availability of digitalized health information, overly optimistic expectations of what data could be collected and analyzed by the federal government, and how meaningful such data would be to decision makers... It is not clear thus far... that BioWatch information alone is "actionable." That is, in several incidents of BioWatch detectors accurately signaling the presence of a pathogen, public health officials were reluctant to take decisive action—to act as though an attack were underway—without confirmatory clinical data. That raises questions about whether BioWatch truly shortens "response time."[72]

In response to such concerns DHS initiated the Biological Warning and Incident Characterization System to provide a better and more rapid determination of the public health effects of bioagent detections by BioWatch.[73] However, considering overall surveillance needs and capabilities, the Director of the Center for Biosecurity, Dr. O'Toole, continued to express doubts, asking, "Does it make sense to invest limited biodefense funds in more advanced BioWatch technology, even as we are now doing? Many public health professionals... noted that assessment of BioWatch data requires limited public health resources that might be otherwise employed to greater effect."[74] And the Congress directed that $2 million be taken out of BioWatch's FY 2008 operating budget to be used for a study by the National Academies of Science on the cost effectiveness of the program's environmental sampling approach versus enhanced monitoring of disease patterns.[75]

HOSPITAL PREPAREDNESS AND SURGE CAPACITY

After widespread criticism of the overall federal response to Hurricane Katrina, the White House issued a report on "lessons learned" in February 2006. Among many other problem areas, that assessment highlighted a number of flaws in the public health system's response to the biggest mass-casualty event since 2001.

> Most local and state public health and medical assets were overwhelmed by the [post-Katrina] conditions, placing even greater challenges on federally deployed personnel. Immediate challenges included the identification, triage, and treatment of acutely sick and injured patients; the management of chronic medical conditions in large numbers of evacuees with special healthcare needs; the assessment, communication, and mitigation of public health risk; and the provision of assistance to state and local health officials to quickly reestablish

health care delivery systems and public health infrastructures. Despite the success of federal, state, and local personnel in meeting this enormous challenge, obstacles at all levels reduced the reach and efficiency of public health and medical support efforts ... These inefficiencies were the products of a fragmented command structure for medical response; inadequate evacuation of patients; weak state and local public health infrastructures; insufficient pre-storm risk communication to the public; and the absence of a uniform electronic health record system.[76]

The HHS hospital preparedness grants program was transferred from the Health Resources and Services Administration to the newly created office of the Assistant Secretary for Preparedness and Response under the terms of the Pandemic and All-Hazards Response Act of 2006.

In October 2007 testimony to Congress, Assistant Secretary for Preparedness and Response William Vanderwagen reported that the program's current focus was on improving hospital surge capacity for mass-casualty events by identifying available beds, utilizing civilian volunteers, planning for alternate care sites, promoting effective resource sharing under surge conditions by developing health-care provider partnerships, providing the highest possible standards of patient care in scarce resource situations, and establishing stockpiles of critical medical equipment and supplies.[77]

To accomplish these objectives, between FY 2002 and 2007 $2.6 billion was appropriated for hospital preparedness grants, though annual funding levels declined after FY 2004. With approximately 5,000 general hospitals in the United States, this averages out to less than $100,000 per hospital per year, less the amounts provided out of the grant total to local health departments. One of the few attempts to calculate the costs of accomplishing the stated objectives of the hospital grants program was made by the Center for Biosecurity, which arrived at a rough estimate of an initial expense of $1 million per hospital ($5 billion total) to make an average-sized facility capable of coping with a mass-casualty event on the scale of the 1918 flu pandemic. In addition, the center projected recurring costs of $200,000 per year per average hospital to maintain the requisite level of preparedness.[78]

The apparent mismatch between goals and means is reflected in a number of negative assessments of hospital preparedness and surge capacity. TFAH reported that "shortfalls exist in facilities, beds, medical supplies, and equipment to respond to major outbreaks," only twenty-five states and the District of Columbia have the capacity to supply sufficient hospital beds for at least two weeks during a "moderately severe" flu pandemic,[79] and "an already over-stretched public health workforce ... remains in most localities ill-prepared to respond to major disasters."[80]

In March 2008 the majority staff of the House Committee on Oversight and Government Reform conducted a survey of hospitals in seven U.S. cities "to determine the real-time capacity of the emergency rooms ... to absorb a sudden influx from a mass casualty event." The survey found that "none of the hospitals surveyed . . . had sufficient emergency care capacity to respond to an attack generating the number of casualties that occurred in [the March 2004 terrorist attacks on commuter trains in] Madrid." More specifically, the staff report noted,

- Almost 60 percent of the emergency rooms were already operating over capacity, "meaning they had no available treatment space in the emergency rooms to accommodate new patients."
- The *combined* number of available treatment spaces in the seven cities was less than the 270 patients sent to a single hospital for emergency care after the Madrid attacks.
- *None* of the hospitals surveyed had sufficient capacity for critical care or inpatient beds to be able to cope with the type and level of casualties experienced at a single Madrid hospital after the 2004 attacks.[81]

The Center for Biosecurity has observed that most hospitals have done minimal disaster planning, have not joined together with other local facilities in establishing regional collaboration plans, and continue to experience difficulty in communicating with other regions and in sharing lessons learned.[82]

In a 2006 review of state preparedness for catastrophic events, DHS found that fewer than half of all states had adequate patient tracking systems, licensing procedures for out-of-state medical volunteers, or mass-fatality management systems.[83] And in separate 2007 surveys only 19 percent of local health department officials indicated they are "highly prepared" for a major emergency,[84] whereas infection control professionals reported that, though three-quarters (76 percent) of hospitals have plans to utilize alternative care sites during emergencies, only one-fifth of these have realistic provisions for staffing such locations.[85]

Dr. O'Toole of the Center for Biosecurity asserted flatly in testimony to Congress, "The U.S. healthcare delivery sector is not equipped or prepared to provide timely medical care to the tens or possibly even hundreds of thousands of casualties that could result from a successful bioattack."[86] A CRS report made a similar point with respect to pandemic influenza, noting, "There is a growing concern that medical surge capacity could be the Achilles' heel of pandemic preparedness."[87]

VACCINES AND OTHER COUNTERMEASURES

The timely provision of vaccine and/or antibiotic drug treatments has long been recognized as vital to efforts to mitigate the effects of pandemic influenza or acts of bioterrorism.

The Strategic National Stockpile was developed in order to ensure that sufficient amounts of vaccines, antibiotics, antitoxins, and other medical supplies would be available for response to mass-casualty events. The Stockpile has acquired medical countermeasures for anthrax and radiological/nuclear agents, and is in the process of obtaining antitoxins for botulinum toxins.[88]

The National Strategy for Pandemic Influenza Implementation Plan established stockpile goals of 40 million doses of pandemic influenza vaccine (sufficient to vaccinate 20 million persons), and 75 million antiviral treatment courses for the disease (sufficient to treat the one-fourth of the U.S. population the plan estimated as likely to become clinically ill during the pandemic). The HHS Pandemic Influenza Plan modified the antiviral stockpile goal to be 81 million treatment courses, 50 million of which are to be held in the Strategic National Stockpile, with the remaining 31 million to be maintained in state stockpiles.[89]

The first U.S. licensing of a H5N1 flu vaccine occurred in April 2007 and it is estimated that by the end of the year 26 million doses will have been manufactured. As of October 2007, 37.5 million courses of influenza antivirals had been purchased for the Strategic National Stockpile, with the remaining 12.5 million due for acquisition over the next twelve months. Also as of that date, the federal government had provided $170 million to subsidize one-fourth of the cost of antiviral purchases for the state stockpiles, which then totaled 15.1 million courses, with the remainder due to be obtained by July 2008.[90] However, a May 2007 survey of state health officials discovered that almost half (twenty-four) of all states did not yet have sufficient nonfederal funding to be able to purchase the planned amounts.[91] An additional concern is that the federal stockpile for influenza contains only 6,000 pediatric antiviral treatment courses for the 73.6 million children in the United States.[92]

Several problems have been observed in the operation of the Strategic National Stockpile. The 2006 TFAH readiness survey found only fifteen states and two cities were rated by CDC at the highest preparedness level ("green") for distributing and administering vaccines and antivirals from the Strategic National Stockpile.[93]

A new methodology was instituted by CDC for measuring states' preparedness to distribute National Stockpile supplies in September 2006. It is not yet clear whether the new results indicate progress over the previous reports. As TFAH's 2007 analysis indicates, the new system continues to rely on evaluation of plans rather than performance assessment, and "states still have not received clear information about the quantities of medications and supplies that are in the Strategic National Stockpile and how effective the federal government would be in delivering supplies to states during a multi-state crisis."[94]

A particular concern about vaccine management is the uncertainty about how vaccines would be made available after an influenza pandemic has begun. Because flu viruses undergo continuous changes, vaccines must be "matched" to the specific strain causing the outbreak in order to maximize their effectiveness. And while the federal government is in the process of stockpiling a pre-pandemic H5N1 vaccine, the current HHS pandemic flu plan provides that during a pandemic, existing commercial providers and distribution mechanisms would be used for "matched" vaccine acquisition. However, as a CRS report observed, "This is the same system that has come under fire during recent shortages of seasonal flu vaccine, because of the difficulties faced by public health officials in trying to locate and redirect available vaccine to priority groups."[95]

Another issue with respect to medical countermeasures is the capacity of the U.S. biopharmacological industry to produce the necessary vaccines and other drugs to meet current and future public health security needs.

In 2006 HHS created the Public Health Emergency Medical Countermeasures Enterprise (PHEMCE) "to provide an integrated, systematic approach to the development and purchase of the necessary vaccines, drugs, therapies, and diagnostic tools for public health emergencies." This was followed in 2007 by the promulgation of a PHEMCE Strategy and Implementation Plan. In a November 2007 progress report, HHS indicated that "significant steps" had been taken to develop and obtain such countermeasures as anthrax vaccine and antitoxin, botulism antitoxin, broad-spectrum antibiotics, filovirus vaccines and therapeutics, and smallpox vaccines and therapeutics.[96]

However, TFAH has concluded, "The U.S. vaccine industry is broken, and there is limited incentive for companies to pursue research and development into new vaccines."[97] Citing a broad consensus among industry representatives and independent experts, the Center for Biosecurity's Dr. O'Toole pointed to continuing problems—even after the changes made in the 2006 legislation—with the BioShield program that had been created to facilitate the development of the necessary countermeasures.

- *Inadequate funding*: The $5.6 billion made available for BioShield "is not sufficient," given that the average development costs alone for a single drug currently average approximately $800 million.
- *A flawed contracting process*: Thus far, the BioShield system has produced a mean time of twenty-seven months from the beginning of the process until an award is made.
- *Insufficient attention to advanced development and clinical testing*: The Biodefense Advanced Research and Development Authority, which "was intended to improve coordination of BioShield activities across government agencies and to bridge the gap between early stage basic research and drug target 'discovery' and late-stage product development and procurement," has also been inadequately funded, receiving $99 million in FY 2007 and $189 million in the administration's FY 2008 request.[98]

Another development limiting the potential effectiveness of public health security countermeasures has been the lag in vaccination of at-risk individuals against existing infectious disease threats, caused in part by increased costs and various other access barriers.[99] For instance, the vaccination rate among seniors for seasonal flu actually decreased in thirteen states between 2005 and 2006, and the median state rate for vaccinating seniors for pneumonia was 65.7 percent in 2006, compared to the 2010 national health goal of 90 percent.[100]

INFORMATION SHARING

Perhaps the most serious deficiency exposed by the 2001 anthrax attacks was in the field of communications, both internal within and between the various governmental agencies involved in the response, and external from governmental authorities to the general public.

The National Response Plan mandated the sharing of information and intelligence about threats and security-related incidents between federal agencies, and established procedures to facilitate the provision of such information to state, local, and relevant private sector entities as well.[101]

Much of this internal communications on homeland security matters is handled through the DHS National Operations Center,[102] which, in the words of a senior DHS official,

> is able to pass real-time information in our Joint Regional Information Exchange system or network out to our state and local partners in coordinated efforts with the FBI. So we now have real-time . . . instant messaging capability where law enforcement and homeland security-type data is passed back and forth between all jurisdiction levels across the country, and we now have placed in the hands of state governors and some of our top 50 urban population centers across the country actual capabilities for them to have . . . provided by the federal government, secure voice equipment and secure video teleconferencing capability that they simply did not have a couple of years ago.[103]

Additional post-2001 homeland security information sharing initiatives have included the expansion of the FBI's Joint Terrorism Task Forces that bring together personnel from all governmental levels, the creation by some states and localities of their own information "fusion" centers, and the establishment of a DHS program to improve the protection of commercially sensitive information provided by private owners of critical assets.[104]

However, since 2005, GAO has regularly "designated information sharing for homeland security a high-risk area because the federal government still faces formidable challenges in analyzing and disseminating key information among federal, state, local, and private partners in a timely, accurate, and useful manner." In renewing the high-risk status in January 2007, GAO reported, "More than 5 years after 9/11, the federal government still lacks an implemented set of policies and processes for sharing terrorism information, but has issued a government-wide strategy on how it will put in place the overall framework, policies, and architecture for sharing with critical partners."[105]

The importance of "clear, effective, and coordinated" internal communication between the whole range of federal, state, local, international, and private sector entities involved in public health security is also recognized in both the National Strategy for Pandemic Influenza[106] and the HHS Pandemic Influenza Plan.[107]

Though few comprehensive analyses have been conducted on the effectiveness of current internal communications efforts in public health security, the various post-2001 biosecurity exercises referred to above raised some serious concerns as to how well this particular shortcoming in the response to the anthrax attacks has been addressed. The official DHS after action summary report for the 2003 TOPOFF 2 exercise made the following observations:

> Communication and coordination issues drove the course and outcome of critical public policy decisions, from raising the threat level to the various disaster/emergency declarations, from the determination of exclusion zones to the re-opening of transportation systems. To the extent that there were problems in these areas, communication issues were likely the primary cause. TOPOFF 2 showed that how people believe communications and coordination is supposed to work based on policy is often not how they work in reality [sic]. What may appear to be clearly defined processes—such as requesting the SNS—in practice become much more difficult.[108]

Two of the leaders of the 2005 trans-Atlantic simulation Atlantic Storm wrote afterwards,

> In most countries, the hospitals, health departments, emergency management agencies, local and regional political leaders, and national government agencies are not optimally organized to communicate with each other about the location and number of victims; to request national vaccine, medicine or equipment assets; or to plan for the distribution of key resources.[109]

The New Jersey Center for Public Health Preparedness after action summary on the 2005 TOPOFF 3 simulation found a number of "communications challenges," including confusion about the casualty count, problems with conference calling, and limited situational awareness at hospitals and other treatment centers.[110]

Dr. Tara O'Toole has expressed particular worry about the latter issue, testifying at one Congressional hearing, "Should there be a covert biological attack on U.S. civilians, it is highly unlikely that the national command structure, or governors, or mayors would have even rudimentary situational awareness."[111] She elaborated on this point at another hearing.

The confusion that inevitably accompanies epidemics—whether they are naturally occurring or the result of a deliberate attack—is not easily resolved. Attaining sufficient "situational awareness" to make informed decisions about what to do will be a major challenge for decision makers at all levels. In the current U.S. health care system, it will probably be extremely difficult to even obtain an accurate, near real-time count of infected victims during a bioattack because rapid diagnostic tests and digital connections between public health are lacking.[112]

PUBLIC COMMUNICATIONS

At least in part based on recognition of the public communications problems experienced during the anthrax incidents of late 2001, the National Response Plan promulgated in 2004 contained an Incident Communications Emergency Policy and Procedures component. The Public Affairs Support Annex to the National Response Plan (NRP) set out the communication plan's goals in the event of major disasters.

> Communications objectives during an Incident of National Significance are focused on delivering information regarding incident facts, health and safety, preparedness, and response/recovery activity and instructions. Citizens are reassured that authorities are executing coordinated response plans and are provided with frequent updates on incident facts and important instructions. Throughout all phases of incident management, public confidence and credibility must be maintained, particularly if WMD [Weapon of Mass Destruction] are involved or threatened.[113]

In seeking to achieve these goals, the plan gave the DHS Office of Public Affairs primary responsibility for leading federal communications efforts; mandated prompt coordination among federal, state, and local authorities; promoted the "immediate involvement of agency subject-matter experts . . . to ensure effective, accurate, and timely incident communications with the public;" and called for the early identification of effective spokespersons, including scientific, technical, and medical experts to make sure "a message is clearly transmitted into common terms and is received by the audience with credibility."[114]

The first major test of the NRP and its communications strategy occurred in the aftermath of Hurricane Katrina in 2005. The White House's February 2006 analysis noted some successes in the early stages of the crisis—via the dissemination of timely and useful weather reports and hurricane track predictions by the National Oceanic and Atmospheric Administration (NOAA) and the National Hurricane Center, but reported significant problems in communications with the public.

> More could have been done by officials at all levels of government. For example, the EAS—a mechanism for federal, state, and local officials to communicate disaster information and instructions—was not utilized by state and

local officials in Louisiana, Mississippi, or Alabama prior to Katrina's landfall. Further, without timely, accurate information or the ability to communicate, public affairs officers at all levels could not provide updates to the media and to the public. It took several weeks before public affairs structures . . . were adequately resourced and operating at full capacity. In the meantime, federal, state, and local officials gave contradictory messages to the public, creating confusion and feeding the perception that government sources lacked credibility . . . The federal public communications and public affairs response proved inadequate and ineffective.[115]

Some minor changes were made in the NRP in May 2006 as a result of the post-Katrina report, but little was done with respect to the public communications provisions.[116]

Turning specifically to the public health side, various efforts concerning pandemic flu preparedness have addressed the issue of communicating with the public. For example, the HHS Pandemic Influenza Plan contains general guidance on pandemic risk communications for federal, state, and local public health communicators.

- When health risks are uncertain, as likely will be the case during an influenza pandemic, people need information about what is known and unknown, as well as interim guidance to formulate decisions to help protect their health and the health of others.
- An influenza pandemic will generate immediate, intense, and sustained demand for information from the public, health-care providers, policy makers, and news media.
- Timely and transparent dissemination of clear, accurate, science-based, culturally competent information about pandemic influenza and the progress of the response can build public trust and confidence.
- Coordination of message development and release of information among federal, state, and local officials is critical to help avoid confusion that can undermine public trust, raise fear and anxiety, and impede response measures.
- Information to public audiences should be technically correct and sufficiently complete to encourage support of policies and official actions.[117]

The Centers for Disease Control and Prevention developed its own pandemic influenza risk communication plan in 2006,[118] and the federal government created a Web site (www.pandemicflu.gov) as an information resource for both the general public and the medical community. On the state level, all fifty states have held summits on pandemic flu.[119] The state influenza preparedness and response plans have addressed public communications to varying degrees. The aforementioned CRS survey of these documents found that thirty-four designated a lead public information officer. However, the CRS report indicated, "Plans did not always explicitly address other aspects of public communication during a pandemic, namely, training and outreach to other responders; monitoring of information from official sources; maintenance of websites and other public information resources; or individual and family preparedness."[120]

In the absence of large-scale pandemic exercises or detailed analyses of the pandemic communications plans, it is difficult to provide an informed assessment of how these strategies would work in practice. TFAH has, however, expressed its judgment about certain deficiencies in overall public health security communications efforts.

> Risk communication strategies are out-of-date. (Many of the standard models for risk communications have not been updated to adjust to today's 24-hour news cycles and the proliferation of Internet, telephonic, radio, cable, and television news outlets.) Limited efforts exist to inform and prepare the public for future health emergencies and to modernize strategies for information dissemination during emergencies. No systematic effort has been made to include the public in emergency planning or to address public concerns.[121]

INTERNATIONAL ACTIVITIES

The impact of the increasing globalization of travel and commerce on the spread of infectious diseases has led public health authorities to increasingly consider the international dimension of public health security. For example, in its 2002 Global Infectious Disease Strategy, CDC observed, "It is not possible to adequately protect the health of our nation without addressing infectious disease problems that occur elsewhere in the world."[122]

The communiqué on the eighth ministerial meeting of the Global Health Security Initiative, involving senior health officials from the United States, a number of other nations, and WHO, held in Washington, DC on November 2, 2007, reported on the group's progress to date.

- The creation of a secure Web site and an operational communication system utilizing videoconferencing to bring together senior officials on short notice.
- The establishment of a network of GHSI [Global Health and Security Initiative] member risk communications specialists to develop and integrate effective risk communications strategies for critical GHSI priorities.
- The significant contribution to the current global level of knowledge of, and preparedness for, a pandemic influenza outbreak.
- The significant progress on reducing the threat of smallpox as a result of intensive work, including a unique worldwide exercise, and the support given to the WHO Secretariat, particularly in the creation of an international stockpile of smallpox vaccine and in the field of planning for the potential need for vaccination.[123]

A potentially important milestone in international public health security occurred in June 2007 when the new WHO International Health Regulations entered into force. The Secretary of HHS's Operations Center was designated as the U.S. center to communicate with WHO on a full-time basis about public health events that could qualify as a potential public health emergency of international concern. The Department of Health and Human Services is also convening an interagency committee to develop an HHS international response plan to "outline and define the appropriate processes to coordinate preparedness and response efforts with international partners."[124]

The U.S. government has taken a number of other actions in recent years to boost global public health preparedness. An October 2007 GAO report focused on programs supporting the key objective of enhancing international infectious disease surveillance capabilities, and identified four principal such efforts: CDC's Global Disease Detection Program (GDD); CDC and USAID's Field Epidemiology Training Programs (FETP); CDC and USAID's Integrated Disease Surveillance and Response Program (IDSR); and DOD's Global Emerging Infectious Surveillance and Response System (GEIS). Combined with related USAID-funded capacity-building projects, these programs received approximately $84 million in the FY 2004–2006 period.[125]

Another GAO analysis, this one on international efforts to combat pandemic flu, reported,

> The United States has played a prominent role in global efforts to improve avian and pandemic influenza preparedness, committing the greatest share of funds and creating a framework for managing its efforts. Through 2006, the United States had committed about $377 million to improve global preparedness for pandemic influenza, about 27 percent of the $1.4 billion committed by all donors.

The same report noted that the National Strategy for Pandemic Influenza Implementation Plan provided a framework for U.S. international activities outlined in the plan and added, "[The Homeland Security Council] reported in December 2006 that all international action items due to be completed by November had been completed, and provided evidence of timely completion for the majority of these items."[126]

Set against these, and other, efforts to improve global health security are a series of ongoing, daunting challenges.

- Nonexistent or inadequate health care facilities (including infectious disease detection and response systems) in many low-income countries in Africa, Asia, and elsewhere.
- Non-existent or inadequate diagnostic tests and communication networks in many areas.
- A lack of funding to implement the new International Health Regulations for global disease surveillance and response.[127]

- Limited resources for WHO, which had an entire biennial budget of $2.8 billion for 2004–2005 ("like a middle-sized hospital in England in total resources," according to former WHO head Gro Harlem Brundtland).[128]
- In the words of a 2007 WHO report, "the inability of affected countries [in the H5N1 avian influenza outbreaks] to sustain an emergency response system over months, if not years."[129]

Citing the "unprecedented" level of funding in recent years for control of diseases that have a disproportionate impact on lower-income nations, the Global Health Security Project at the Stimson Center asserted that these investments had yielded an "uncertain return."

Unintended consequences of the public health funding windfall for developing nations include onerous and duplicative reporting requirements, sequestering of limited facilities and personnel, and corruption. Current metrics to determine programmatic success usually focus on disease-specific processes (such as the number of bednets distributed to combat malaria) rather than broader security or development goals.[130]

FUNDING AND ACCOUNTABILITY

Though federal spending for public health security went up exponentially after 2001, many questions remain about the adequacy, effectiveness, and allocation of these additional dollars.

With particular reference to the public health infrastructure capacity grants for state, local, and hospital preparedness, the 2006 TFAH readiness survey reported, "After the initial rounds of [federal] funds to support public health preparedness, the programs have already experienced cuts, even before many basic preparedness goals could be met. These cuts threaten to halt or even reverse progress that has been achieved." The same report found that thirty-three states had actually reduced their public health spending in 2003 compared to 2002, and though by 2006 most states had maintained or somewhat increased their public health budgets compared to the previous year, "the [state] funding falls far short of the estimated levels needed to reach an acceptable level of preparedness, according to most public health experts. For example, the Public Health Foundation estimates an additional $10 billion is needed to reach the minimum preparedness requirements."[131]

A *Washington Post* survey of public health experts found many who felt that current federal pandemic flu preparedness efforts "have left too much of the responsibility and the cost of preparing to a health care system that even in normal times is stretched to the breaking point," thus representing an "unfunded mandate." Dan Hanfling, director of emergency management for Northern Virginia Inova Health Systems, which was directly involved in the response to the 2001 anthrax attacks in the Washington, DC area, stated,

"The amounts of funding still pale in comparison to the tremendous need that exists... It makes our current state of readiness tenuous at best."[132]

Action on FY 2008 appropriations for HHS, as Table 7.2 indicates, has largely conformed to the patterns of recent years, with the administration proposing reductions in public health infrastructure programs and increases in spending for pandemic influenza preparedness, whereas the Congress sought to restore some (but not all) of the cuts in the former while cutting a portion of the proposed increases in the latter.[133]

President Bush vetoed the first version of the Labor-HHS-Education appropriations bill on November 13, 2007, citing what he regarded as "excessive spending" on certain health care, education, and job training programs.[134] Most of the FY 2008 appropriation measures, including the Labor-HHS-Education bill, were ultimately incorporated into the Consolidated Appropriations Act of 2008, which made many of the cuts sought by the President and was signed into law on December 26, 2007.[135]

In addition to the amounts of funding, some independent analysts have questioned the effectiveness of the sums provided. The Global Health Security Project raised concerns about the actual impact of current spending approaches.

> Assumptions that programs developed to address specific disease threats, such as potential use of a biological weapon, would benefit public health generally by building a "dual-use" infrastructure appear exaggerated. Available evidence suggests that a lack of long-term goals and fluctuating political pressures can channel public health resources into programmatic stovepipes with limited value beyond specific disease scenarios, draining rather than building local capacities and engendering a false sense of security among policymakers.[136]

GAO's 2007 progress report on DHS concluded the department had not achieved the performance goal of providing assistance to state and local governments to develop all-hazards plans and capabilities, stating, "DHS did not provide us with evidence on the extent to which its assistance to state and local governments has focused on all-hazards, rather than just terrorism preparedness and response or hazard mitigation." The Government Accountability Office also indicated DHS had not documented "that its assistance... has helped those government agencies develop all-hazards capabilities."[137]

Underlying concerns about the effectiveness and allocation of public health security spending is the question of accountability. In most of the specific areas discussed above, progress has been made at least as measured by *inputs* into the various systems: more money, more labs, more vaccine, and so forth. Yet, when put to the test, whether real as in the case of Hurricane Katrina, or simulated as in the various biosecurity drills like the TOPOFF series, serious *performance* flaws have been discerned.

TABLE 7.2
FY 2008 Appropriations for Selected HHS Programs (in $ millions)

Program	FY 07	FY 08 Adm.	FY 08 House	FY 08 Senate	FY 08 Final
CDC Total	**6,266**	**5,983**	**6,458**	**6,435**	**6,376**
Global Health	330	380	381	334	371
Terrorism Preparedness/Response	1,496	1,504	1,599	1,632	1,497
State/Local Capacity grants	*824*	*698*	*735*	*760*	*746*
Biosurveillance Initiative	*78*	*88*	*81*	*79*	*63*
PHSSEF Fund Total	**717**	**1,754**	**1,705**	**1,730**	**729**
ASPR Hospital Preparedness grants	474	414	451	439	420
ASPR Advanced R&D	54	189	140	189	102
Pandemic Influenza Preparedness	0	948	948	888	75

Notes:

1. FY 07 = FY 07 appropriated level. FY 08 Adm = President's FY 08 budget proposal. FY 08 House = FY 08 House-passed funding level. FY 08 Senate = FY 08 Senate-passed funding level. FY 08 FINAL = FY 08 appropriated level (PL 110-161). CDC Total includes funds made available under Section 241 of the Public Health Services Act.

2. CDC Global Health includes global AIDS program and international pandemic influenza activities.

3. PHSSEF = Public Health and Social Services Emergency Fund.

4. ASPR = Assistant Secretary for Preparedness and Response.

Sources: U.S. House, *Making Appropriations for the Departments of Labor, Health and Human Services, and Education, and Related Agencies for the Fiscal Year Ending September 30, 2008, Conference Report to Accompany HR 3043,* 110th Congress, 1st session (Washington, DC, November 5, 2007), H. Report 110-424; and *Public Law 110-161, Consolidated Appropriations Act, 2008, Division G: Labor-Health and Human Services-Education and Related Agencies, FY 2008* (Washington, DC, December 26, 2007).

In attempting to determine why this has been so, one possible answer was supplied in the 2006 TFAH readiness report.

> Five years after September 11, there is still little information publicly available to evaluate how states' preparedness capabilities have improved and what vulnerabilities remain. The lack of concrete data has raised concerns among Members of Congress, the GAO, and HHS, as well as independent analysts and watchdog groups. This means Americans do not have information about how well their communities and states are prepared, and do not know whether their tax dollars are being spent efficiently. It also makes it difficult for Congress to know where it should invest limited federal funds to address vulnerabilities and to hold states accountable for their use of these funds.

After noting recent efforts by CDC and other HHS components to establish clearer "performance measures," the report went on to cite continuing inadequacies in these measures.

- Self-reported information from states that cannot be verified objectively or by external evaluators;
- Releasing data only in aggregate form, rather than on a state-by-state basis, which denies the public and policy makers information about how prepared their communities are and how well the funds are being used;
- Process versus outcomes, such as evaluating time frames for activities rather than the quality and impact of the information; and
- Basic capabilities instead of how a state would be able to cope with a mass emergency when the regular functions would be quickly overwhelmed.[138]

HSPD-21

In an attempt to "transform our national approach to protecting the health of the American people against all disasters," on October 18, 2007 President Bush issued Homeland Security Presidential Directive 21 (HSPD-21), which established a National Strategy for Public Health and Medical Preparedness. In distinguishing itself from previous efforts, the directive stated:

> Present public health and medical preparedness plans incorporate the concept of "surging" existing medical and public health capabilities in response to an event that threatens a large number of lives. The assumption that conventional public health and medical systems can function effectively in catastrophic health events has, however, proved to be incorrect in real-world situations. Therefore, it is necessary to transform the national approach to health care in the context of a catastrophic health event in order to enable U.S. public health and medical systems to respond effectively to a broad range of incidents.

To aid in this transformation, the strategy called for the establishment of a new discipline of disaster health that "will provide a foundation for doctrine, education, training, and research and will integrate preparedness into the public health and medical communities."

More specifically, HSPD-21 focused on "the four most critical components of public health and medical preparedness...biosurveillance, countermeasure distribution, mass casualty care, and community resilience."

- *Biosurveillance*: The plan calls for the development of "an operational national epidemiologic surveillance system for human health, with international connectivity where appropriate, that is predicated on State, regional, and community-level capabilities and creates a networked system to allow for two-way communications flow between and among Federal, State, and local government public health authorities, and clinical health-care providers." The system is "to provide early warning and ongoing characterization of disease outbreaks in near real-time," and is to utilize electronic health information systems "to the extent feasible."
- *Countermeasure Stockpiling and Distribution*: "Recognizing that state and local government authorities have the primary responsibility to protect their citizens," HSPD-21 calls upon HHS to "develop templates, using a variety of tools and including private sector resources when necessary, that provide minimum operational plans to enable communities to distribute and dispense countermeasures to their populations within 48 hours after a decision to do so."
- *Mass-Casualty Care*: With the goal of "develop[ing] a disaster medical capability that can immediately re-orient and coordinate existing resources within all sectors...during a catastrophic health event," the strategy provides for HHS, in coordination with the Departments of Defense, Veterans Affairs, and Homeland Security, and in consultation with state, local, and other health authorities, to develop "a concept plan that identifies and coordinates all federal, state, and local government and private sector public health and medical disaster response resources, and identifies options for addressing critical deficits" in mass-casualty care.
- *Community Resilience*: "Where local civic leaders, citizens, and families are educated regarding threats and are empowered to mitigate their own risk, where they are practiced in responding to events, where they have social networks to fall back upon, and where they have familiarity with local public health and medical systems, there will be community resilience that will significantly attenuate the need for additional assistance. The Federal Government must formulate a comprehensive plan for promoting community public health and medical preparedness to assist state and local authorities in building resilient communities in the face of potential catastrophic health events."

Additionally, HSPD-21 calls for the following: DHS to provide an unclassified briefing for governors and the city and county leaders representing the nation's fifty largest metropolitan areas "that clearly outlines the scope of the risks to public health posed by relevant threats and catastrophic health events;" HHS to develop means by which to coordinate federal grant, training, and education programs related to public health and medical preparedness; the Institute of Medicine to lead a process "to facilitate the development of national disaster public health and medicine doctrine and system design and to develop a strategy for long-term enhancement of disaster public health and medical capacity, and the propagation of disaster public health and medicine education and training;" HHS to include the "principles and actions in this directive" and its implementation plan in the National Health Security Strategy required under the Pandemic and All-Hazards Preparedness Act; and a newly created Public Health and Medical Preparedness Task Force to develop the implementation plan.

To carry out all of these objectives, the new strategy sets out a series of deadlines for task completion.[139]

The plan received an initial positive response from at least some of those who had been critical of previous planning efforts. For example, the Center for Biosecurity called HSPD-21 "an important and commendable development in national biodefense policy. It offers clear strategic direction and is in keeping with the best professional judgments of many medical, public health, disaster response and community engagement experts in and out of government."[140]

On the other hand, a number of major questions about current public health security efforts appear to be either unaddressed or compounded by the new strategy.

How are the laudable objectives of this (and other federal plans and strategies) to be paid for? Indeed, HSPD-21 makes explicit that its provisions are to be implemented "subject to the availability of appropriations and within the current projected spending levels for Federal health entitlement programs."[141]

How will the accountability concerns raised by TFAH be addressed, given the strategy's reliance on the same type of compliance mechanisms (such as the use of timelines rather than impact analyses) critiqued by that organization?

How will its objectives actually be formulated and achieved, given that key parts of the strategy, including those concerning countermeasures, mass-casualty preparedness, and community resilience are, at present, essentially "plans to plan?"

How will the fundamental question of "who is in charge" be resolved, whether with respect to the roles of HHS versus DHS in major disasters, or between the federal government and states and localities on such questions as vaccine distribution during pandemics?

Though it is supposed to be incorporated into the upcoming National Health Security Strategy, how will this plan be coordinated with other major plans and strategies, including the National Response Plan/Framework, the National Strategy for Pandemic Influenza, and the WHO International Health Regulations?

CHAPTER 8

Conclusion

Over six years have passed since multiple envelopes containing anthrax spores were mailed in New Jersey, and it has been five years since the reemergence of the H5N1 avian influenza virus in Hong Kong. In the United States, federal, state, and local governmental authorities and the public health community have devoted large amounts of attention and resources to improving the ability of the public health system to respond to biological terrorism and naturally occurring pandemics. And yet, virtually all assessments, both within and outside the government, have concluded that the system is far from ready to cope with either eventuality.

In spite of improvements in many areas, such as communications equipment, training exercises, laboratory capacity, the Strategic National Stockpile, and international disease reporting authorities and systems, and of a plethora of new planning and organizational arrangements, major deficiencies continue to exist in such critical areas as workforce preparedness, surveillance and diagnostic systems, mass-casualty capacity, vaccine production and distribution, internal and external communications protocols, international health care capacity, and program accountability.

In sum, there have been plenty of strategies, plans, and organizational schemes, but not enough "funded mandates," priority-setting, and, above all, leadership.

PUBLIC HEALTH SECURITY IN THE 21ST CENTURY

The list of unfunded or underfunded mandates in public health security is a long one, as it is in other areas of homeland security.[1] Serious mismatches exist between the aspirations and resources of a number of these programs, including in hospital preparedness, vaccine production capacity, public health workforce readiness, disease surveillance systems, and international health security activities.

Perhaps most importantly, each of the key "foundation" plans and strategies that are to serve as the basis for public health security policy are all but silent on the question of implementation costs and funding sources. Thus, neither the 2005 National Strategy for Pandemic Influenza, nor the National Health Security Strategy required by the Pandemic and All-Hazards Preparedness Act of 2006, nor Homeland Security Presidential Directive 21 from October 2007, nor, at the international level, WHO's 2005 International Health Regulations, make any provision as to how the actions they call for are to be financed.

In its "Final Report on 9/11 Commission Recommendations," issued in December 2005, the Commission's successor, the 9/11 Public Discourse Project (9/11 PDP), observed

> A draft National Infrastructure Protection Plan [NIPP] (November 2005) spells out a methodology and process for critical infrastructure assessments. No risk and vulnerability assessments [were] actually made; no national priorities established; no recommendations made on allocation of scarce resources... It is time that we stop talking about setting priorities, and actually set some.[2]

Though GAO and the National Research Council have documented some progress in these fields, the judgments of the 9/11 PDP about the NIPP's shortcomings in risk assessment and priority-setting appear to still apply to the key strategies and plans for public health security, whether directed at bioterrorism or pandemics.

As cited previously, GAO has concluded that "it is unclear the extent to which DHS will be able to use [Sector-Specific Plans] to identify security gaps and critical interdependencies across the sectors," and that "gaps and deficiencies in [the National Strategy for Pandemic Influenza] are particularly troubling because they can affect the usefulness of the planning documents to those with key roles to play and affect their ability to effectively carry out their responsibilities." Additionally, a National Research Council committee indicated DHS' current Bioterrorism Risk Assessment "does not fully support any of the components of risk analysis."

Another impediment to priority-setting—noted by the Trust for America's Health (TFAH)—is the absence of useful performance information about the various elements of the public health security system, thus depriving policy makers of essential information for determining "where [they] should invest limited federal funds to address vulnerabilities."

Finally, priority-setting has been hindered by fragmentation and stovepiping both within the public health system and among those who govern, oversee, and help to fund that system.

- A large portion of federal public health funding continues to be provided through targeted grants, with such new programs as those for pandemic influenza joining the lengthy list of previously created public health stovepipes. The Stimson Center's Global Health Security Project has reported "Available evidence suggests... [these] programmatic stovepipes [have] limited value beyond specific disease scenarios, draining rather than building local capacities and engendering a false sense of security among policymakers."
- The fragmented public health security system observed in September 2001 by the Government Accountability Office (GAO) has little changed, with the exception of the creation of the Department of Homeland Security. This has resulted in the addition of another major federal player, with its own objectives, personnel, state and local connections and funding streams.
- The multiplicity of congressional committees and subcommittees involved in the oversight and funding of various aspects of public health security has produced the same sort of "dysfunctional" Congressional performance in this arena as was cited by the 9/11 Commission with respect to intelligence and homeland security.[3]
- Though reliable data are limited, available evidence indicates that there continues to be wide disparities in the public health security capabilities and needs among and within the states. For instance, the 2006 readiness survey by TFAH, which used ten indicators of state preparedness,[4] found that only one state (Oklahoma) met the desired performance objective on all ten measures, and only one other (Kansas) did so on nine of the ten. Another twenty-three states achieved the goal on seven or eight of the objectives, whereas twenty-five states plus the District of Columbia had scores of six or less.[5]

Employing a slightly different set of measures, the 2007 TFAH report noted "significant progress among the states in those areas where data are available." It continued, "Not all areas of preparedness, however, can be measured by the [chosen] indicators... because data from all levels of government are still insufficient. Even within these indicators, some important geographic disparities are identified that affect the nation's ability to protect Americans from emergency health threats."[6]

Intertwined with the funding and priority-setting problems has been the issue of leadership. The unique challenges to the effective exercise of that leadership within the fragmented American system were summed up in the 2007 "A Healthier America: A New Vision and Agenda," prepared by TFAH and other organizations.

> In a public health system as decentralized as ours, national leadership is essential to ensure that disaster and emergency threats are properly assessed and that standards for preparedness are set and maintained. At the same time, state and local governmental leadership, supported by sufficient federal funding, is needed to create and sustain local response capacity.[7]

Serious obstacles have emerged to the attainment of these objectives at the federal and non-federal levels. In the former case, the difficulties center on the large (and compared to the pre-2001 situation, growing) number of federal departments, agencies, and offices having responsibility for some aspect of public health security.

At least eight federal agencies and two federal offices currently have significant public health responsibilities,[8] but the question of leadership primarily involves three entities: the Office of Health Affairs, which was given chief responsibility for DHS medical emergency activities by the Post-Katrina Emergency Management Reform Act of 2006; the HHS Assistant Secretary for Preparedness and Response (ASPR), which was established by the Pandemic and All-Hazards Preparedness Act of 2006 and made responsible for coordinating public health preparedness and response programs for all disasters; and the Centers for Disease Control and Prevention (CDC), which, as part of its traditional public health role, is to coordinate the national response to pandemics and other health emergencies with state and local health authorities. The first two of these have undergone considerable evolution in recent years, reaching their current structure and responsibilities under the separate 2006 legislation after having been present in different, and frequently changing, forms prior to that time. And though CDC has retained its basic pre-2001 form and functions, the agency underwent a major internal reorganization in 2005 that produced considerable turmoil within it. Thus all three of the key federal public health security entities have faced considerable challenges in fulfilling their rapidly evolving leadership responsibilities.

A more serious impediment to effective federal leadership from the three organizations is the largely unresolved question of how their intersecting roles, assigned by different legislative and administrative instruments, are to function in practice, especially in cases of actual emergencies. After citing a number of deficiencies in the public health response to Hurricane Katrina, the White House after action report on that disaster noted "the coordination of Federal assets within and across agencies was poor," due in part to "a fragmented command structure for medical response."[9] Though the laws establishing the Office of Health Affairs (OHA) and ASPR were designed to remedy such shortcoming, there is little evidence thus far that the basic problem of who is to be in charge has been solved.

A final critical flaw in federal leadership was also highlighted by the 2006 White House report on the response to Katrina.

> The Federal government cannot and should not be the Nation's first responder. State and local governments are best positioned to address incidents in their jurisdictions and will always play a large role in disaster response. But Americans have a right to expect that the Federal government will effectively respond to a catastrophic incident. When local and State governments are overwhelmed or incapacitated by an event that has reached catastrophic proportions, only the Federal government has the resources and capabilities to respond.

The report went on to recite the changes that had occurred within the Federal Emergency Management Agency (FEMA) since its incorporation into DHS, which moved it away from its previous community-oriented organization toward greater centralization of focus and resources, and which resulted in "weakness of our regional planning and coordination structures." The "lesson learned" from this was, "The Federal government should work with its homeland security partners in revising existing [response and preparedness] plans, ensuring a functional operational structure."[10]

In spite of subsequent intentions to address this situation (for example, in the congressionally mandated requirements in the National Health Security Strategy for bolstering state and local public health capacity), once again the available evidence indicates that difficulties remain. The Trust for America's Health's 2006 readiness survey and 2007 vision statement, for instance, reported a number of continuing impediments to state and local preparedness, including inadequacies in federal leadership.

The latest effort to revise the National Response Plan, which would include its redesignation as the National Response Framework, revealed persistent dissatisfaction with federal attempts to better coordinate with nonfederal partners in the field of homeland security. The release of a draft version during the summer of 2007 produced a number of negative reactions from state and local officials, and outside observers. For example, the president of the state emergency management directors association observed that, as a result of the exclusion of state and local officials from the drafting process in this case, he had "never experienced a more polarized environment between state and federal governments," and that the document appeared to be more of an attempt to shift any blame for future disaster response away from federal authorities to state officials. Professor John R. Harrald of the George Washington University Institute for Crisis, Disaster and Risk Management commented that DHS appeared "to be guided by a desire to ensure centralized control of what is an inherently decentralized process . . . Response to catastrophic events requires collaboration and trust in a broad network of organizations."[11]

In response to such criticisms, DHS revised the draft proposal by more clearly defining the state role and better integrating planning for man-made and natural disasters. When the new framework was announced in January 2008, it was much better received by state officials,[12] but the episode is illustrative of ongoing challenges in federal–state relations with respect to homeland security.

RECOMMENDATIONS

Many useful suggestions have been made for improving public health security.[13] And, as demonstrated by the numerous actions taken by both executive agencies and Congress since 2001, policy makers have been actively attempting to fix existing problems. However, it is the view here that current reform efforts will continue to produce the very mixed results reported on in the previous chapter unless and until attention is given to rectifying the overarching, systemic problems of funding, priority-setting, and leadership.

First of all, it is recommended that the key frameworks for U.S. public health security—especially HSPD-21 and the forthcoming National Health Security Strategy—be amended to include cost estimates for the programs and policies they envision as well as the accompanying anticipated funding mechanisms (such as Congressional appropriations, federal fees, and state/local/private sector cost-sharing). This is similar to the 9/11 Commission proposal that the federal plan for transportation security should include a "budget and funding to implement the effort,"[14] but, significantly, this was one of the few 9/11 Commission recommendations that failed to receive congressional approval, in any form, in either the 2004 or 2007 legislation enacted to implement the Commission's suggestions.[15]

In addition, this "public health security budget" should be updated as needed, and should be reflected in the President's annual budget submission to Congress. Any departures from it should be explicitly cited and explained in both the President's budget and in subsequent congressional actions.

This approach would not only tackle the problem of unfunded mandates head-on, but would also address the issues of priority-setting and leadership by lodging primary responsibility (and accountability) clearly with those empowered by the American people to make the key national security decisions: the President and the members of Congress.

Second, in a further attempt to improve priority-setting and leadership, the executive branch and Congress should move as expeditiously as possible to transfer all public health security programs from the Department of Homeland Security (primarily the department's biosurveillance and biological countermeasures programs within the Office of Health Affairs and FEMA's Metropolitan Medical Response System) to HHS, where the vast majority of such programs already reside.

Such a consolidation would facilitate the integration of planning and execution of bioterrorism and natural disease control programs (as called for by Anthony Cordesman).[16] It would also divest DHS of program responsibilities where the department's progress to date has been "limited," according to GAO,[17] and allow for concentration of oversight and appropriations responsibilities (and thus accountability) in the congressional panels devoted to health programs[18] while removing the roles of the authorization and appropriations committees and subcommittees in both houses that deal with DHS.

It is true that this proposal runs somewhat counter to the laudable notions embodied in the Homeland Security Act of 2002, which created DHS to be the lead agency in coordinating the national preparedness for and response to domestic emergencies (including acts of bioterrorism), and the recommendation of the 9/11 Commission that called for Congress to "create a single, principal point of oversight and review for homeland security" in each house.[19] But the August 2007 GAO assessment of DHS reveals that the department is very far from realizing the original goals set out for it.

> While DHS has made progress in transforming its component agencies into a fully functioning department, it has not yet addressed key elements of the transformation process, such as developing a comprehensive strategy for agency transformation and assuring that management systems and functions are integrated. This lack of a comprehensive strategy and management systems and functions limits DHS's ability to carry out its homeland security responsibilities in an effective, risk-based way.[20]

Removal of the public health-related programs, which are a very small part of DHS' current efforts, should allow the department to concentrate on improvements in other fields where it has greater overall responsibility and expertise (such as transportation and border security) and in the critical discipline of risk assessment (which has a very important role to play in guiding public health security activities) while making sure that the resources made available for public health security are put to their most effective use.

As for congressional oversight, the objective of consolidating jurisdiction for homeland security programs into single committees in the House and Senate remains unmet, with little done to advance further in that direction than when the 9/11 Commission wrote in 2004, "Few things are more difficult to change in Washington than congressional Committee jurisdiction and prerogatives."[21] Under these circumstances, concentrating public health security functions within HHS will, as a practical matter, allow these programs to receive more centralized and responsible oversight. At the same time, in order to appropriately discharge their security responsibilities the health authorizing and appropriations panels will need to devote more attention and resources to monitoring the performance of the public health programs.

Third, renewed emphasis must be placed on enhancing state and local public health capacities. This objective is reflected in one of HSPD-21's "most critical components of public health and medical preparedness . . . community resilience," which is to be achieved by "promoting community public health and medical preparedness to assist state and local authorities in building resilient communities in the face of potential catastrophic health events." Yet, the primary means by which this goal is to be pursued under the directive is via development of "a plan to promote comprehensive community medical preparedness."[22]

A number of other indicators point, in fact, to a diminution in federal attention to the state and local role in recent years.

- The lack of consultation with nonfederal authorities in development of DHS' draft National Response Framework.
- Steady declines in funding since FY 2003 for the two major federal support programs for state and local public health readiness: CDC's state and local capacity grants and HHS' hospital preparedness grants.
- Reductions since FY 2005 in the overall budget for CDC, the lead federal agency in supporting state and local public health efforts.

In some ways, current federal public health security policy seems to be repeating one of the critical mistakes that seriously hindered the national response to Hurricane Katrina: the atrophying of FEMA's community-based focus after its absorption into DHS. Such an error in the public health arena would be particularly egregious because the overwhelming responsibility and capacity for health emergencies do now, and under any conceivable future scenario will continue to, rest at the state and local level. Furthermore, public trust—so vital in minimizing panic and otherwise mitigating the consequences in disasters (as recognized very clearly by HSPD-21)—is considerably higher in those authorities than their federal counterparts.

The Harvard School of Public Health survey, taken during the anthrax crisis in October 2001, that found CDC Director Jeffrey Koplan to be the most trusted federal official during the attack (with 48 percent expressing a "great deal" or "quite a lot" of confidence in him) discovered significantly more faith in almost all of the non-federal authorities tested. The proportions of those who indicated "a great deal" or "quite a lot" of trust in each of these individuals were as follows:

Your own doctor	77 percent
The director of your local fire department	61 percent
The director of your local hospital	53 percent
The director of your state or local police department	53 percent
The director of your state or local health department	52 percent
The governor of your state	48 percent[23]

In recognition of these realities and needs, it is recommended that funding be increased for the state and local capacity and hospital preparedness grant programs. Absent more detailed analysis, the Center for Biosecurity's estimate for hospital preparedness needs of $5 billion initially, followed by $1 billion annually for maintenance purposes, can serve as a guide for the latter.

Also, amidst all of the organizational changes and additional bureaucratic layers that have been or are proposed to be erected in the field of emergency health preparedness, the position of the CDC as the preeminent federal public health agency and the chief contact point for state and local authorities must not be allowed to erode. This means not only adequate budgets but also independent, nonpoliticized leadership and lines of authority for the agency.

Finally, because of continuing problems in the consultation and collaboration process, the HHS-led "Intergovernmental Public Health Coordinating Council composed of representatives of state, tribal, and local health directors and persons representing the general public" called for by TFAH should be established.[24]

In addition to the above suggestions for improving public health security budgeting, organization, and state and local capacity, a number of useful suggestions for further enhancing federal oversight and accountability have been put forward by TFAH.

- HHS and CDC should develop new evidence-based benchmarks and objective standards for public health preparedness to replace the process-oriented measures now in use.
- All levels of government must do a better job of incorporating the lessons learned from preparedness drills into program planning.
- The federal government should link public health preparedness grants to awardees' performance in meeting specified benchmarks.
- The various health security plans, including the National Strategy for Pandemic Influenza and the impending National Health Security Strategy, "should clearly designate the official in charge of public health preparedness and specify how various departments, state and local officials, and first responders are to collaborate in the event of a public health emergency."[25]

Another area deserving increased attention is that of international public health security assistance. With the large stake the United States has in the global economy and its potential vulnerability of exposure to diseases originating abroad because of that extensive involvement, the limited American investment in international public health security to date falls far short of what is needed. It is certainly true that the United States has done more in this regard than any other nation and is clearly recognized as the global leader in the field. And documentation of funding needs has been even more inadequate on the international level than domestically.

Nevertheless, as the WHO's 2007 World Health Report observes, "It cannot be over-emphasized that a truly effective international preparedness and response mechanism cannot be managed nationally. Global cooperation, collaboration, and investment are necessary to ensure a safer future." The WHO report went on to make several recommendations, most of which were somewhat general and none of which contained suggested funding levels.

- Full implementation of the 2005 International Health Regulations by all countries.
- Improved global cooperation in surveillance and outbreak alert and response.

- Improved sharing of knowledge, technologies, and materials, including viruses and other laboratory samples.
- Expanded international assistance for public health capacity-building in all countries.
- Increased cross-sector (health, agriculture, trade, and tourism) collaboration within national governments.
- Increased resources, at both the national and international levels, for "the training of public health personnel, the advancement of surveillance, the building and enhancing of laboratory capacity, the support of response networks, and the coordination and progression of prevention campaigns."[26]

As a first step in trying to bring the means provided into closer alignment with the international community's goals and expectations for global health security, it is recommended that the actions called for in the 2005 International Health Regulations (IHR) be subjected to the same kind of cost-estimating and funding source identification suggested above for HSPD-21 and the National Health Security Strategy. Though such a process is likely to prove even more difficult at the international level, identification of the implementation costs would greatly facilitate efforts to quantify the need for assistance and thus to help translate worthy objectives into concrete achievements.

This work has focused on the U.S. public health system and its ability to cope with the major threats of infectious disease and bioterrorism, with some attention to the international dimensions of these subjects. However, there are a number of other important components involved in public health security that have received little or no attention.

The key role of law enforcement in responding to the anthrax attacks and conducting the subsequent criminal investigation was discussed, as was, briefly, the somewhat contentious subject of law enforcement and public health communication and coordination during that investigation. However, when considered in its fullest aspect, including not only the FBI but police forces at all levels and border and customs control officials, it is clear that law enforcement is integrally involved in the effort to prevent and mitigate biological disasters, especially those caused by terrorist action. Among the key law enforcement functions in promoting public health security are keeping order during emergencies, enforcing restrictions on access to biological agents and advanced equipment, and identifying and apprehending "bio-offenders."[27]

And as Barry Kellman, Special Advisor to the Interpol Program on Prevention of Bio-crimes, has written.

Can [public health] preparedness measures, even if substantially upgraded, keep us safe from human malevolence? ... Intentionally inflicted disease differs from natural disease precisely because the bio-offender has strategic agility. The attacker can choose where to pierce society's preparedness, even pierce it repeatedly... Given the range of available agents, the agent-specific nature of most defenses, the long time needed to develop new vaccines, and how easily an attacker can achieve surprise, protecting large populations against numerous threat agents is a dauntingly expensive undertaking that might readily be eluded.[28]

On the threat side, dangers other than bioterrorism and infectious disease among humans present major challenges to public health.

- Food-borne diseases, such as salmonella and E. coli, which can cause serious harm to humans if ingested.
- Animal-borne diseases, such as rabies, that can spread to humans. (Both SARS and the H5N1 avian flu originated in this category.)
- Water-borne diseases from contaminated water.
- Harmful chemical agents, such as poisonous gases or pesticides, which have toxic effects on people, animals, and/or plants.
- Radiological materials, such as those used in nuclear power plants or certain medical devices, that are toxic if directly exposed to living organisms.

Furthermore, all of these dangers can arise from either natural or accidental causes, or from deliberate acts of terrorism.[29]

Although it must certainly be a key part of any comprehensive approach to protecting the public, public health security itself is but one of many claimants to national attention and resources, in competition with such other needs as education, social security, housing, and economic development, not to mention other facets of homeland security and national defense.

The resolution of such competing claims is necessarily a part of the political process, and in the American system ultimate responsibility rests with our elected officials. Here, one of the key findings of the 1988 assessment of public health by the Institute of Medicine remains pertinent. The report called attention to the often unrecognized but key role of the political process in the evolution of the public health system, and the challenges this posed.

Decision-making in public health, as in other areas, is driven by crises, hot issues, and the concerns of organized interest groups. Decisions are made largely on the basis of competition, bargaining, and influence rather than comprehensive analysis... Public health has had great difficulty accommodating itself to these political dynamics... Too frequently during its investigations, the committee heard legislators and members of the general public castigate public health professionals as paper-shufflers, out of touch with reality, and caught up in red tape... Many public health professionals who talked with us seemed to regard politics as a contaminant of an ideally rational decision-making process rather than as an essential element of democratic governance. We saw much evidence of isolation and little evidence of constituency building, citizen participation, or continuing (as opposed to crisis-driven) communications with elected officials or with the community at large.[30]

Disconnections like this one abound today in many relationships involved in public health security, not only between the public health and political worlds, but also between the public health realm and law enforcement, the homeland security bureaucracy, and others. It is recommended that priority attention be devoted to bridging these gaps, which is at least as much of an attitudinal as a policy challenge. As one example of what is needed here, expanded cross-discipline training among law enforcement and public health workers could help reduce the kinds of communications and "cultural" problems that hampered the interaction of these two key disciplines during the response to the anthrax attacks.

From the colonial era until the early twentieth century, control of infectious disease was a major concern in the United States, with the evolution of local, state, and then federal policies and bureaucracies to combat what was then the country's leading cause of death. The emergence of the discipline of bacteriology at the end of that period, with its identification of the sources and treatments of many of those diseases, initiated a long period of declining death rates, which in time led to a diminution of governmental (especially federal) attention and resources directed toward public health security over the last quarter of the 20th century.

Events at the turn of the twenty-first century, including a reemergent threat from infectious diseases and the anthrax attacks of 2001, thrust concerns about the public health system back at the forefront of the federal government's agenda. Yet, the resulting funding, laws, organizations, and reorganizations have not, so far, produced the improvements desired by either policy makers or the public health community. Indeed, many of the problems identified prior to 2001 persist and involve such key components of the public health system as its workforce, communications capabilities, and mass-casualty capacity.

As of this writing (August 2008), the anthrax case may have been solved, there has not been another major bioterrorism incident and the H5N1 avian influenza virus has not yet entered into the widespread and sustained transmission among humans that would mark the onset of an epidemic. Under these circumstances, it remains to be seen whether the recent interest will be sustained for long enough for an appropriate level of public health security to be identified and achieved.

There is little doubt that the nation is far better prepared now to cope with a biodisaster that mimics the 2001 anthrax attacks in scope and method of attack. The larger question, however, is how well prepared it will be if history does not repeat itself so precisely when the next major disaster strikes.

NOTES

CHAPTER 1

1. Centers for Disease Control and Prevention, *CDC Influenza Pandemic Operation Plan (OPLAN)* (Atlanta, December 20, 2006), p. 20.

2. Derived from the Greek word meaning "all of the people," a pandemic is an epidemic of human disease that is very widespread geographically, crossing international borders, and affects a large number of people. Sarah A. Lister, Congressional Research Service, The Library of Congress "Pandemic Influenza: Domestic Preparedness Efforts," RL33145 (Washington, DC, November 10, 2005), p. 3.

3. Lister, "Pandemic Influenza," p. 6.

4. Thomas V. Inglesby, Tara O'Toole, Donald A. Henderson, et al., "Anthrax as a Biological Weapon: Updated Recommendations for Management," in Henderson, Inglesby and O'Toole, eds., *Bioterrorism: Guidelines for Medical and Public Health Management* (Chicago, IL: AMA Press, 2002), p. 64.

5. Ibid., pp. 65, 70.

6. World Health Organization, *Public Health Response to Biological and Chemical Weapons: WHO Guidance*, second edition (Geneva: WHO, 2004), pp. 236–237.

7. Inglesby, O'Toole, Henderson, et al., "Anthrax as a Biological Weapon," p. 66.

8. National Commission on Terrorist Attacks Upon the United States (9/11 Commission), *The 9/11 Commission Report: The Final Report of the National Commission on Terrorist Attacks Upon the United States*, authorized edition (New York: W.W. Norton, 2004), pp. 1–14, 311, 552n188.

9. Ibid., p. xv.

10. Marilyn W. Thompson, *The Killer Strain: Anthrax and a Government Exposed* (New York: HarperCollins Publishers, 2003), pp. 66–67.

11. Department of Health and Human Services, "Secretary Thompson Testifies on Bioterrorism," news release, October 3, 2001.

12. Leonard A. Cole, *The Anthrax Letters: A Medical Detective Story* (Washington, DC: Joseph Henry Press, 2003), pp. 115–117.

13. These and all of the other recovered anthrax letters were in the Postal Service's "blue eagle," stamped envelopes available in Postal Service vending machines. GAO, *U.S. Postal Service: Better Guidance Is Needed to Ensure an Appropriate Response to Anthrax Contamination*, GAO-04-239 (Washington, DC, September 9, 2004), p. 26n45.

14. FBI, "Amerithrax: Linguistic/Behavioral Analysis," news release, November 9, 2001.

15. Daniel B. Jernigan, Pratima L. Raghunathan, et al., "Investigations of Bioterrorism-Related Anthrax, United States, 2001: Epidemiologic Findings," *Emerging Infectious Diseases*, vol. 8, No. 10, October 2002, p. 1023; Cole, *The Anthrax Letters*, pp. 38–41.

16. Ibid., pp. vii–viii, 52–53.

17. Ibid., pp. 52–54.

18. AMI published a number of tabloids, including the *National Enquirer*, the *Star*, the *Globe*, the *Sun*, and the *National Examiner*. Cole, *The Anthrax Letters*, p. 36.

19. The identification of the *National Enquirer* as the likely Florida addressee was inferred from the fact that an "anthrax trail" was later discovered leading through the post office that served Lantana, Florida, which had been the location of the *Enquirer* until January 2001. Andrew C. Revkin and Dana Canedy, "Anthrax Pervades Florida Site, and Experts See Likeness to That Sent to Senators," *New York Times*, December 5, 2001.

20. Jernigan, Raghunathan, et al., "Investigations of Bioterrorism-Related Anthrax," p. 1023.

21. With respect to the victims of the 2001 anthrax attacks, names are only used in cases where the individual's identity has been widely reported.

22. Cole, *The Anthrax Letters*, pp. 38–41.

23. Eric Liption and Jim Rutenberg, "Anthrax Inquiries Expand in Three States," *New York Times*, October 14, 2001.

24. Traeger MS, Wiersma ST, Rosenstein NE, Malecki JM, Shepard CW, Raghunatahn PL, "First Case of Bioterrorism-Related Inhalational Anthrax in the United States, Palm Beach County, Florida, 2001," *Emerg Infect Dis* [serial online] Oct. 2002; 8. Available from: URL: http://www.cdc.gov/ncidod/EID/vol8no10/02-03454.htm

25. Ed Lake, "The Florida Anthrax Cases," April 15, 2003, available online at www.anthraxinvestigation.com/Florida.html.

26. Jernigan, Raghunathan, "Investigations of Bioterrorism-Related Anthrax," pp. 1021, 1024.

27. Traeger, Wiersma, et al., "First Case of Bioterrorism-Related Inhalational Anthrax."

28. Cole, *The Anthrax Letters*, pp. 4–9; and Thompson, *The Killer Strain*, p. 62.

29. Cole, *The Anthrax Letters*, pp. 9, 15; and Thompson, *The Killer Strain*, p. 62.

30. Cole, *The Anthrax Letters*, pp. 13–15; and Thompson, *The Killer Strain*, pp. 62–63.

31. Department of Health and Human Services, "Secretary Thompson Testifies on Bioterrorism Preparedness."

32. This chapter utilizes the specific definitions employed by CDC in classifying anthrax diagnoses as either "confirmed" or "suspected:" "A confirmed case of anthrax was defined as clinically compatible illness (cutaneous, inhalational, or gastrointestinal) that was either (1) laboratory confirmed by isolation of B. *anthracis* from a patient's clinical specimens, or (2) associated with other laboratory evidence of B. *anthracis* infection based on at least two supportive tests. A suspected case of anthrax was defined as a clinically compatible illness with no alternative diagnosis and no isolation of B. *anthracis*, but with either (1) laboratory evidence of B. *anthracis* by one supportive laboratory test, or (2) an epidemiologic link to an environmental B. *anthracis* exposure." Traeger, Wiersma, et al., "First Case of Bioterrorism-Related Inhalational Anthrax."

33. Department of Health and Human Services, "Public Health Message Regarding Anthrax Case," news release, October 4, 2001.

34. Patricia Thomas, *The Anthrax Attacks* (New York: Century Foundation, 2003), p. 16.

35. Cole, *The Anthrax Letters*, p. 17.

36. Traeger, Wiersma, et al., "First Case of Bioterrorism-Related Inhalational Anthrax."

37. Cole, *The Anthrax Letters*, pp. 17, 21.

38. Traeger, Wiersma, et al., "First Case of Bioterrorism-Related Inhalational Anthrax."

39. Traeger, Wiersma, et al., "First Case of Bioterrorism-Related Inhalational Anthrax;" and Cole, *The Anthrax Letters*, pp. 22–31.

40. Centers for Disease Control and Prevention, "Update: Public Health Message Regarding Florida Anthrax Case," news release, October 7, 2001.

41. Cole, *The Anthrax Letters*, p. 33.

42. Traeger, Wiersma, et al., "First Case of Bioterrorism-Related Inhalational Anthrax."

43. Cole, *The Anthrax Letters*, p. 33.

44. GAO, *U.S. Postal Service: Better Guidance Is Needed to Ensure an Appropriate Response to Anthrax Contamination*, pp. 16–17.

45. Thomas, *The Anthrax Attacks*, p. 19.

46. Thompson, *The Killer Strain*, pp. 100–101.

47. Cole, *The Anthrax Letters*, pp. 51–52.

48. Jernigan, Raghunathan, "Investigations of Bioterrorism-Related Anthrax," p. 1021.

49. Cole, *The Anthrax Letters*, pp. 30, 53.

50. Ibid., p. 54.

51. FBI, "Amerithrax: Linguistic/Behavioral Analysis," and Judith Miller and David Johnston, "Anthrax Investigators Open Letter Sent to Senator Leahy," *New York Times*, December 6, 2001.

52. Jernigan, Raghunathan, "Investigations of Bioterrorism-Related Anthrax," p. 1023.

53. Cole, *The Anthrax Letters*, pp. 55–56.

54. Jernigan, Raghunathan, "Investigations of Bioterrorism-Related Anthrax," p. 1021; and Cole, *The Anthrax Letters*, pp. 81–82, 85.

55. Thompson, *The Killer Strain*, pp. 109–110; Centers for Disease Control and Prevention, "Update: Investigation of Bioterrorism-Related Anthrax and Interim Guidelines for Exposure Management and Antimicrobial Therapy, October 2001," *MMWR Weekly*, October 26, 2001, http://www.cdc.gov/mmwr/preview/mmwrhtml/mm5042a1.htm; and Cole, *The Anthrax Letters*, p. 55.

56. Thompson, *The Killer Strain*, p. 109.

57. Centers for Disease Control and Prevention, "Update: Investigation of Bioterrorism-Related Anthrax;" and Jernigan, Raghunathan, "Investigations of Bioterrorism-Related Anthrax," p. 1021.

58. Cole, *The Anthrax Letters*, p. 59; and Jernigan, Raghunathan, "Investigations of Bioterrorism-Related Anthrax," pp. 1021, 1024.

59. Richard Morin and Claudia Deane, "Poll Shows Anthrax Sparks Broad Concern," *Washington Post*, October 16, 2001, p. A06.

60. Cole, *The Anthrax Letters*, p. 92; and Jernigan, Raghunathan, "Investigations of Bioterrorism-Related Anthrax," pp. 1021, 1024.

61. Thompson, *The Killer Strain*, p. 166.

62. National Research Council, National Academy of Sciences, *Reopening Public Facilities After A Biological Attack* (Washington, DC: National Academies Press, 2005), p. 68.

63. Cole, *The Anthrax Letters*, pp. 74–75; and Jernigan, Raghunathan, "Investigations of Bioterrorism-Related Anthrax," p. 1021.

64. White House, "Director Ridge, Leaders Discuss Homeland Security," transcript, October 18, 2001, http://www.whitehouse.gov/news/releases/2001/11/print/20011018-1.html.

65. Cole, *The Anthrax Letters*, p. 75.

66. Cole, *The Anthrax Letters*, p. 53; and Centers for Disease Control and Prevention, "Update: Investigation of Bioterrorism-Related Anthrax."

67. Centers for Disease Control and Prevention, "Update: Investigation of Bioterrorism-Related Anthrax;" and Jernigan, Raghunathan, "Investigations of Bioterrorism-Related Anthrax," p. 1021.

68. White House, "Director Ridge Briefs Media at Week's End," transcript, October 19, 2001, http://www.whitehouse.gov/news/releases/2001/10/print/20011019-7.html.

69. Centers for Disease Control and Prevention, "Update: Investigation of Bioterrorism-Related Anthrax."

70. Cole, *The Anthrax* Letters, p. 66; Centers for Disease Control and Prevention, "Update: Investigation of Bioterrorism-Related Anthrax;" and Jernigan, Raghunathan, "Investigations of Bioterrorism-Related Anthrax," p. 1021.

71. Centers for Disease Control and Prevention, "Update: Investigation of Bioterrorism-Related Anthrax;" and Jernigan, Raghunathan, "Investigations of Bioterrorism-Related Anthrax," p. 1021.

72. White House, "Director Ridge Discusses Anthrax Situation," transcript, October 22, 2001, http://www.whitehouse.gov/news/releases/2001/10/print/20011023-1.html.

73. Cole, *The Anthrax Letters*, pp. 66–67; Centers for Disease Control and Prevention, "Update: Investigation of Bioterrorism-Related Anthrax;" and Jernigan, Raghunathan, "Investigations of Bioterrorism-Related Anthrax," p. 1021.

74. Centers for Disease Control and Prevention, "Update: Investigation of Bioterrorism-Related Anthrax."

75. White House, "Director Ridge Discusses Anthrax Situation."

76. Cole, *The Anthrax Letters*, pp. 54, 67; Centers for Disease Control and Prevention, "Update: Investigation of Bioterrorism-Related Anthrax;" and Jernigan, Raghunathan, "Investigations of Bioterrorism-Related Anthrax," p. 1021.

77. Jernigan, Raghunathan, "Investigations of Bioterrorism-Related Anthrax," p. 1023.

78. White House, "Gov. Ridge, Medical Authorities Discuss Anthrax," transcript, October 25, 2001, http://www.whitehouse.gov/news/releases/2001/10/print/20011025-4.html.

79. Traeger, Wiersma, et al., "First Case of Bioterrorism-Related Inhalational Anthrax."

80. Jernigan, Raghunathan, "Investigations of Bioterrorism-Related Anthrax," p. 1021.

81. Ibid.

82. Thompson, *The Killer Strain*, pp. 160–161; and Bushra Mina, J. P. Dym, Frank Kuepper, Raymond Tso, et al., "Fatal Inhalational Anthrax With Unknown Source of Exposure in 61-Year-Old Woman in New York City," in Henderson, Inglesby, and O'Toole, eds., *Bioterrorism: Guidelines for Medical and Public Health Management* (Chicago, IL: AMA Press, 2002), pp. 33–39.

83. Thomas, *The Anthrax Attacks*, pp. 30–31.

84. Mina, Dym, Kuepper, Tso, et al., "Fatal Inhalational Anthrax," p. 40.

85. Thompson, *The Killer Strain*, p. 163; and Lydia Barakat, Howard Quentzel, John Jernigan, David Kirschke, et al., "Fatal Inhalational Anthrax in a 94-Year-Old Connecticut Woman," in Henderson, Inglesby, and O'Toole, eds., *Bioterrorism: Guidelines for Medical and Public Health Management* (Chicago, IL: AMA Press, 2002), pp. 43–46.

86. Barakat, Quentzel, Jernigan, Kirschke, et al., "Fatal Inhalational Anthrax," p. 48.

87. Thompson, *The Killer Strain*, pp. 165–167.

88. Thompson, *The Killer Strain*, pp. 172–173; and Cole, *The Anthrax Letters*, pp. 90–91.

89. Jernigan, Raghunathan, "Investigations of Bioterrorism-Related Anthrax," pp. 1021–1022.

90. Anthony S. Fauci, "Foreword," in Henderson, Inglesby, and O'Toole, eds., *Bioterrorism: Guidelines for Medical and Public Health Management* (Chicago, IL: AMA Press, 2002), p. vi.

91. Jernigan, Raghunathan, "Investigations of Bioterrorism-Related Anthrax," pp. 1025–1026.

92. Fauci, "Foreword," p. v.

CHAPTER 2

1. White House, "Fact Sheet Addressing the Threat of Emerging Infectious Diseases," news release, June 12, 1996, available online at http://www.fas.org/irp/offdocs/pdd_ntsc7.htm.

2. Both the 1976 and 1977 outbreaks were thought to have the potential to become pandemics but neither spread sufficiently to reach that status. Lister, "Pandemic Influenza: Domestic Preparedness Efforts," p. 6.

3. Andrew Dobson and E. Robin Carper, "Infectious Diseases and Human Population History," *Bioscience*, February 1996, vol. 46, No. 2, p. 119.

4. Brian Williams, "Infectious Diseases in History," http://urbanrim.org.uk/diseases.htm.

5. Dobson and Carper, "Infectious Diseases and Human Population History," p. 120.

6. Lister, "Pandemic Influenza," p. 6.

7. Dobson and Carper, "Infectious Diseases and Human Population History," p. 121.

8. Between 1877 and 1884, the bacteriologic agents responsible for anthrax, tuberculosis, diphtheria, typhoid, and yellow fever were discovered.

9. Committee for the Study of the Future of Public Health, Institute of Medicine, *The Future of Public Health* (Washington, DC: The National Academies Press, 1988), p. 63.

10. Bernard Guyer, Mary Anne Freedman, Donna M. Strobino, and Edward J. Sondik, "Annual Summary of Vital Statistics: Trends in the Health of Americans During the 20th Century," *Pediatrics*, vol. 106, No. 6, December 2000, p. 1307.

11. National Intelligence Council, *The Global Infectious Disease Threat and Its Implications for the United States*, NIE 99-17D (Washington, DC: National Intelligence Council, January 2000); available online at http://www.fas.org/irp/threat/nie99-17d.htm.

12. Jennifer Brower and Peter Chalk, *The Global Threat of New and Reemerging Infectious Diseases: Reconciling U.S. National Security and Public Health Policy* (Santa Monica, CA: RAND Corporation, 2003), pp. 14–16.

13. Ibid., pp. 17–20.

14. Ibid., pp. 20–21.

15. Ibid., pp. 21–23.

16. Ibid., pp. 23–25.

17. Ibid., pp. 26–28.

18. National Intelligence Council, *The Global Infectious Disease Threat and Its Implications for the United States.*

19. Brower and Chalk, *The Global Threat of New and Reemerging Infectious Diseases*, pp. 13–14.

20. National Intelligence Council, *The Global Infectious Disease Threat and Its Implications for the United States.*

21. *World Health Organization, World Health Report 2007—A Safer Future: Global Public Health Security in the 21st Century* (Geneva: WHO, 2007), pp. 12–13, 59.

22. Anthony H. Cordesman, *The Challenge of Biological Terrorism* (Washington, DC: CSIS, 2005), pp. 12–13; and Monterrey Institute of International Studies, Center

for Nonproliferation Studies, "Chronology of State Use and Biological and Chemical Weapons Control," http://cns.miis.edu/research/cbw/pastuse.htm.

23. Cordesman, *The Challenge of Biological Terrorism*, p. 13; and Monterrey Institute of International Studies, "Chronology of State Use and Biological and Chemical Weapons Control."

24. Amy E. Smithson and Leslie-Anne Levy, *Ataxia: The Chemical and Biological Terrorism Threat and the U.S. Response*, The Henry L. Stimson Center, Report No. 35 (Washington, DC, October 2000), pp. 43, 46–47.

25. Barry Kellman, *Bioviolence: Preventing Biological Terror and Crime* (Cambridge: Cambridge University Press, 2007), pp. 59–61.

26. Kellman, *Bioviolence*, pp. 57–59.

27. Ibid., pp. 202–204.

28. Ibid., p. 66.

29. The Commission on the Intelligence Capabilities of the United States Regarding Weapons of Mass Destruction, *Report to the President of the United States* (Washington, DC, March 31, 2005), pp. 505–506.

30. Kellman, *Bioviolence*, p. 66.

31. W. Seth Carus, Center for Counterproliferation Research, "Bioterrorism and Biocrimes: Illicit Use of Biological Agents Since 1900," working paper (Washington, DC: National Defense University, February 2001), pp. 8, 11.

32. Cordesman, *The Challenge of Biological Terrorism*, p. 15; and Carus, "Bioterrorism and Biocrimes," p. 7.

33. Advisory Panel to Assess Domestic Response Capabilities for Terrorism Involving Weapons of Mass Destruction, *First Annual Report to the President and the Congress: I. Assessing the Threat* (Washington, DC, December 15, 1999), pp. 8–9.

34. National Commission on Terrorist Attacks Upon the United States (9/11 Commission), *The 9/11 Commission Report: The Final Report of the National Commission on Terrorist Attacks Upon the United States*, authorized ed. (New York: W.W. Norton, 2004), pp. 151, 380.

35. The Commission on the Intelligence Capabilities of the United States Regarding Weapons of Mass Destruction, *Report to the President of the United States*, p. 505.

36. World Health Organization, Public Health Response to Biological and Chemical Weapons: WHO Guidance (Geneva: WHO, 2004), p. 26.

37. Tara O'Toole, Thomas V. Inglesby, and Donald A. Henderson, "Why Understanding Biological Weapons Matters to Medical and Public Health Professionals," in Henderson, Inglesby, and O'Toole, eds., *Bioterrorism: Guidelines for Medical and Public Health Management* (Chicago, IL: AMA Press, 2002), p. 1.

38. World Health Organization, *Public Health Response to Biological and Chemical Weapons*, p. 26.

39. Ibid., pp. 236–274.

40. Ibid., pp. 217–225.

41. National Intelligence Council, *The Global Infectious Disease Threat and Its Implications for the United States*.

42. World Health Organization, *WHO Global Influenza Preparedness Plan* (Geneva: WHO, 2005), p. 2.

43. World Health Organization, *World Health Report 2007*, p. 47.

44. Cordesman, *The Challenge of Biological Terrorism*, pp. 141–142, 195–198.

45. Centers for Disease Control and Prevention, *CDC Influenza Pandemic Operation Plan (OPLAN)*, December 20, 2006, pp. 19–20.

46. Cordesman, *The Challenge of Biological Terrorism*, p. 3.

47. The Commission on the Intelligence Capabilities of the United States Regarding Weapons of Mass Destruction, *Report to the President of the United States*, p. 506.

48. Central Intelligence Agency, *Attachment A: Unclassified Report to Congress on the Acquisition of Technology Relating to Weapons of Mass Destruction and Advanced Chemical Munitions, 1 July through 31 December 2003* (Washington, DC, 2004), p. 7, www.cia.gov/cia/reports/721_reports/pdfs/721report_july_dec2003.pdf.

49. Center for Biosecurity, University of Pittsburgh Medical Center, *Testimony of Tara O'Toole at "Hearing on Bioterrorism Preparedness and the Role of DHS Chief Medical Officer," U.S. House of Representatives, Committee on Appropriations, Subcommittee on Homeland Security*, March 29, 2007.

50. Milton Leitenberg, *Assessing the Biological Weapons and Bioterrorism Threat* (Carlisle, PA: Strategic Studies Institute, U.S. Army War College, 2005), pp. 87–88.

51. Cordesman, *The Challenge of Biological Terrorism*, p. 141.

52. 9/11 Commission, *Testimony of Gerald Dillingham*, First Public Hearing, New York City, May 1, 2003; and 9/11 Commission, *The Final Report*, p. 391.

53. R. William Johnstone, *9/11 and the Future of Transportation Security* (Westport, CT: Praeger Security International, 2006), pp. 115–118.

54. Gary A. Ackerman and Kevin S. Moran, The Weapons of Mass Destruction Commission, "Bioterrorism and Threat Assessment," No. 22 (Stockholm, Sweden, November 2004), pp. 4, 6.

55. Committee on Methodological Improvements to the Department of Homeland Security's Biological Agent Risk Analysis, National Research Council, *Interim Report on Methodological Improvements to the Department of Homeland Security's Biological Risk Analysis* (Washington, DC: National Academies Press, 2007), p. 4.

56. *Ibid.*, pp. 6–7.

57. Colin McInnes, Nuffield Trust Global Programme on Health, Foreign Policy and Security, *Health, Security and the Risk Society* (London: The Nuffield Trust, 2005), p. 11.

58. Ibid., p. 6.

59. Quoted in Joel Achenbach, "Threat Level Gray: When the Danger Is Relative, Assessing Risks Can Be Well, Risky," *Washington Post*, February 8, 2004.

60. McInnes, *Health, Security and the Risk Society*," p. 19.

CHAPTER 3

1. "Public health focuses on the prevention of disease within populations, while health care focuses on the treatment of disease in individuals." Eileen Salinsky, "Public Health Emergency Preparedness: Fundamentals of the System," National Health Policy Forum Background Paper (Washington, DC: George Washington University, April 3, 2002), p. 2.

2. Elin Gursky, *Drafted to Fight Terror: U.S. Public Health on the Front Lines of Biological Defense* (Arlington, VA: ANSER, August 2004), p. 30; and Centers for Disease Control and Prevention, "Achievements in Public Health, 1900–1999: Changes in the Public Health System," *MMWR Weekly*, December 24, 1999, http://www.cdc.gov/mmwr/preview/mmwrhtml/mm4850a1.htm.

3. Salinsky, "Public Health Emergency Preparedness," p. 3.

4. Gursky, *Drafted to Fight Terror*, p. 30; and Centers for Disease Control and Prevention, "Achievements in Public Health."

5. Gursky, *Drafted to Fight Terror*, pp. 30–31.

6. Centers for Disease Control and Prevention, *CDC's Origins and Malaria* (Atlanta, GA: April 23, 2004), http://www.cdc.gov/malaria/history/history_cdc.htm.

7. Gursky, *Drafted to Fight Terror*, p. 30.

8. Salinsky, "Public Health Emergency Preparedness," pp. 3–4.

9. Centers for Disease Control and Prevention, "Achievements in Public Health."

10. Salinsky, "Public Health Emergency Preparedness," p. 4.

11. Sarah A. Lister, Congressional Research Service, "An Overview of the U.S. Public Health System in the Context of Emergency Preparedness," RL31719 (Washington, DC, March 17, 2005), pp. 4–5.

12. Thirty-six states have separate environmental health agencies, and at least seven handle emergency medical services outside the state health agency. Salinsky, "Public Health Emergency Preparedness," pp. 22–23.

13. Salinsky, "Public Health Emergency Preparedness," pp. 15–16.

14. Salinsky, "Public Health Emergency Preparedness," p. 24.

15. GAO, *Public Health Response to Anthrax Incidents*, GAO-04-152 (Washington, DC, October 15, 2003), p. 7.

16. Lister, "An Overview of the U.S. Public Health System," pp. 5, 7.

17. Lister, "An Overview of the U.S. Public Health System," pp. 7–8.

18. Committee on Assuring the Health of the Public in the 21st Century, Institute of Medicine, *The Future of the Public's Health in the 21st Century* (Washington, DC: The National Academies Press, 2002), p. 19.

19. Centers for Disease Control and Prevention, *Public Health's Infrastructure: A Status Report Prepared for the Appropriations Committee of the United States Senate*, March 2001, Appendix D, pp. 23–24, www.phppo.cdc.gov.

20. Lister, "An Overview of the U.S. Public Health System," pp. 8–9.

21. Patricia Thomas, *The Anthrax Attacks* (New York: The Century Foundation, 2003), p. 11.

22. Salinsky, "Public Health Emergency Preparedness," App. A, pp. 35–36.

23. Salinsky, "Public Health Emergency Preparedness," pp. 18–19; and Lister, "An Overview of the U.S. Public Health System," pp. 13–14.

24. Centers for Medicare & Medicaid Services, Office of the Actuary, National Health Statistics Group, "Table 2. National Health Expenditures Aggregate Amounts and Average Annual Percent Change by Type of Expenditure: Selected Calendar Years 1960–2005."

25. Committee for the Study of the Future of Public Health, Institute of Medicine, *The Future of Public Health* (Washington, DC: The National Academies Press, 1988), pp. 57–58.

26. Committee for the Study of the Future of Public Health, *The Future of Public Health*, p. 61.

27. Gursky, *Drafted to Fight Terror*, p. 35.

28. Committee for the Study of the Future of Public Health, *The Future of Public Health*, p. 63.

29. Gursky, *Drafted to Fight Terror*, p. 35.

30. Committee for the Study of the Future of Public Health, *The Future of Public Health*, pp. 65–68.

31. World Health Organization, *International Health Regulations (1969)*, (Geneva: WHO, 1983), p. 5.

32. Committee on International Science, Engineering and Technology Policy, National Science and Technology Council, *Global Microbial Threats in the 1990s* (Washington, DC, September 1995), http://clinton2.nara.gov/WH/EOP/OSTP/CISET/exsum.html.

33. Centers for Disease Control and Prevention, "Addressing Emerging Infectious Disease Threats: A Prevention Strategy for the United States, Executive Summary," *MMWR Weekly*, April 15, 1994, http://wonder.cdc.gov/wonder/prevguid/m0031393/m0031393.asp.

34. Canada, France, Germany, Italy, Japan, United Kingdom, and the United States.

35. Committee on International Science, Engineering and Technology Policy, *Global Microbial Threats in the 1990s*.

36. Jennifer Brower and Peter Chalk, *The Global Threat of New and Reemerging Infectious Diseases* (Santa Monica, CA: RAND, 2003), p. 75; and White House, "Fact Sheet Addressing the Threat of Emerging Infectious Diseases," news release, June 12, 1996, available online at http://www.fas.org/irp/offdocs/pdd_ntsc7.htm.

37. Centers for Disease Control and Prevention, "Preventing Emerging Infectious Diseases: A Strategy for the 21st Century, Overview of the Updated CDC Plan," *MMWR Weekly*, September 11, 1998, http://www.cdc.gov/mmwr/preview/mmwrhtml/00054779.htm.

38. Brower and Chalk, *The Global Threat of New and Reemerging Infectious Diseases*, p. 76.

39. Though the United States observed the Protocol's provisions, it was not formally ratified by the U.S. Senate until April 1975. Department of State, *Convention on the Prohibition of the Development, Production and Stockpiling of Bacteriological (Biological) and Toxin Weapons and on Their Destruction*, narrative, http://www.state.gov/t/ac/trt/4718.htm.

40. World Health Organization, *Public Health Response to Biological and Chemical Weapons: WHO Guidance*, 2nd ed. (Geneva: WHO, 2004), pp. 109–110.

41. Department of State, *Convention*; and World Health Organization, *Public Health Response*, pp. 110–112.

42. Leonard A. Cole, *The Anthrax Letters: A Medical Detective Story* (Washington, DC: Joseph Henry Press, 2003), pp. 227–228.

43. Elizabeth Fee and Thomas Brown, "Preemptive Biopreparedness: Can We Learn Anything from History?" *American Journal of Public Health*, 91, No. 5 (May 2001), pp. 721, 723.

44. Thomas, *The Anthrax Attacks*, p. 9.

45. An all-hazards system is one that is capable of responding to and protecting individuals from the full spectrum of potential emergencies, including bioterrorism, naturally occurring disease threats, and natural disasters. It is based on the recognition that preparing for one threat can have benefits that will assist the system in preparing for other potential emergencies. Trust for America's Health, "Ready or Not? Protecting the Public's Health from Diseases, Disasters, and Bioterrorism 2006" (Washington, DC, December 2006), p. 5.

46. Cole, *The Anthrax Letters*, p. 125; and Thomas, *The Anthrax Attacks*, p. 9.

47. On April 19, 1995 a cargo truck carrying two tons of ammonium nitrate and fuel oil was detonated in front of the Alfred P. Murrah Federal Building. One hundred sixty-eight people were killed and hundreds more injured. Timothy McVeigh was captured less than two hours after the bombing, and was subsequently tried, convicted, and executed for carrying out the bombing. Terry Nichols was charged and convicted of assisting McVeigh, and is currently serving multiple life sentences in prison. Authorities believe the bombers, both of whom were U.S. citizens, were sympathetic with domestic, anti-government hate groups, and undertook the crime to avenge the deaths that resulted from the 1993 federal siege of the Branch Dravidian compound in Waco, Texas. Tim Talley, Associated Press, "Experts Fear Oklahoma City Bombing Lessons Forgotten," *San Diego Union-Tribune*, April 17, 2006.

48. GAO, *Bioterrorism: Federal Research and Preparedness Activities*, GAO-01-915 (Washington, DC, September 2001), pp. 32–33.

49. Lister, "An Overview of the U.S. Public Health System," p. 35.

50. NDMS is a national public–private network of health-care providers created in 1984 to provide rapid medical response, evacuation, and hospital care as a backup to local resources in the event of a catastrophic disaster. Amy E. Smithson and Leslie-Anne Levy, *Ataxia: The Chemical and Biological Terrorism Threat and the U.S. Response*, The Henry L. Stimson Center, Report No. 35 (Washington, DC: October 2000), pp. 114–115.

51. Smithson and Levy, *Ataxia*, p. 125.

52. Smithson and Levy, *Ataxia*, pp. 125–126.

53. Lister, "An Overview of the U.S. Public Health System," p. 17.

54. GAO, *Bioterrorism*, p. 6; Frank J. Cilluffo, Sharon L. Cardash, and Gordon N. Lederman, *Combating Chemical, Biological, Radiological, and Nuclear Terrorism: A Report of the CSIS Homeland Defense Project* (Washington, DC: CSIS Press, 2001), p. 35; and Smithson and Levy, *Ataxia*, pp. 120–121.

55. Cole, *The Anthrax Letters*, p. 126.

56. GAO, *Bioterrorism*, p. 33.

57. Lister, "An Overview of the U.S. Public Health System," p. 38.

58. Smithson and Levy, *Ataxia*, p. 120.

59. Lister, "An Overview of the U.S. Public Health System," pp. 17, 40–41.

60. The General Accounting Office was renamed as the Government Accountability Office, effective July 7, 2004, in order to "better reflect the modern professional services organization GAO has become." The change was made by the *GAO Human Capital Reform Act of 2004* (PL 108-271, 118 Stat. 811). To avoid confusion, this organization will generally be referred to as GAO elsewhere in this work.

61. GAO, *Bioterrorism*, p. 2.

62. GAO, *Public Health Response to Anthrax Incidents*, p. 30.

63. GAO, *Bioterrorism*, p. 34.

64. Cilluffo, Cardash, and Lederman, *Combating Chemical, Biological, Radiological, and Nuclear Terrorism*, p. 35; and GAO, *Bioterrorism*, p. 13.

65. The other component of TOPOFF 2000 was a simulated chemical attack in Portsmouth, NH. A concurrent exercise, called National Capital Region 2000, concerned a simulated radiological attack in the Washington, DC area.

66. GAO, *Bioterrorism*, p. 13.

67. Tara O'Toole, Michael Mair, and Thomas V. Inglesby, "Shining Light on 'Dark Winter,' " *Clinical Infectious Diseases*, 2002: 34 (April 2002), pp. 972–994.

68. Fee and Brown, "Preemptive Biopreparedness," p. 725.

69. Committee for the Study of the Future of Public Health, *The Future of Public Health*, p. 1.

70. Committee for the Study of the Future of Public Health, *The Future of Public Health*, p. 3.

71. Centers for Disease Control and Prevention, *Public Health's Infrastructure*, p. iii.

72. GAO, *Bioterrorism*, pp. 4, 14; Advisory Panel to Assess Domestic Response Capabilities for Terrorism Involving Weapons of Mass Destruction, *Second Annual Report to the President and the Congress—II: Toward a National Strategy for Combating Terrorism* (Santa Monica, CA: RAND, December 15, 2000), p. 32; and Brower and Chalk, *The Global Threat of New and Reemerging Infectious Diseases*, p. 100.

73. GAO, *Bioterrorism*, pp. 4, 16.

74. Jonathan R. Davis and Joshua Lederberg, eds., *Public Health Systems and Emerging Infections: Assessing the Capabilities of the Public and Private Sectors: Workshop Summary* (Washington, DC: National Academy Press, 2000), p. 12.

75. Davis and Lederberg, eds., *Public Health Systems and Emerging Infections*, p. 6.

76. Bernard Turnock and Christopher Atchison, "Governmental Public Health in the United States: The Implications of Federalism," *Health Affairs* 21, No. 6 (November–December 2002), p. 75.

77. Eileen Salinsky, "Will the Nation Be Ready for the Next Bioterrorism Attack? Mending Gaps in the Public Health Infrastructure," National Health Policy Forum Issue Brief, No. 776 (Washington, DC: George Washington University, June 12, 2002), p. 5.

78. GAO, *Health Workforce: Ensuring Adequate Supply and Distribution Remains Challenging*, GAO-01-1042T (Washington, DC, August 1, 2001), p. 3.

79. GAO, *Emerging Infectious Diseases: National Surveillance System Could Be Strengthened*, GAO/T-HEHS-99-62 (Washington, DC, February 25, 1999), p. 2.

80. Brower and Chalk, *The Global Threat of New and Reemerging Infectious Diseases*, p. 96; and Davis and Lederberg, eds., *Public Health Systems and Emerging Infections*, pp. 4–5.

81. Centers for Disease Control and Prevention, *Public Health's Infrastructure*, pp. 3, 7–8.

82. Smithson and Levy, *Ataxia*, p. 252.

83. Davis and Lederberg, eds., *Public Health Systems and Emerging Infections*, p. 5.

84. O'Toole, Mair, and Inglesby, "Shining Light on 'Dark Winter,' " p. 981.

85. Centers for Disease Control and Prevention, *Public Health's Infrastructure*, p. 8.

86. Davis and Lederberg, eds., *Public Health Systems and Emerging Infections*, pp. 4, 9.

87. Smithson and Levy, *Ataxia*, pp. 271–274.

88. Centers for Disease Control and Prevention, *Public Health's Infrastructure*, pp. 8–9.

89. GAO, *Bioterrorism*, pp. 22–23.

90. Smithson and Levy, *Ataxia*, p. 262.

91. GAO, *Bioterrorism*, p. 23; and Smithson and Levy, *Ataxia*, p. 227.

92. Smithson and Levy, *Ataxia*, p. 265.

93. Institute of Medicine, *Chemical and Biological Terrorism: Research and Development to Improve Civilian Medical Response* (Washington, DC: National Academies Press, 1999), p. 101.

94. Smithson and Levy, *Ataxia*, p. 266.

95. Smithson and Levy, *Ataxia*, pp. 245, 247.

96. GAO, *Emerging Infectious Diseases: National Surveillance System Could Be Strengthened*, p. 2.

97. Davis and Lederberg, eds., *Public Health Systems and Emerging Infections*, pp. 4, 7.

98. Salinsky, "Will the Nation Be Ready for the Next Bioterrorism Attack?" p. 8.

99. Brower and Chalk, *The Global Threat of New and Reemerging Infectious Diseases*, pp. 97–98.

100. Smithson and Levy, *Ataxia*, p. 259.

101. GAO, *Bioterrorism*, p. 23.

102. O'Toole, Mair, and Inglesby, "Shining Light on "Dark Winter,' " p. 981.

103. Kathleen S. Swendiman and Jennifer K. Elsea, Congressional Research Service, "Federal and State Quarantine and Isolation Authority," RL33201 (Washington, DC, December 12, 2005), pp. 3–5.

104. Smithson and Levy, *Ataxia*, pp. 268–269.

105. O'Toole, Mair, and Inglesby, "Shining Light on "Dark Winter,' " p. 982.

106. Committee on Assuring the Health of the Public in the 21st Century, *The Future of the Public's Health in the 21st Century*, pp. 24–26.

107. For purposes of these calculations, government public health expenditures include funding for epidemiological surveillance, inoculations, immunization/vaccination services, disease-prevention programs, the operation of public health labs, and related functions. Excluded are expenditures for research, facilities, and equipment, which are in other accounts. Centers for Medicare & Medicaid Services, Office of the Actuary, National Health Statistics Group, *National Health Expenditures Accounts: Definitions, Sources, and Methods Used in the NHEA 2005*, p. 14.

108. Centers for Medicare & Medicaid Services, Office of the Actuary, National Health Statistics Group, "National Health Expenditures by Type of Service and Source of Funds: Calendar Years 2006–1960" (Washington, DC, 2008).

109. U.S. Senate, Committee on Appropriations, *Report to Accompany S. 1650, Departments of Labor, Health and Human Services, Education, and Related Agencies Appropriation Bill, 2000,* 106th Cong., 1st session. (Washington, DC, September 29, 1999), S. Report 106-166, p. 244.

110. Brower and Chalk, *The Global Threat of New and Reemerging Infectious Diseases,* pp. 94–95.

111. Turnock and Atchison, "Governmental Public Health in the United States," pp. 72–74.

112. Centers for Disease Control and Prevention, *Public Health's Infrastructure,* p. 12.

CHAPTER 4

1. Thomas V. Inglesby, Tara O'Toole, Donald A. Henderson, et al., "Anthrax as a Biological Weapon: Updated Recommendations for Management," in Henderson, Inglesby and O'Toole, eds., *Bioterrorism: Guidelines for Medical and Public Health Management* (Chicago, IL: AMA Press, 2002), pp. 63, 70.

2. Leonard A. Cole, *The Anthrax Letters: A Medical Detective Story* (Washington, DC: Joseph Henry Press, 2003), p. 110.

3. Marilyn W. Thompson, *The Killer Strain: Anthrax and a Government Exposed* (New York: HarperCollins Publishers, 2003), pp. 178–179.

4. Jay C. Butler, Mitchell L. Cohen, Cindy R. Friedman, Robert M. Scripp, and Craig G. Watz, "Collaboration between Public Health and Law Enforcement: New Paradigms and Partnerships for Bioterrorism Planning and Response," *Emerging Infectious Diseases,* vol. 8, No. 10, October 2002, p. 1153.

5. For example, in March of 2002 FBI Director Mueller reported that as of that date, approximately 4,000 FBI agents—accounting for over a third of the Bureau's workforce, were still working on the 9/11 investigation. (CNN, "FBI: 4,000 Agents Still Probe September 11," March 6, 2002, available online at http://archives.cnn.com/2002/US/03/06/inv.fbi.terrorism/index.html.) This compared to thirty-five FBI agents and fifteen postal inspectors assigned full time to the Amerithrax investigation. (Marilyn W. Thompson, "The Pursuit of Steven Hatfill," *Washington Post,* September 14, 2003, p. W06.)

6. Thompson, *The Killer Strain,* pp. 121–122.

7. FBI, "Statement of Director Mueller on FBI Investigations into Anthrax Exposures and Suspected Anthrax Exposures," news release, October 16, 2001.

8. Lois R. Ember, "Anthrax Sleuthing: Science Aids a Nettlesome FBI Criminal Probe," *Chemical & Engineering News,* vol. 84, No. 49, December 4, 2006, p. 47; and White House, "Director Ridge Briefs Media at Week's End," transcript, October 19, 2001, http://www.whitehouse.gov/news/releases/2001/10/print/20011019-7.html.

9. White House, "Director Ridge Discusses Anthrax Situation," transcript, October 22, 2001, http://www.whitehouse.gov/news/releases/2001/10/print/20011023-1.html.

10. Ibid.

11. The Ames strain is one of eighty-nine strains, or families, of *Bacillus anthracis,* the bacterium that causes anthrax. It was cultured by the Texas Veterinary Medical

Diagnostic Laboratory in College Station, Texas, which transferred it to USAMRIID in 1981 as part of the Army's effort to obtain as many strains of anthrax as possible to aid in the development and testing of vaccines. It was mistakenly named as the Ames strain after the return address of Ames, Iowa, which appeared on the container in which it had been shipped to USAMRIID. Ember, "Anthrax Sleuthing," p. 51.

12. White House, "Gov. Ridge, Medical Authorities Discuss Anthrax," transcript, October 25, 2001, http://www.whitehouse.gov/news/releases/2001/10/print/20011025-4.html.

13. White House, "Ridge, Thompson Hold Briefing," transcript, October 29, 2001, http://www.whitehouse.gov/news/releases/2001/10/print/20011029-4.html.

14. Guy Gugliotta and Gary Matsumoto, "FBI's Theory on Anthrax Is Doubted," *Washington Post*, October 28, 2002.

15. Ember, "Anthrax Sleuthing," p. 50; and Gugliotta and Matsumoto, "FBI's Theory on Anthrax Is Doubted."

16. Ember, "Anthrax Sleuthing," p. 50.

17. White House, "Wednesday's Homeland Security Briefing," transcript, November 7, 2001, http://www.whitehouse.gov/news/releases/2001/11/print/20011107-1.html.

18. In January 1998, Theodore Kaczynski pleaded guilty to being the Unabomber and was sentenced to life imprisonment without parole. Though he was formally charged and convicted of four bombings that killed two and maimed two others, he accepted responsibility for a total of sixteen bombings that killed three and injured twenty-nine over a period of seventeen years. CNN, "Kaczynski Admits He Is Unabomber, Sentenced to Life Without Parole," news release, January 22, 1998, http://www.cnn.com/US/9801/22/unabomb.plea/

19. Thompson, *The Killer Strain*, pp. 123–124.

20. FBI, "Amerithrax: Linguistic/Behavioral Analysis," news release, November 9, 2001.

21. CNN, "FBI Profiler: We Will Catch Anthrax Mailer," news release, November 17, 2001, http://archives.cnn.com/2001/US/11/16/anthrax.profiler/index.html.

22. Thompson, *The Killer Strain*, p. 171.

23. Steve Fainaru and Ceci Connolly, "Memo on Florida Case Roils Anthrax Probe," *Washington Post*, March 29, 2002, p. A03; and CNN, "Report Raises Question of Anthrax, Hijacker Link," CNN.com, March 23, 2002.

24. Cole, *The Anthrax Letters*, pp. 189–190.

25. Cole, *The Anthrax Letters*, p. 90; and White House, "Ridge, Thompson Hold Briefing."

26. Ember, "Anthrax Sleuthing," pp. 50–51.

27. Cole, *The Anthrax Letters*, pp. 90–91; and Ember, "Anthrax Sleuthing," pp. 47–51.

28. Cole, *The Anthrax Letters*, pp. 201–202; and Judith Miller and David Johnston, "Anthrax Investigators Open Letter Sent to Senator Leahy," *New York Times*, December 6, 2001.

29. Reuters, "Focus of U.S. Anthrax Probe Is Domestic—Ridge," January 13, 2002; and Cole, *The Anthrax Letters*, p. 188.

30. Barbara Hatch Rosenberg, "Analysis of the Anthrax Attacks," (Washington, DC: Federation of American Scientists, February 5, 2002), http://www.fas.org/bwc/

news/anthraxreport.htm, available online at http://scoop.co.nz/stories/print.html? path=HL0206/S00180.htm.

31. CNN, "FBI Asks Microbiologists for Help on Anthrax," February 5, 2002, available online at http://archives.cnn.com/2002/US/02/04/inv.fbi.anthrax/index.html.

32. Rosenberg, "Analysis of the Anthrax Attacks."

33. Thompson, *The Killer Strain*, pp. 203–205.

34. David Tell, "Remember Anthrax? Despite the Evidence, the FBI Won't Let Go of Its 'Lone American' Theory," *The Weekly Standard*, vol. 007, issue 32, April 29, 2002.

35. CNN, "Anthrax Terror Remains a Mystery,' March 27, 2002, available online at http://archives.cnn.com/2002/US/03/26/anthrax.investigation/index.html.

36. Cole, *The Anthrax Letters*, pp. 93, 192–194; Thompson, *The Killer Strain*, p. 201; and Thompson, "The Pursuit of Steven Hatfill."

37. Cole, *The Anthrax Letters*, pp. 194–195.

38. Thompson, "The Pursuit of Steven Hatfill."

39. CNN, "Hatfill's Former Apartment Searched Again," September 13, 2002, available online at: http://archives.cnn.com/2002/US/09/13/hatfill.search/index.html.

40. Gugliotta and Matsumoto, "FBI's Theory on Anthrax Is Doubted."

41. Thompson, "The Pursuit of Steven Hatfill" and CNN, "Anthrax 'person of interest' sues Ashcroft, FBI," August 27, 2003, available online at http://archives.cnn.com/2003/LAW/08/26/lawsuit.hatfill/index.html.

42. CNN, "Anthrax 'Person of Interest' sues Ashcroft, FBI."

43. Allan Lengel, "Little Progress in FBI Probe of Anthrax Attacks," *Washington Post*, September 16, 2005, p. A01.

44. Ember, "Anthrax Sleuthing," p. 47.

45. Douglas J. Beecher, "Forensic Application of Microbiological Culture Analysis To Identify Mail Intentionally Contaminated with *Bacillus anthracis* Spores," *Applied and Environmental Microbiology*, vol. 72, No. 8, August 2006, p. 5309.

46. Ember, "Anthrax Sleuthing," pp. 47–48, 51.

47. FBI, *Amerithrax Fact Sheet—September 2006*, http://www.fbi.gov/amerithrax_factsheet.htm.

48. Allan Lengel and Joby Warrick, "FBI Is Casting A Wider Net In Anthrax Attacks," *Washington Post*, September 25, 2006, p. A01.

49. David Willman, "Apparent Suicide in Anthrax Case," *Los Angeles Times*, August 1, 2008.

50. Joby Warrick, "Documents List Essential Clues," *Washington Post*, August 7, 2008, p. A17.

51. Carrie Johnson, Del Quentin Wilber and Dan Eggen, "Government Asserts Ivins Acted Alone," *Washington Post*, August 7, 2008, p. A01.

52. Butler, Cohen, et al., "Collaboration between Public Health and Law Enforcement," pp. 1152–1154.

53. Ibid., p. 1154.

54. Cole, *The Anthrax Letters*, p. 131.

55. GAO, *Bioterrorism: Public Health Response to Anthrax Incidents of 2001*, GAO-04-152 (Washington, DC, October 15, 2003), pp. 16–17.

56. Judith Miller and Sheryl Gay, "More Checked for Anthrax; U.S. Officials Acknowledge Underestimating Mail Risks," *New York Times*, October 25, 2001.

57. White House, "Gov. Ridge, Medical Authorities Discuss Anthrax."

58. Ember, "Anthrax Sleuthing," pp. 49–50.

59. GAO, *Bioterrorism*, p. 17.

CHAPTER 5

1. Amy E. Smithson and Leslie-Anne Levy, *Ataxia: The Chemical and Biological Terrorism Threat and the U.S. Response*, The Henry L. Stimson Center, Report No. 35 (Washington, DC: October 2000), p. 252.

2. As previously, this Chapter utilizes the specific definitions employed by CDC in classifying anthrax diagnoses as either "confirmed" or "suspected." Traeger MS, Wiersma ST, Rosenstein NE, Malecki JM, Shepard CW, and Raghunatahn PL, "First Case of Bioterrorism-Related Inhalational Anthrax in the United States, Palm Beach County, Florida, 2001," *Emerg Infect Dis* [serial online] Oct. 2002; 8. Available from: URL: http://www.cdc.gov/ncidod/EID/vol8no10/02-03454.htm.

3. Daniel B. Jernigan, Pratima L. Raghunathan, et al., "Investigations of Bioterrorism-Related Anthrax, United States, 2001: Epidemiologic Findings," *Emerging Infectious Diseases*, vol. 8, No. 10, October 2002, pp. 1021, 1024.

4. Leonard A. Cole, *The Anthrax Letters: A Medical Detective Story* (Washington, DC: Joseph Henry Press, 2003), pp. 4–7, 15.

5. Traeger, Wiersma, et al., "First Case of Bioterrorism-Related Inhalational Anthrax."

6. Centers for Disease Control and Prevention, "Update: Public Health Message Regarding the Florida Anthrax Case," news release, October 7, 2001; and Cole, *The Anthrax Letters*, p. 33.

7. Traeger, Wiersma, et al., "First Case of Bioterrorism-Related Inhalational Anthrax."

8. Marilyn W. Thompson, *The Killer Strain: Anthrax and a Government Exposed* (New York: HarperCollins Publishers, 2003), pp. 101–103.

9. Cole, *The Anthrax Letters*, pp. 50–52; and Centers for Disease Control and Prevention, "Update: Investigation of Bioterrorism-Related Anthrax and Interim Guidelines for Exposure Management and Antimicrobial Therapy, October 2001," *MMWR Weekly*, October 26, 2001, http://www.cdc.gov/mmwr/preview/mmwrhtml/mm5042a1.htm.

10. Jernigan, Pratima L. Raghunathan, et al., "Investigations of Bioterrorism-Related Anthrax," p. 1021.

11. Centers for Disease Control and Prevention, "Update: Investigation of Bioterrorim-Related Anthrax," and Jernigan, Pratima L. Raghunathan, et al., "Investigations of Bioterrorism-Related Anthrax," p. 1021.

12. Tara O'Toole, Thomas V. Inglesby, and Donald A. Henderson, "Why Understanding Biological Weapons Matters to Medical and Public Health Professionals," in Henderson, Inglesby and O'Toole, eds., *Bioterrorism: Guidelines for Medical and Public Health Management* (Chicago, IL: AMA Press, 2002), p. 3.

13. David Brown, "Agency With Most Need Didn't Get Anthrax Data," *Washington Post*, February 11, 2002, p. A03.

14. Ibid., p. A03.

15. Cole, *The Anthrax Letters*, pp. 75, 78; Jernigan, Pratima L. Raghunathan, et al., "Investigations of Bioterrorism-Related Anthrax," p. 1021; and Centers for Disease Control and Prevention, "Update: Investigation of Bioterrorim-Related Anthrax."

16. Centers for Disease Control and Prevention, "Update: Investigation of Bioterrorim-Related Anthrax;" and GAO, *U.S. Postal Service: Better Guidance Is Needed to Ensure an Appropriate Response to Anthrax Contamination*, GAO-04-239 (Washington, DC, September 9, 2004), p. 20.

17. White House, "Director Ridge Discusses Anthrax Situation," transcript, October 22, 2001, http://www.whitehouse.gov/news/releases/2001/10/print/20011023-1.html.

18. White House, "Ridge, Thompson Hold Briefing," transcript, October 29, 2001, http://www.whitehouse.gov/news/releases/2001/10/print/20011029-4.html.

19. Jernigan, Pratima L. Raghunathan, et al., "Investigations of Bioterrorism-Related Anthrax," pp. 1021, 1024.

20. Cole, *The Anthrax Letters*, p. 130.

21. Jernigan, Pratima L. Raghunathan, et al., "Investigations of Bioterrorism-Related Anthrax," pp. 1023–1024.

22. Ibid., p. 1024.

23. Ibid., pp. 1024–1025.

24. Ibid., pp. 1025–1026.

25. Ibid., p. 1026.

26. Thomas V. Inglesby, Tara O'Toole, and Donald A. Henderson, "Anthrax as a Biological Weapon: Updated Recommendations for Management," in Henderson, Inglesby and O'Toole, eds., *Bioterrorism: Guidelines for Medical and Public Health Management*, pp. 80–81; and Cole, *The Anthrax Letters*, p. 27.

27. Thompson, *The Killer Strain*, p. 100; Cole, *The Anthrax Letters*, pp. 51, 53, 75–76; and Centers for Disease Control and Prevention, "Update: Investigation of Bioterrorim-Related Anthrax."

28. Abigail Freedman, Olubunmi Afonja, Mary Wu Chang, Farzad Mostashari, et al., "Cutaneous Anthrax Associated With Microangiopathic Hemolytic Anemia and Coagulopathy in a 7-Month-Old Infant," in Henderson, Inglesby and O'Toole, eds., *Bioterrorism: Guidelines for Medical and Public Health Management*, pp. 53–58.

29. Cole, *The Anthrax Letters*, pp. 4, 23–25, 28.

30. Centers for Disease Control and Prevention, "Update: Investigation of Bioterrorim-Related Anthrax;" and Cole, *The Anthrax Letters*, pp. 65, 82, 85–87.

31. Centers for Disease Control and Prevention, "Update: Investigation of Bioterrorim-Related Anthrax;" and Cole, *The Anthrax Letters*, p. 84.

32. Centers for Disease Control and Prevention, "Update: Investigation of Bioterrorim-Related Anthrax;" and Cole, *The Anthrax Letters*, pp. 65–67.

33. Jernigan, Pratima L. Raghunathan, et al., "Investigations of Bioterrorism-Related Anthrax," pp. 1021, 1024.

34. Bushra Mina, J. P. Dym, Frank Kuepper, Raymond Tso, et al., "Fatal Inhalational Anthrax with Unknown Source of Exposure in 61-Year-Old Woman in New

York City," in Henderson, Inglesby and O'Toole, eds., *Bioterrorism: Guidelines for Medical and Public Health Management*, pp. 33–38.

35. Lydia Barakat, Howard Quentzel, John Jernigan, David Kirschke, et al., "Fatal Inhalational Anthrax in a 94-Year-Old Connecticut Woman," in Henderson, Inglesby, and O'Toole, eds., *Bioterrorism: Guidelines for Medical and Public Health Management*, pp. 43–46.

36. Jernigan, Pratima L. Raghunathan, et al., "Investigations of Bioterrorism-Related Anthrax," p. 1025.

37. Ibid., p. 1023.

38. Inglesby, O'Toole, and Henderson, "Anthrax as a Biological Weapon," in Henderson, Inglesby and O'Toole, eds., *Bioterrorism: Guidelines for Medical and Public Health Management*, p. 88.

39. Ibid., pp. 78–79; and Thompson, *The Killer Strain*, p. 184.

40. Cole, *The Anthrax Letters*, p. 33.

41. Ibid., p. 52.

42. Centers for Disease Control and Prevention, "Update: Investigation of Bioterrorim-Related Anthrax."

43. National Research Council, National Academies of Science, *Reopening Public Facilities After A Biological Attack* (Washington, DC: National Academies Press, 2005), p. 68.

44. GAO, *U.S. Postal Service*, pp. 4, 19–20.

45. Ibid., pp. 18–19.

46. Cole, *The Anthrax Letters*, p. 79; Centers for Disease Control and Prevention, "Update: Investigation of Bioterrorism-Related Anthrax;" and GAO, *U.S. Postal Service*, pp. 4, 20.

47. GAO, *U.S. Postal Service*, pp. 20–22; and Centers for Disease Control and Prevention, "Update: Investigation of Bioterrorism-Related Anthrax."

48. GAO, *U.S. Postal Service*, p. 21n32.

49. Frank Gottron, Congressional Research Service, "The U.S. Postal Service Response to the Threat of Bioterrorism Through the Mail," RL31280 (Washington, DC, February 11, 2002), p. 4.

50. GAO, *Bioterrorism: Public Health Response to Anthrax Incidents of 2001*, p. 9.

51. Michael M. Simpson, Congressional Research Service, "Anthrax-Contaminated Facilities: Preparations and a Standard for Remediation," RL33191 (Washington, DC, December 16, 2005), p. 2.

52. Cole, *The Anthrax Letters*, pp. 165–166.

53. National Research Council, *Reopening Public Facilities After A Biological Attack*, pp. 66, 68.

54. Thompson, *The Killer Strain*, p. 185.

55. GAO, *U.S. Postal Service: Better Guidance Is Needed to Ensure an Appropriate Response to Anthrax Contamination*, pp. 1–2.

56. Ibid., p. 2; and Melissa Campanelli, "NJ Post Office That Handled Anthrax-Laced Letters Reopens," *DM News*, March 15, 2005, http://www.dmnews.com/cms/trackback/32195-1.

57. Office of Inspector General, United States Postal Service, "Management Advisory: Contract Management for the Curseen-Morris Facility Cleanup and Modification," memo, March 31, 2004, p. 2 n2.

58. National Research Council, *Reopening Public Facilities After A Biological Attack*, p. 63.

59. MARCOR, "AMI Building Declared Anthrax-Free After MARCOR Remediation Decontamination," news release, February 13, 2007, http://www.marcor.com/index.cfm/do/article.display/articleID/34.

60. GAO, *Bioterrorism: Public Health Response to Anthrax Incidents of 2001*, GAO-04-152 (Washington, DC, October 15, 2003), pp. 24–26.

61. Patricia Thomas, *The Anthrax Attacks* (New York: The Century Foundation, 2003), pp. 15–16.

62. Thomas, *The Anthrax Attacks*, pp. 16–20.

63. Ibid., pp. 20–22.

64. Ibid., p. 7.

65. Dana Milbank, "Government's Anthrax Muddle: Many Voices, Few Facts," *Washington Post*, October 18, 2001, p. A13.

66. Thomas, *The Anthrax Attacks*, pp. 23–24; and Thompson, *The Killer Strain*, p. 98.

67. Milbank, "Government's Anthrax Muddle."

68. White House, "Director Ridge, Leaders Discuss Homeland Security," transcript, October 18, 2001, http://www.whitehouse.gov/news/releases/2001/10/print/20011018-1.html.

69. Thomas, *The Anthrax Attacks*, pp. 24–25.

70. White House, "Director Ridge Discusses Anthrax Situation," October 22, 2001.

71. GAO, *Bioterrorism: Public Health Response to Anthrax Incidents of 2001*, pp. 26–27.

72. Thomas, *The Anthrax Attacks*, p. 27.

73. Ibid., p. 29.

74. White House, "Director Ridge, Medical Authorities Discuss Anthrax," transcript, October 25, 2001, http://www.whitehouse.gov/news/releases/2001/10/print/20011025-4.html.

75. Thomas, *The Anthrax Attacks*, p. 30.

76. Ibid., pp. 28, 30–31.

77. GAO, *U.S. Postal Service: Better Guidance Is Needed to Ensure an Appropriate Response to Anthrax Contamination*, p. 5.

78. Though both of these, as well as a number of other antibiotics, were found to be effective against the anthrax employed in the 2001 attacks, CDC made the change because of doxycycline's fewer side effects, lower cost, and greater availability. GAO, *U.S. Postal Service: Better Guidance Is Needed to Ensure an Appropriate Response to Anthrax Contamination*, pp. 31n54, 71.

79. This move was in recognition of uncertainties within the agency about the optimal length of treatment. GAO, *U.S. Postal Service: Better Guidance Is Needed to Ensure an Appropriate Response to Anthrax Contamination*, p. 31.

80. Ibid., pp. 30–32, 72.

81. GAO, *Bioterrorism: Public Health Response to Anthrax Incidents of 2001*, pp. 1–2.

82. Ibid., pp. 21–22; Partnership for Public Service, *Homeland Insecurity: Building the Expertise to Defend America from Bioterrorism*, (Washington, DC, 2003), pp. 11–12; and Cole, *The Anthrax Letters*, p. 132.

83. CDC processed over 5,400 anthrax-related specimens in its own labs, and helped other labs in managing more than 70,000 additional samples. Partnership for Public Service, *Homeland Insecurity*, p. 12.

84. Julie L. Gerberding, "Lessons Being Learned: The Challenges and Opportunities," in Institute of Medicine, *Biological Threats and Terrorism: Assessing the Science and Response Capabilities* (Washington, DC: National Academies Press, 2002), pp. 150–151.

85. Partnership for Public Service, *Homeland Insecurity*, p. 12; and GAO, *Bioterrorism: Public Health Response to Anthrax Incidents of 2001*, pp. 21–22.

86. GAO, *Bioterrorism: Public Health Response to Anthrax Incidents of 2001*, p. 28.

87. Ibid., pp. 4, 11–13.

88. Ibid., pp. 14–15.

89. Richard Morin and Claudia Deane, "Poll Shows Anthrax Sparks Broad Concern," *Washington Post*, October 16, 2001, A06.

90. Thomas, *The Anthrax Attacks*, pp. 35–37; Harvard School of Public Health, "Survey Shows Americans Not Panicking over Anthrax, but Starting to Take Steps to Protect Themselves Against Possible Bioterrorist Attacks," news release, November 8, 2001, http://www.hsph.harvard.edu/news/press-releases/2001-releases/press11082001.html.

91. GAO, *Bioterrorism: Public Health Response to Anthrax Incidents of 2001*, p. 2.

92. Jernigan, Pratima L. Raghunathan, et al., "Investigations of Bioterrorism-Related Anthrax," p. 1027.

93. GAO, *Bioterrorism: Public Health Response to Anthrax Incidents of 2001*, pp. 22–23.

94. Cole, *The Anthrax Letters*, pp. 220–221.

95. CNN.com, "Expert: Government gets 'D' on anthrax response," November 7, 2001, http://archives.cnn.com/2001/HEALTH/conditions/11/06/bioterrorism.conference/index.html.

96. GAO, *Bioterrorism: Public Health Response to Anthrax Incidents of 2001*, p. 19.

97. Gerberding, "Lessons Being Learned," p. 150.

98. Partnership for Public Service, *Homeland Insecurity*, p. 12.

99. Eileen Salinsky, "Will the Nation Be Ready for the Next Bioterrorism Attack? Mending Gaps in the Public Health Infrastructure," *NHPF Issue Brief No. 776* (Washington, DC: George Washington University, June 12, 2002), p. 3.

100. GAO, *Bioterrorism: Public Health Response to Anthrax Incidents of 2001*, p. 18.

101. Ibid., pp. 15–16.

102. Ibid., pp. 24–25.

103. Gerberding, "Lessons Being Learned," pp. 151–152.

104. GAO, *Bioterrorism: Public Health Response to Anthrax Incidents of 2001*, pp. 26–27.

105. Cole, *The Anthrax Letters*, p. 221.

106. Harvard School of Public Health, "Survey Shows Americans Not Panicking Over Anthrax, but Starting to Take Steps to Protect Themselves Against Bioterrorist Attacks," news release, November 8, 2001, http://www.hsph.harvard.edu/news/press-releases/2001-releases/press11082001.html.

107. Harvard School of Public Health/Robert Wood Johnson Foundation Survey Project on Americans' Response to Biological Terrorism, October 24–28, 2001, http://www.hsph.harvard.edu/news/press-releases/2001-releases/press11082001.html.

108. Partnership for Public Service, *Homeland Insecurity*, p. 12.

109. National Commission on Terrorist Attacks Upon the United States (9/11 Commission), *The 9/11 Commission Report: Final Report of the National Commission on Terrorist Attacks Upon the United States*, Authorized Edition (New York: W.W. Norton & Company, 2004), pp. 339–348.

110. GAO, *U.S. Postal Service: Better Guidance Is Needed to Ensure an Appropriate Response to Anthrax Contamination*, p. 27.

CHAPTER 6

1. White House, "Executive Order Establishing Office of Homeland Security," October 8, 2001, http://www.whitehouse.gov/news/releases/2001/10/print/20011008-2.html.

2. Ibid.

3. Department of Health and Human Services, "Secretary Thompson Testifies on HHS Readiness and Role of Vaccine Research and Development," transcript, October 23, 2001, http://www.hhs.gov/news/press/2001pres/20011023.html.

4. Leonard A. Cole, *The Anthrax Letters* (Washington, DC: Joseph Henry Press, 2003), p. 118.

5. Global Health Security Initiative, "GHSI Background, Overview: Global Health Security Initiative (GHSI)," http://www.ghsi.ca/english/background.asp.

6. Funding for the federal response to 9/11 was largely provided in three supplemental appropriations measures: 2001 Emergency Supplemental Appropriations Act for Recovery From and Response to Terrorist Attacks on the United States (PL 107-38), Department of Defense and Emergency Supplemental Appropriations Act for Recovery From and Response to Terrorist Attacks, 2002 (PL 107-117), and 2002 Supplemental Appropriations Act for Further Recovery From and Response to Terrorist Attacks on the United States (PL 107-206). The major legislative vehicle was the Aviation and Transportation Security Act (ATSA, PL 107-71), which was signed into law on November 19, 2001 and, among other things, established a Transportation Security Administration within the Department of Transportation that was to be responsible for the security of all modes of transportation. Congressional Budget Office, "Letter to the Honorable John M. Spratt Jr. regarding federal costs associated with the terrorist attacks of September 11, 2001," August 29, 2002; and R. William Johnstone, *9/11 and the Future of Transportation Security* (Westport, CT: Praeger Security International, 2006), p. 48.

7. Johnstone, *9/11 and the Future of Transportation Security*, pp. 49–53.

8. Sarah A. Lister, Congressional Research Service, "An Overview of the U.S. Public Health System in the Context of Emergency Preparedness," RL31719 (Washington, DC, March 17, 2005), pp. 17, 19–20; U.S. House, Committee on Appropriations, *Conference Report to Accompany HR 3061, Making Appropriations for the Departments of Labor, Health and Human Service, and Education, and Related Agencies for the Fiscal Year Ending September 30, 2002,* 107th Cong., 1st session (Washington, DC, December 19, 2001), H. Report 107-342, p. 116; U.S. House, Committee on Appropriations, *Conference Report to Accompany HR 3338, Making Appropriations for the Department of Defense for the Fiscal Year Ending September 30, 2002,* 107th Cong., 1st session (Washington, DC, December 19, 2001), H. Report 107-350, pp. 85–86; and Department of Health and Human Services, FY2004 Budget in Brief, (Washington, DC, 2003), pp. 93–94.

9. These sums include programs that were subsequently transferred to the Department of Homeland Security, including the National Pharmaceutical Stockpile, the Smallpox Vaccine program, and the Office of Emergency Response, Department of Health and Human Services, Fiscal Year 2004 Budget in Brief, pp. 93–94.

10. Department of Health and Human Services, Fiscal Year 2004 Budget in Brief, pp. 93–94; and Lister, "An Overview of the U.S. Public Health System," pp. 17, 19–20.

11. Kathleen S. Swendiman and Jennifer K. Elsea, Congressional Research Service, "Federal and State Quarantine and Isolation Authority," RL33201 (Washington, DC, December 12, 2005), p. 10.

12. Eileen Salinsky, "Will the Nation Be Ready for the Next Bioterrorism Attack? Mending Gaps in the Public Health Infrastructure," National Health Policy Forum Issue Brief, No. 776 (Washington, DC: George Washington University, June 12, 2002), p. 4.

13. Lister, "An Overview of the U.S. Public Health System," p. 15; and U.S. House, Committee on Energy and Commerce, *Conference Report to Accompany HR 3448, Public Health Security and Bioterrorism Preparedness and Response Act of 2002,* 107th Cong., 2nd session (Washington, DC, May 21, 2002), H. Report 107-481, p. 4.

14. U.S. House, *Conference Report to Accompany HR 3448,* p. 5.

15. Lister, "An Overview of the U.S. Public Health System," pp. 15–16.

16. Ibid., p. 16.

17. U.S. House, *Conference Report to Accompany HR 3448,* pp. 13–14.

18. Lister, "An Overview of the U.S. Public Health System," pp. 23, Appendix C.

19. Johnstone, *9/11 and the Future of Transportation Security,* p. 48.

20. White House, "Analysis for the Homeland Security Act of 2002," June 18, 2002, http://www.whitehouse.gov/deptofhomeland/analysis/

21. Lister, "An Overview of the U.S. Public Health System," pp. 9–10, 16.

22. Ibid., p. 22.

23. Centers for Disease Control and Prevention, "Outbreak of Severe Acute Respiratory Syndrome—Worldwide, 2003," *MMWR Weekly,* March 21, 2003, http://www.cdc.gov/mmwr/preview/mmwrhtml/mm5211a5.htm.

24. World Health Organization, Regional Office for the Western Pacific, "SARS," http://www.wpro.who.int/health_topics/sars/

25. Centers for Disease Control and Prevention, "SARS Update—May 19, 2004," news release, May 19, 2004, http://www.cdc.gov/ncidod/sars/situation/may19.htm.

26. Centers for Disease Control and Prevention, "Current SARS Situation, May 3, 2005," http://www.cdc.gov/ncidod/sars/situation.htm.

27. The Century Foundation, *Breathing Easier? Report of the Century Foundation Working Group on Bioterrorism Preparedness* (New York: The Century Foundation Press, 2004), pp. 16–18.

28. Influenza strains are named based on which of fifteen separate hemagglutinin (H) and of nine different neuraminidase (N) antigens are present on the surface of the virus. Sarah A. Lister, Congressional Research Service, "Pandemic Influenza: Domestic Preparedness Efforts," RL33145 (Washington, DC, November 10, 2005), p. 4.

29. World Health Organization, "Avian Influenza ('bird flu')—Fact Sheet, January 2006," http://www.who.int/csr/disease/avian_influenza/avianinfluenza_fact sheetJan2006; and Robert G. Webster, Malik Peiris, Honglin Chen, and Yi Guan, "H5N1 Outbreaks and Enzootic Influenza," *Emerging Infectious Diseases*, vol. 12, No. 1, January 2006, pp. 3–4.

30. Centers for Disease Control and Prevention, "Avian Influenza: Current Situation," Fact Sheet, July 15, 2007, p. 1.

31. World Health Organization, "Cumulative Number of Confirmed Human Cases of Avian Influenza A/(H5N1) Reported to WHO," Fact Sheet, August 16, 2007, http://www.who.int/csr/disease/avian_influenza/country/cases_table_ 2007_08_16/

32. World Health Organization, *WHO Global Influenza Preparedness Plan* (Geneva, 2005), p. 1.

33. Ibid., pp. 1–2.

34. World Health Organization, *The World Health Report 2007: A Safer Future* (Geneva: WHO, 2007), p. vii.

35. Ibid., p. 13.

36. Lister, "Pandemic Influenza," pp. 11–12; and Department of Homeland Security, *National Response Plan* (Washington, DC, December 2004), pp. 43–44.

37. White House, Homeland Security Council, *National Strategy for Pandemic Influenza* (Washington, DC, November 2005).

38. Lister, "Pandemic Influenza," p. 13.

39. White House, Homeland Security Council, *National Strategy for Pandemic Influenza Implementation Plan* (Washington, DC, May 2006), p. i.

40. PandemicFlu.gov, *National Strategy for Pandemic Influenza Implementation Plan: Summary of Progress, December 2006*, http://pandemicflu.gov/plan/federal/ strategyimplementationplan.htm.

41. Lister, "Pandemic Influenza," pp. 12, 14; and Department of Health and Human Services, *HHS Pandemic Influenza Plan* (Washington, DC, November 2005), p. 2.

42. Department of Health and Human Services, *HHS Pandemic Influenza Plan*, pp. 2, 9–11, 27.

43. Centers for Disease Control and Prevention, *CDC Influenza Pandemic Operation Plan (OPLAN)* (Atlanta, December 20, 2006), pp. 11–12.

44. Ibid., pp. 12–13, 15.

45. Lister, "Pandemic Influenza," pp. 15–16.

46. Sarah A. Lister, Congressional Research Service, "An Overview of the U.S. Public Health System in the Context of Emergency Preparedness," RL31719 (Washington, DC, March 17, 2005), pp. 17–18, 43–44.

47. Ibid., pp. 34–35, 47.

48. Frank Gottron, Congressional Research Service, "Project BioShield," RS21507 (Washington, DC, June 10, 2005), pp. 1–4.

49. Donald F. Kettl and Steven Kellman, IBM Center for the Business of Government, "The Government of the Future: Dr. Julie Gerberding at the CDC," *Reflections on 21st Century Management* (New York, 2007), pp. 18–20.

50. Trust for America's Health, "Ready or Not? Protecting the Public's Health in the Age of Bioterrorism 2004, Executive Summary" (Washington, DC, December 2004), p. 3.

51. Trust for America's Health, "Ready or Not? Protecting the Public's Health from Diseases, Disasters, and Bioterrorism 2005, Executive Summary" (Washington, DC, December 2005), pp. 2, 6.

52. Ibid., p. 4.

53. Lister, "An Overview of the U.S. Public Health System," pp. 21–26.

54. Isolation measures restrict the movement of *infected* individuals, whereas quarantines limit the movement of individuals *exposed to* a communicable disease. Lister, "Pandemic Influenza," pp. 21–23.

55. Ibid., pp. 17–32.

56. Lister, "The Pandemic and All-Hazards Preparedness Act," p. 3.

57. "Katrina Chronology," *Washington Post*, September 4, 2005.

58. Johnstone, *9/11 and the Future of Transportation Security*, pp. 142–143.

59. Sarah A, Lister, Congressional Research Service, "The Pandemic and All-Hazards Preparedness Act (PL 109-417): Provisions and Changes to Preexisting Law," RL33589 (Washington, DC, January 25, 2007), p. 3.

60. Ibid., pp. 1–2.

61. Ibid., pp. 9–10.

62. Ibid., pp. 13–19.

63. Ibid., pp. 30–32.

64. Ibid., pp. 11–13, 15, 20–21, 25, 27–28.

65. Trust for America's Health, "Ready or Not? Protecting the Public's Health from Diseases, Disasters and Bioterrorism 2006" (Washington, DC, December 2006), p. 4.

66. Advisory Panel to Assess Domestic Response Capabilities for Terrorism Involving Weapons of Mass Destruction, *Second Annual Report to the President and the Congress—II: Toward a National Strategy for Combating Terrorism* (Santa Monica, CA: RAND, December 15, 2000), p. 32.

67. Elin Gursky, *Progress and Peril: Bioterrorism Preparedness Dollars and Public Health* (New York: The Century Foundation, 2003), p. 45.

68. Elin Gursky, *Drafted to Fight Terror: U.S. Public Health on the Front Lines of Biological Defense* (Arlington, VA: ANSER, August 2004), pp. 34–35.

69. The Century Foundation, *Breathing Easier? Report of the Century Foundation Working Group on Bioterrorism Preparedness* (New York: The Century Foundation Press, 2004), pp. 14–15.

70. Lister, "An Overview of the U.S. Public Health System," pp. 26–27.

71. Trust for America's Health, "Ready or Not? Protecting the Public's Health from Diseases, Disasters and Bioterrorism 2006," pp. 2, 4.

CHAPTER 7

1. Trust for America's Health, "A Healthier America: A New Vision and Agenda," (Washington, DC, September 2007), pp. 2, 34.

2. Centers for Disease Control and Prevention, *Statement of Julie L. Gerberding on the President's FY 2008 Budget Request for the Centers for Disease Control and Prevention, Testimony before U.S. House of Representatives Committee on Appropriations, Subcommittee on Labor, Health and Human Services, Education, and Related Agencies*, March 9, 2007, p. 4.

3. Center for Biosecurity, University of Pittsburgh Medical Center, *Testimony of Tara O'Toole on "Six Years After Anthrax: Are We Better Prepared to Respond to Bioterrorism?" Testimony before U.S. Senate Committee on Homeland Security and Governmental Affairs*, October 23, 2007, p. 1.

4. Trust for America's Health, "Ready or Not? Protecting the Public's Health from Diseases, Disasters, and Bioterrorism 2007," (Washington, DC, December 2007), p. 73.

5. Harris Interactive, "CDC, FAA, NIH, FBI, and USDA Get the Highest Ratings of Thirteen Federal Government Agencies," The Harris Poll # 10, news release, February 6, 2007.

6. Center for Biosecurity, University of Pittsburgh Medical Center, *Anthrax Appraisal 5 Years Later: Top 10 Accomplishments and Remaining Challenges* (Baltimore, MD, September 22, 2006), http://www.upmc-cbn.org/report_archive/2006/09_September_2006/cbnreport_0922.

7. Center for Biosecurity, *Anthrax Appraisal 5 Years Later*; and Department of Health and Human Services, *Statement by Gerald W. Parker on Emergency Preparedness, Testimony before U.S. House of Representatives Committee on Appropriations, Subcommittee on Labor, Health and Human Services, Education, and Related Agencies*, March 9, 2007.

8. Center for Biosecurity, *Anthrax Appraisal 5 Years Later*.

9. Centers for Disease Control and Prevention, *Statement of Julie L. Gerberding on the President's FY 2008 Budget Request for the Centers for Disease Control and Prevention*, March 9, 2007.

10. Trust for America's Health, "Ready or Not? Protecting the Public's Health from Diseases, Disasters, and Bioterrorism 2006" (Washington, DC, December 2006), pp.3, 11.

11. Center for Biosecurity, *Anthrax Appraisal 5 Years Later*.

12. Ibid.

13. Department of Health and Human Services, *Statement by Gerald W. Parker on Emergency Preparedness*, March 9, 2007.

14. U.S. House, Committee on Homeland Security, "Letter to Secretary Michael O. Leavitt," news release, September 10, 2007.

15. Center for Biosecurity, University of Pittsburgh Medical Center, *Testimony of Tara O'Toole*, October 23, 2007, pp. 3–4.

16. Trust for America's Health, "Ready or Not? Protecting the Public's Health from Diseases, Disasters, and Bioterrorism 2007," p. 23.

17. Center for Biosecurity, *Anthrax Appraisal 5 Years Later.*

18. Trust for America's Health, "Ready or Not? Protecting the Public's Health from Diseases, Disasters, and Bioterrorism 2007," p. 13.

19. Trust for America's Health, "A Healthier America: A New Vision and Agenda," p. 12.

20. Center for Biosecurity, University of Pittsburgh Medical Center, *Testimony of Tara O'Toole at "Hearing on Bioterrorism Preparedness and the Role of the DHS Chief Medical Officer" Testimony before U.S. House of Representatives Committee on Appropriations, Subcommittee on Homeland Security,* March 29, 2007, p. 4.

21. GAO, *Influenza Pandemic: Further Efforts Are Needed to Ensure Clearer Federal Leadership Roles and an Effective National Strategy,* GAO-07-781 (Washington, DC, August 14, 2007), pp. 5–6.

22. Center for Biosecurity, *Testimony of Tara O'Toole,* October 23, 2007, p. 3.

23. R. William Johnstone, *9/11 and the Future of Transportation Security* (Westport, CT: Praeger Security International, 2006), pp. 54–63.

24. Trust for America's Health, "Ready or Not? Protecting the Public's Health from Diseases, Disasters, and Bioterrorism 2007," p. 6.

25. GAO, *Department of Homeland Security: Progress Report on Implementation of Mission and Management Functions,* GAO-07-454 (Washington, DC, August 2007), p. 133.

26. GAO, *Critical Infrastructure Sector Plans Complete and Sector Councils Evolving,* GAO-07-1075T (Washington, DC, July 12, 2007), Highlights.

27. Ibid., pp. 3, 5, 17.

28. Committee on Methodological Improvements to the Department of Homeland Security's Biological Agent Risk Analysis, National Research Council, *Interim Report on Methodological Improvements to the Department of Homeland Security's Biological Risk Analysis* (Washington, DC: National Academies Press, 2007), p. 1.

29. Ibid., p. 7.

30. GAO, *Department of Homeland Security: Progress Report on Implementation of Mission and Management* Functions, p. 166.

31. Department of Health and Human Services, *Statement of Radm. William C. Vanderwagen on Pandemic Influenza: HHS Progress in National Preparedness Efforts, Testimony before U.S. Senate Committee on Homeland Security and Governmental Affairs, Subcommittee on State, Local, and Private Sector Preparedness and Integration,* October 3, 2007, p. 1.

32. GAO, *Influenza Pandemic: Further Efforts Are Needed to Ensure Clearer Federal Leadership Roles and an Effective National Strategy,* pp. 6–7.

33. Ibid., pp. 7–8.

34. Johnstone, *9/11 and the Future of Transportation Security,* pp. 112–113.

35. Center for Biosecurity, University of Pittsburgh Medical Center, "Comments from the Center for Biosecurity of UPMC on the National Strategy for Pandemic Influenza Implementation Plan," *Biosecurity and Bioterrorism,* vol. 4, No. 3, 2006, pp. 320–324.

36. Holmberg, S.D., Layton, C.M., Ghneim, G.S., and Wagener, D.K., "State Plans for Containment of Pandemic Influenza," *Emerging Infectious Diseases*, vol. 12, No. 9, September 2006, pp. 1414–1415.

37. Sarah A. Lister and Holly Stockdale, Congressional Research Service, "Pandemic Influenza: An Analysis of State Preparedness and Response Plans," RL34190 (Washington, DC, September 24, 2007), p. 22.

38. National Association of County and City Health Officials, *Federal Funding for Public Health Emergency Preparedness: Implications and Ongoing Issues for Local Health Departments* (Washington, DC, August 2007), pp. 10–11.

39. Trust for America's Health, "Ready or Not? Protecting the Public's Health from Diseases, Disasters, and Bioterrorism 2006," pp. 2, 4, 11.

40. Centers for Disease Control and Prevention, *Public Health Preparedness: Mobilizing State by State* (Atlanta, GA, February 2008), pp. 4–5.

41. American Public Health Association, *The Public Health Workforce Shortage: Left Unchecked, Will We Be Protected?* Issue Brief (Washington, DC, September 2006), p. 3.

42. National Association of County and City Health Officials, *Federal Funding for Public Health Emergency Preparedness*, pp. 6–7.

43. Trust for America's Health, "Ready or Not? Protecting the Public's Health from Diseases, Disasters, and Bioterrorism 2007," p. 77.

44. Ibid., p. 37.

45. GAO, *Department of Homeland Security: Progress Report on Implementation of Mission and Management Functions*, pp. 128–129.

46. Ibid., p. 128.

47. TOPOFF 4, from October 15 to 19, 2007, involved the simulated detonation of "dirty bombs" with radiological materials in Guam, Oregon and Arizona. Mark Brabrook, "TOPOFF 4," *EMSE 232 Disaster Newsletter*, vol. 13, No. 3, December 2007, http://www.seas.gwu.edu/~emse232/december2007_23.html.

48. Department of Homeland Security, *Top Officials (TOPOFF) Exercise Series: TOPOFF 2, After Action Summary for Public Release* (Washington, DC, December 19, 2003), p. 1.

49. Daniel S. Hamilton and Bradley T. Smith, "Atlantic Storm," *EMBO Reports*, vol. 7, No. 1, 2006, p. 4.

50. Eileen Sullivan, "TOPOFF: Largest Terror Exercise in U.S. History," Associated Press, October 3, 2007.

51. Department of Homeland Security, *TOPOFF 2, After Action Summary for Public Release*, pp. 3–7; Hamilton and Smith, "Atlantic Storm," pp. 5–8; and New Jersey Center for Public Health Preparedness at UMDNJ, *TOPOFF 3 After Action Report (AAR) of the New Jersey Center for Public Health Preparedness (NJCPHP) at UMDNJ* (New Brunswick, NJ, May 24, 2005), pp. 5–6.

52. Ibid., pp. 4–5.

53. New Jersey Center for Public Health Preparedness at UMDNJ, *TOPOFF 3 After Action Report*, p. 6.

54. Sullivan, "TOPOFF: Largest Terror Exercise in U.S. History," October 3, 2007.

55. GAO, *Influenza Pandemic: Further Efforts Are Needed to Ensure Clearer Federal Leadership Roles and an Effective National Strategy*, p. 6.

56. Sarah A. Lister, Congressional Research Service, "Pandemic Influenza: Domestic Preparedness Efforts," RL33145 (Washington, DC, February 20, 2007), p. 19.

57. Centers for Disease Control and Prevention, *Statement of Julie L. Gerberding on the President's FY 2008 Budget Request for the Centers for Disease Control and Prevention*, March 9, 2007.

58. Lister and Stockdale, "Pandemic Influenza: An Analysis of State Preparedness and Response Plans," pp. 11, 11n36.

59. Trust for America's Health, "Ready or Not? Protecting the Public's Health from Diseases, Disasters, and Bioterrorism 2007," pp. 27, 30.

60. Trust for America's Health, "Ready or Not? Protecting the Public's Health from Diseases, Disasters and Bioterrorism 2006," p. 3.

61. Center for Biosecurity, *Anthrax Appraisal 5 Years Later*.

62. Associated Press, "U.S. Labs Mishandling Deadly Germs," October 2, 2007, http://www.msnbc.com/id/21096974/print/1/displaymode/1098.

63. Centers for Disease Control and Prevention, *Public Health Preparedness*, p. 3.

64. Trust for America's Health, "Ready or Not? Protecting the Public's Health from Diseases, Disasters, and Bioterrorism 2007," p. 31.

65. Trust for America's Health, "Ready or Not? Protecting the Public's Health from Diseases, Disasters and Bioterrorism 2006," p. 4.

66. Trust for America's Health, "A Healthier America: A New Vision and Agenda," p. 11.

67. Centers for Disease Control and Prevention, *Public Health Preparedness*, p. 4.

68. Center for Biosecurity, *Testimony of Tara O'Toole*, October 23, 2007, p. 3; and Lister, "Pandemic Influenza: Domestic Preparedness Efforts," February 20, 2007, p. 22.

69. Trust for America's Health, "Ready or Not? Protecting the Public's Health from Diseases, Disasters and, Bioterrorism 2007," p. 6.

70. GAO, *Department of Homeland Security: Progress Report on Implementation of Mission and Management Functions*, pp. 168–169.

71. Spencer S. Hsu, "New York Presses To Deploy More Bioweapons Sensors," *Washington Post*, January 9, 2008, p. A03.

72. Center for Biosecurity, *Testimony of Tara O'Toole*, October 23, 2007, pp. 6, 8.

73. GAO, *Department of Homeland Security: Progress Report on Implementation of Mission and Management Functions*, p. 168.

74. Center for Biosecurity, *Testimony of Tara O'Toole*, October 23, 2007, p. 8.

75. Hsu, "New York Presses To Deploy More Bioweapons Sensors."

76. White House, *The Federal Response to Hurricane Katrina: Lessons Learned* (Washington, DC, February 2006), pp. 58–59.

77. Department of Health and Human Services, Statement of Radm. William C. Vanderwagen on Pandemic Influenza: HHS Progress in National Preparedness Efforts, pp. 5–6.

78. Center for Biosecurity, University of Pittsburgh Medical Center, *Comments from Thomas Inglesby at Roundtable on All-Hazards Medical Preparedness and*

Response, before U.S. Senate Subcommittee on Bioterrorism and Public Health Preparedness (Baltimore, MD, April 5, 2006), pp. 3–4.

79. Trust for America's Health, "Ready or Not? Protecting the Public's Health from Diseases, Disasters, and Bioterrorism 2006," pp. 2, 4, 11.

80. Trust for America's Health, "A Healthier America: A New Vision and Agenda," p. 13.

81. The cities chosen for the survey included five deemed to be at greatest risk of terrorist attack (New York City, Los Angeles, Washington, DC, Chicago, and Houston), plus the two hosts of the 2008 Presidential nominating conventions (Denver and Minneapolis). The Madrid attacks had previously been utilized by CDC as an appropriate standard for gauging mass casualty preparedness because they generated the kind of surge anticipated after a major terrorist attack, with almost 1,000 patients transported to area hospitals on the day of the attacks. U.S. House, Committee on Oversight and Government Reform, majority staff, "Hospital Emergency Surge Capacity: Not Ready for the Predictable Surprise," 110th Congress, 1st session (Washington, DC, May 2008), pp. i–iii, 1.

82. Center for Biosecurity, *Testimony of Tara O'Toole*, March 29, 2007, p. 4.

83. Department of Homeland Security, *Nationwide Plan Review, Phase 2 Report* (Washington, DC, June 16, 2006), pp. 27–28.

84. National Association of County and City Health Officials, *Federal Funding for Public Health Emergency Preparedness*, p. 5.

85. Trust for America's Health, "Ready or Not? Protecting the Public's Health from Diseases, Disasters, and Bioterrorism 2007," p. 63.

86. Center for Biosecurity, *Testimony of Tara O'Toole*, March 29, 2007, p. 3.

87. Lister and Stockdale, "Pandemic Influenza: An Analysis of State Preparedness and Response Plans," p. 18.

88. Department of Health and Human Services, *Statement by Gerald W. Parker on Emergency Preparedness*, March 9, 2007.

89. Department of Health and Human Services, *Statement of Radm. William C. Vanderwagen on Pandemic Influenza: HHS Progress in National Preparedness Efforts*, pp. 6, 10.

90. Ibid., pp. 9–10.

91. Lister and Stockdale, "Pandemic Influenza: An Analysis of State Preparedness and Response Plans," pp. 14–15.

92. Trust for America's Health, "Ready or Not? Protecting the Public's Health from Diseases, Disasters, and Bioterrorism 2007," p. 7.

93. Trust for America's Health, "Ready or Not? Protecting the Public's Health from Diseases, Disasters, and Bioterrorism 2006," pp. 4, 11.

94. Trust for America's Health, "Ready or Not? Protecting the Public's Health from Diseases, Disasters and Bioterrorism 2007," pp. 7, 21.

95. Lister and Stockdale, "Pandemic Influenza: An Analysis of State Preparedness and Response Plans," pp. 12–14.

96. Department of Health and Human Services, *Pandemic and All-Hazards Preparedness Act Progress Report* (Washington, DC, November 2007), pp. 2–3.

97. Trust for America's Health, "Ready or Not? Protecting the Public's Health from Diseases, Disasters, and Bioterrorism 2006," p. 4.

98. Center for Biosecurity, *Testimony of Tara O'Toole*, October 23, 2007, pp. 4–6.

99. Trust for America's Health, "A Healthier America: A New Vision and Agenda," p. 11.

100. Trust for America's Health, "Ready or Not? Protecting the Public's Health from Diseases, Disasters, and Bioterrorism 2006," pp. 2, 11.

101. Department of Homeland Security, *National Response Plan* (Washington, DC, December 2004), pp. 46–49.

102. This was originally called the Homeland Security Operations Center until the name was changed in the May 2006 revisions to the National Response Plan. Department of Homeland Security, *Notice of Change to the National Response Plan*, version 5.0 (Washington, DC, May 25, 2006), p. 3.

103. Department of Homeland Security, "Transcript of Background Briefing with Senior DHS Officials on TOPOFF 3," news release, April 8, 2005.

104. GAO, *High Risk Series: An Update*, GAO-07-310 (Washington, DC, January 2007), p. 47.

105. GAO, *High Risk Series: An Update*, p. 47.

106. White House, Homeland Security Council, *National Strategy for Pandemic Influenza* (Washington, DC, November 2005), p. 4.

107. Department of Health and Human Services, *HHS Pandemic Influenza Plan* (Washington, DC, November 2005), p. 34.

108. Department of Homeland Security, *TOPOFF 2, After Action Summary for Public Release*, p. 9.

109. Hamilton and Smith, "Atlantic Storm," p. 8.

110. New Jersey Center for Public Health Preparedness at UMDNJ, *TOPOFF 3 After Action Report*, pp. 6–7.

111. Center for Biosecurity, *Testimony of Tara O'Toole*, October 23, 2007, p. 3.

112. Center for Biosecurity, *Testimony of Tara O'Toole*, March 29, 2007, p. 3.

113. Department of Homeland Security, *National Response Plan, Public Affairs Support Annex* (Washington, DC, December 2004), p. PUB-7.

114. Department of Homeland Security, *National Response Plan, Public Affairs Support Annex*, pp. PUB-2, 7–8.

115. White House, *The Federal Response to Hurricane Katrina*, p. 60.

116. Department of Homeland Security, *Notice of Change to the National Response Plan*, pp. 1–4.

117. Department of Health and Human Services, *HHS Pandemic Influenza Plan*, p. 11.

118. Centers for Disease Control and Prevention, *Statement of Julie L. Gerberding on the President's FY 2008 Budget Request for the Centers for Disease Control and Prevention*, March 9, 2007.

119. Trust for America's Health, "Ready or Not? Protecting the Public's Health from Diseases, Disasters, and Bioterrorism 2006," p. 4.

120. Lister and Stockdale, "Pandemic Influenza: An Analysis of State Preparedness and Response Plans," pp. 17–18.

121. Trust for America's Health, "Ready or Not? Protecting the Public's Health from Diseases, Disasters, and Bioterrorism 2006," p. 4, 52.

122. Centers for Disease Control and Prevention, *Protecting the Nation's Health in an Era of Globalization: CDC's Global Infectious Disease Strategy, Executive Summary* (Atlanta, GA, 2002), http://www.cdc.gov/globalidplan/3-exec_summary.htm.

123. Global Health Security Initiative, "Ministerial Statements: Communiqué— Eighth Ministerial Meeting of the Global Health Security Initiative, Washington, DC, November 2, 2007," http://www.ghsi.ca/english/statementWashington2007.asp.

124. Department of Health and Human Services, *Pandemic and All-Hazards Preparedness Act Progress Report*, pp. 9–10.

125. GAO, *Global Health: U.S. Agencies Support Programs to Build Overseas Capacity for Infectious Disease Surveillance*, GAO-08-138T (Washington, DC, October 4, 2007), p. 3.

126. GAO, *Influenza Pandemic: Efforts to Forestall Onset Are Under Way; Identifying Countries at Highest Risk Entails Challenges*, GAO-07-604 (Washington, DC, June 2007), pp. 4–5.

127. Penny Hitchcock, Allison Chamberlain, Megan Van Wagoner, Thomas V. Inglesby, and Tara O'Toole, "Challenges to Global Surveillance Response to Infectious Disease Outbreaks of International Importance," *Biosecurity and Bioterrorism*, vol. 5, No. 3, 2007, pp. 221–222.

128. Hamilton and Smith, "Atlantic Storm," p. 6.

129. World Health Organization, *World Health Report 2007: A Safer Future* (Geneva: WHO, 2007), p. 49.

130. Global Health Security Project, Henry L. Stimson Center, "Unprecedented Investment—Uncertain Return," http://www.stimson.org/print.cfm?SN=GH200701291197.

131. Trust for America's Health, "Ready or Not? Protecting the Public's Health from Diseases, Disasters, and Bioterrorism 2006," pp. 33, 35, 37.

132. Christopher Lee, "U.S. Flu Outbreak Plan Criticized," *Washington Post*, February 2, 2008, p. A03.

133. U.S. House, *Making Appropriations for the Departments of Labor, Health and Human Services, Education, and Related Agencies for the Fiscal Year Ending September 30, 2008, Conference Report to Accompany HR 3043*, 110th Congress, 1st session (Washington, DC, November 5, 2007), H. Report 110-424, pp. 134–135, 389, 406–407.

134. White House, "President Bush Vetoes the Departments of Labor, Health and Human Services, Education, and Related Agencies Appropriations Act, 2008," news release, November 13, 2007, http://www.whitehouse.gov/news/releases/2007/11/20071113-6.html.

135. Public Law 110-161, *Consolidated Appropriations Act, 2008* (Washington, DC, December 26, 2007).

136. Global Health Security Project, "Unprecedented Investment—Uncertain Return."

137. GAO, *Department of Homeland Security: Progress Report on Implementation of Mission and Management Functions*, p. 147.

138. Trust for America's Health, "Ready or Not? Protecting the Public's Health from Diseases, Disasters, and Bioterrorism 2006," p. 38.

139. White House, "Homeland Security Presidential Directive/HSPD-21: Public Health and Medical Preparedness," news release, October 18, 2007, http://www.whitehouse.gov/news/releases/2007/10/20071018-10.html.

140. Michael Mair and Crystal Franco, Center for Biosecurity, University of Pittsburgh Medical Center, *HSPD-21: National Strategy for Public Health and Medical Preparedness* (Baltimore, MD, October 2007), http://www.upmc-biosecurity.org/se/util/display_mod.cfm?MODULE=SEv35/mod/

141. White House, "Homeland Security Presidential Directive/HSPD-21."

CHAPTER 8

1. For example, for transportation security, see R. William Johnstone, *9/11 and the Future of Transportation Security* (Westport, CT: Praeger Security International, 2006), p. 113.

2. 9/11 Public Discourse Project, *Final Report on 9/11 Commission Recommendations* (Washington, DC, December 5, 2005), p. 1.

3. National Commission on Terrorist Attacks Upon the United States (9/11 Commission), *The 9/11 Commission Report: The Final Report of the National Commission on Terrorist Attacks Upon the United States*, Authorized Edition (New York: W.W. Norton, 2004), pp. 419–421.

4. The ten were: "green" status for SNS delivery, sufficient high-security labs, sufficient lab scientists to test for anthrax or plague, year-round lab-based influenza surveillance, two weeks hospital bed capacity in the event of a "moderate" pandemic, seasonal flu vaccination rates for seniors, number of seniors who have received a pneumonia vaccination, compatibility with CDC's National Electronic Disease Surveillance System, nursing workforce, and public health services funding changes. Trust for America's Health, "Ready or Not? Protecting the Public's Health from Diseases, Disasters, and Bioterrorism 2006," (Washington, DC, December 2006), p. 11.

5. Trust for America's Health, "Ready or Not? Protecting the Public's Health from Diseases, Disasters, and Bioterrorism 2006," p. 10.

6. Trust for America's Health, "Ready or Not? Protecting the Public's Health from Diseases, Disasters, and Bioterrorism 2007," p. 3.

7. Trust for America's Health, "A Healthier America: A New Vision and Agenda," (Washington, DC, September 2007), p. 35.

8. Trust for America's Health, "Ready or Not? Protecting the Public's Health from Diseases, Disasters, and Bioterrorism 2006," p. 7.

9. White House, *The Federal Response to Hurricane Katrina: Lessons Learned* (Washington, DC, February 2006), pp. 58–59.

10. Ibid., pp. 52–54.

11. Spencer S. Hsu, "States Feel Left Out of Disaster Planning," *Washington Post*, August 8, 2007, p. A01.

12. Spencer S. Hsu, "DHS To Unveil New Disaster Response Plan," *Washington Post*, January 19, 2008, p. A03.

13. For examples, see: Trust for America's Health, "A Healthier America," pp. 27–38; World Health Organization, *World Health Report 2007: A Safer Future* (Geneva: WHO, 2007), pp. 66–67; Center for Biosecurity, University of Pittsburgh Medical Center, "Comments from the Center for Biosecurity of UPMC on the National Strategy for Pandemic Influenza: Implementation Plan," *Biosecurity and Bioterrorism*, vol. 4, No. 3, 2006, pp. 320–324; and Anthony Cordesman, *The Challenge of Biological Terrorism* (Washington, DC: CSIS, 2005), pp. 62–65, 108–111, 137–139, 150–151, 164–170.

14. 9/11 Commission, *Final Report*, p. 391.

15. Johnstone, *9/11 and the Future of Transportation Security*, pp. 49–53; and U.S. House, Committee on Homeland Security, *Implementing Recommendations of the 9/11 Commission Act of 2007, Conference Report to accompany HR 1*, 110th Congress, 1st session (Washington, DC, July 25, 2007), H. Report 110-259.

16. Cordesman, *The Challenge of Biological Terrorism*, p. 150.

17. GAO, *Department of Homeland Security: Progress Report on Implementation of Mission and Management Functions*, GAO-07-954 (Washington, DC, August 2007), pp. Highlights, 125–126, 164.

18. House Committee on Energy and Commerce, Senate Committee on Health, Education, Labor, and Pensions, and House and Senate Appropriations Subcommittees on Labor-HHS-Education.

19. 9/11 Commission, *Final Report*, p. 421.

20. GAO, *Department of Homeland Security: Progress Report on Implementation of Mission and Management Functions*, Highlights.

21. 9/11 Commission, *Final Report*, p. 419.

22. White House, "Homeland Security Presidential Directive/HSPD-21," news release, October 18, 2007.

23. Harvard School of Public Health/Robert Wood Johnson Foundation Survey Project on Americans' Response to Biological Terrorism, October 24–28, 2001.

24. Trust for America's Health, "A Healthier America: A New Vision and Agenda," p. 6.

25. Trust for America's Health, "Ready or Not? Protecting the Public's Health from Diseases, Disasters, and Bioterrorism 2007," p. 86.

26. World Health Organization, *World Health Report 2007: A Safer Future*, pp. 66–67.

27. Barry Kellman, *Bioviolence: Preventing Biological Terror and Crime* (Cambridge: Cambridge University Press, 2007), pp. 96–97.

28. Kellman, *Bioviolence*, p. 163.

29. Trust for America's Health, "Ready or Not? Protecting the Public's Health from Diseases, Disasters, and Bioterrorism 2006," p. 5.

30. Committee for the Study of the Future of Public Health, Institute of Medicine, *The Future of Public Health* (Washington, DC: The National Academies Press, 1988), pp. 4–5.

INDEX

About the Author

R. WILLIAM JOHNSTONE served on the staff of the 9/11 Commission, after working for over twenty years as a Congressional staff member. He is the author of *9/11 and the Future of Transportation Security*. Johnstone is a consultant on homeland and national security matters.

DATE DUE